GW00889897

CHINA'S ECONOMIC STATECRAFT

Co-optation, Cooperation and Coercion

Series on Contemporary China   (ISSN: 1793-0847)

Series Editors: Joseph Fewsmith *(Boston University)*
Zheng Yongnian *(East Asian Institute, National University of Singapore)*

*To view the complete list of the published volumes in the series, please visit:
http://www.worldscientific.com/series/scc

Series on Contemporary China – Vol. 39

CHINA'S ECONOMIC STATECRAFT

Co-optation, Cooperation and Coercion

Mingjiang Li

S. Rajaratnam School of International Studies, NTU, Singapore

 **World Scientific**

NEW JERSEY · LONDON · SINGAPORE · BEIJING · SHANGHAI · HONG KONG · TAIPEI · CHENNAI · TOKYO

Published by

World Scientific Publishing Co. Pte. Ltd.
5 Toh Tuck Link, Singapore 596224
USA office: 27 Warren Street, Suite 401-402, Hackensack, NJ 07601
UK office: 57 Shelton Street, Covent Garden, London WC2H 9HE

Library of Congress Cataloging-in-Publication Data
Names: Li, Mingjiang, author.
Title: China's economic statecraft : co-optation, cooperation, and coercion /
  [edited by] Mingjiang Li, S. Rajaratnam School of International Studies, NTU, Singapore.
Description: New Jersey : World Scientific, [2017] | Series: Series on contemporary China,
  ISSN 1793-0847 | Includes index.
Identifiers: LCCN 2016054693 | ISBN 9789814713467 (hard cover)
Subjects: LCSH: China--Foreign economic relations. | China--Foreign relations. |
  China--Economic policy.
Classification: LCC HF1604 .C45265 2017 | DDC 337.51--dc23
LC record available at https://lccn.loc.gov/2016054693

British Library Cataloguing-in-Publication Data
A catalogue record for this book is available from the British Library.

Desk Editor: Tay Yu Shan

Typeset by Stallion Press
Email: enquiries@stallionpress.com

Printed in Singapore

Contents

About the Editor

Mingjiang Li is an Associate Professor at the S. Rajaratnam School of International Studies (RSIS), Nanyang Technological University, Singapore. He is also the Coordinator of the China Program at RSIS. He received his Ph.D in Political Science from Boston University. His main research interests include China-ASEAN relations, Sino-U.S. relations, Asia-Pacific security, and domestic sources of Chinese foreign policy. He is the author (including editor and co-editor) of 12 books. His recent books are *New Dynamics in US-China Relations: Contending for the Asia Pacific* (lead editor, Routledge, 2014) and *Mao's China and the Sino-Soviet Split* (Routledge, 2012). He has published papers in various peer-reviewed journals including the *Journal of Strategic Studies*, *Global Governance*, *Cold War History*, *Journal of Contemporary China*, the *Chinese Journal of International Politics*, the *Chinese Journal of Political Science*, *China: An International Journal*, *China Security*, *Harvard Asia Quarterly*, *Security Challenges*, and *the International Spectator*.

List of Contributors

Ana Cristina Alves is Assistant Professor at the School of Humanities and Social Sciences, Nanyang Technological University, Singapore, where she lectures courses on China-Africa relations and Chinese Foreign Policy. Previously she worked at the South African Institute of International Affairs in Johannesburg as Senior Researcher in the Global Powers in Africa programme. She holds a Ph.D in International Relations from the London School of Economics. Her doctoral dissertation was a comparative study of China's engagement in the oil industry in Angola and Brazil. She has published widely on China-Africa relations and China's relations with Portuguese speaking countries, including 'China's Regional Forums in the Developing World: Socialisation and the "Sinosphere"' (co-authored), *Journal of Contemporary China* (2016).

Gerald Chan is Professor of Politics and International Relations at the University of Auckland, New Zealand. He is life member of Clare Hall, Cambridge, and Senior Research Fellow in the New Zealand Contemporary China Research Centre at Victoria University of Wellington. He holds the East Asian Institute Fellowship in Seoul in 2015–16 working on 'China's high-speed rail diplomacy'. His latest book is *China Engages Global Governance* (Routledge, 2013, ppk, co-authored with Pak K. Lee and Lai-Ha Chan). His articles include: 'Capturing China's international identity,' *Chinese Journal of International Politics* (2014); 'China and small states in food security governance,' *African and Asian Studies* (2015); and 'China eyes ASEAN,' *Journal of Asian Securities and International Affairs* (2015). Gerald obtained his Ph.D in Chinese politics and history from

Griffith University in Australia and his MA in International Relations from the University of Kent, UK. He has taught for 15 years at Victoria University of Wellington, and has held visiting or short-term positions in many universities, including the Chinese University of Hong Kong, Cambridge University, the National University of Singapore, Nanyang Technological University, Singapore, and Kobe-Gakuin University in Japan. He sits on the editorial or advisory board of many academic journals.

Xiaohe Cheng is an Associate Professor at the School of International Studies and Deputy Director of the Center for China's International Strategic Studies, Renmin University of China. His main research focuses on China's foreign relations in general and China's relations with the United States and some neighboring countries in particular. Dr. Cheng once worked for China Institutes of Contemporary International Relations for nine years and served as a Visiting Research Fellow at the Fairbank Center of Harvard University (1997–1998). He also taught China's Politics & Foreign Policies in Dublin College University (2007) and China's Foreign Relations in University of Michigan at Ann Arbor (2009). His recently published articles mainly cover China's relations with the Korean Peninsula and the Indian Subcontinent. Dr. Cheng did his undergraduate works in International Politics in Fudan University, Shanghai, and earned his Ph.D in Political Science from Boston University.

Xue Gong is a Ph.D candidate at the S. Rajaratnam School of International Studies (RSIS), Nanyang Technological University, Singapore. Her major research interests include China's economic diplomacy, Chinese business-government relations, and international political economy. She has published one journal article, two book reviews and has presented widely on China's economic activities in several international conferences such as Midwest Political Science Association of United States (MPSA) and International Studies Association (ISA).

Kwei-Bo Huang is an Associate Professor at the Department of Diplomacy, National Cheng Chi University (NCCU) in Taipei City, as well as Executive Director of NCCU's Vincent Siew International Exchange Program. He was founding director of NCCU International Master's Program in International Studies (IMPIS). Currently, he is also Secretary-General of the Taiwan-based Association of Foreign Relations (AFR). Huang was a Fulbright Visiting Scholar at the China Studies Program of the School of Advanced International Studies (SAIS), Johns Hopkins University, as well as a Visiting Fellow at the Brookings Institution Center for East Asia Policy Studies (CEAPS). He served as chairperson of the Research and Planning Committee of the ROC. Ministry of Foreign Affairs between 2009 and 2011. With research interests in US foreign policy and decision making, Cross-Strait relations, public diplomacy, and international conflict management, Huang earned his master's degree from the Department of Political Science of the George Washington University, and his doctorate in Government and Politics, University of Maryland, College Park.

Kheng Swe Lim is a research analyst at the China Programme at the S. Rajaratnam School of International Studies, Nanyang Technological University, Singapore. He holds a Master's in East Asian Studies from Harvard University, and a Bachelor's in Foreign Service from Georgetown University. His work focuses on the development of a more rigorous theoretical and conceptual understanding of the interaction of security and economics concerns, or the 'security-economic nexus', in the Asia Pacific, in particular with regard to Sino-Southeast Asian relations.

Roman Muzalevsky works for iJet International where he focuses on analysis of security trends and global affairs. He has authored 100 articles on Eurasian affairs, the book *Central Asia's Shrinking Connectivity Gap: Implications for US Strategy* (2014), and three policy monographs: *From Frozen Ties to Strategic Engagement: US-Iranian Relations in 2030* (2015); *China's Rise and Reconfiguration of Central Asia's Geopolitics: A Case for US Pivot to Eurasia* (2015); and *Unlocking India's Strategic Potential in Central Asia* (2015). He received his MA in International Affairs with concentration in Security and Strategy Studies from Yale. He can be contacted at muzalevsky@hotmail.com.

William J. Norris is currently an Assistant Professor of Chinese Foreign and Security policy at the Bush School of Government and Public Service at Texas A&M University where he teaches graduate-level courses in Chinese domestic politics, East Asian security, and Chinese foreign policy. He is also a non-resident Associate with the Nuclear Policy Program at the Carnegie Endowment for International Peace in Washington D.C. He completed his doctoral work in the Security Studies Program in the Department of Political Science at Massachusetts Institute of Technology where he specialized in the confluence of economics and security, focusing on the role of economics in contemporary Chinese grand strategy. His recent work examines the use of commercial sector actors to achieve national foreign policy objectives in the context of Chinese grand strategy. His most recent book is entitled *Chinese Economic Statecraft: Commercial Actors, Grand Strategy, and State Control* (Ithaca, NY: Cornell University Press 2016).

Xiaoyu Pu is an Assistant Professor of Political Science at the University of Nevada, Reno. Previously, he was a Postdoctoral Research Fellow in the Princeton-Harvard China and the World Program. He received his Ph.D in political science from Ohio State University. His research has appeared in *International Security, the China Quarterly, Chinese Journal of International Politics, Asian Affairs*, as well as in the edited volumes. He serves on the editorial boards of *Foreign Affairs Review* (Beijing) and *Global Studies Journal* (Hong Kong).

Reuben Wong is Director of Studies at the College of Alice and Peter Tan (CAPT). He also holds the Jean Monnet Chair (European Integration & Foreign Policy), focusing on EU-China research at the National University of Singapore. Reuben's publications have focused on EU and French foreign policy. They include *The Europeanization of French Foreign Policy: France and the EU in East Asia* (Palgrave Macmillan, 2006), *National and European Foreign Policies?* (co-edited with Christopher Hill, Routledge, 2011), and journal articles in the *Cambridge Review of International Affairs, Politique Européenne, Asia Europe Journal*, the *Journal of Contemporary China Studies*, and *EU External Affairs Review*. He has held visiting positions at Cambridge University, the LSE, the Stimson Center (Washington, DC), and the East Asian Institute (Singapore). His current research interests include the EU's relations with China, ASEAN regionalism, and the politics of disability rights. A Fulbright Scholar (2009), he serves on the Council of the Singapore Institute of International Affairs (SIIA), the EU Centre Singapore, and is Senior Research Affiliate in the EU-China programme of the College of Europe in Bruges. He speaks French, Chinese and some Spanish. He consults and does media interviews on EU foreign policy, international relations, and Singapore politics. He raises four children to help arrest Singapore's declining total fertility rate.

Hongzhou Zhang is an Associate Research Fellow with the China Programme at the S. Rajaratnam School of International Studies (RSIS), Nanyang Technological University, Singapore. He is also a Center for Strategic and International Studies (CSIS) Pacific Forum Young Leader. His main research interests include China and regional resources security (food, water and energy), agricultural and rural development, China's fishing policies and maritime security. He has contributed papers to peer reviewed journals such as the *Marine Policy, Pacific Review, WIREs Water, the Copenhagen Journal of Asia Studies, Harvard Asia Quarterly, the ISPI Analysis* and *Southeast Asia Studies*, edited volumes, RSIS Working papers and Policy Reports. He has also published Op-Ed in the *Straits Times, Yale-Global Online, the Diplomat, ChinaDialogue, the Global Times, Today, Lianhe Zaobao, the Nation, the Jakarta Post, Fair Observer* and others.

Introduction

Mingjiang Li*

After nearly 40 years of reforms and opening up, China has become the second largest economy in the world, the biggest international trader, the holder of the largest amount of foreign reserves, and one of the most rapidly growing economies. The international society has exhibited mixed reactions toward China's growing economic clout. Many countries regard China's economic growth as an opportunity for their long-term prosperity. Some countries are anxious about China's economic influence fearing that Beijing may decide to use its economic leverages for the pursuit of its strategic, political, and security objectives at the expense of their interests.

During the Cold War era, China categorically denounced Western powers' policy of using coercive economic means, such as embargo and sanctions in international politics, as imperialist crimes. Since the end of the Cold War, China's criticism of international sanctions has gradually weakened, although in principle Beijing is still opposed to this type of economic statecraft. In the past decade or so, the term economic statecraft has gained popularity in China, both in official documents and in scholarly writings. In many cases, the Chinese understand the term economic statecraft or economic diplomacy as employing foreign economic policies

*A few chapters in this edited volume have appeared in *Harvard Asia Quarterly* 16, 1 (2014) or are adapted from the papers in that issue. The editor thanks the journal for permitting these papers to be included in this volume.

for the attainment of economic interests. But increasingly, there is greater awareness that foreign economic policies can and should be used for the pursuit of other objectives.

In history, China has primarily used economic statecraft in the positive sense, providing benefits and assistance to help influence other countries' foreign policy. A Chinese government white paper states that China has provided a total of 256 billion yuan financial aid mostly to other developing countries from 1950 to 2009, including 106 billion yuan of free aid, 76.5 billion yuan of interest-free loans, and 73.5 billion yuan of preferential loans. In addition, Beijing has also provided significant assistance in the form of infrastructure projects, agricultural technologies, medical teams, and human resources training programs to foreign governments.[1] China's positive economic statecraft has helped China develop strong relations with countries in the developing world, raise its international status, and contend with Western countries on issues such as human rights. After the Tiananmen incident in 1989, Beijing has, to some extent, effectively used its purchasing power and domestic market share as a leverage to divide and rule among Western countries that were critical of China's human rights situation. China's economic power helped Beijing in breaking the diplomatic isolation in much of the 1990s. However, it is fair to say that China has only occasionally used its economic clout in an explicitly coercive manner.

However, many observers believe that China is gradually changing its approach to economic statecraft and is increasingly prepared to use coercive economic tools in its foreign relations. Their assessment is based on some instances of China using economic punishments against other countries in recent years. For instance, import restrictions on salmon from Norway after a Nobel Peace Prize was awarded to a Chinese political dissident and reduction of rare earth exports to Japan in the aftermath of a territorial dispute with Japan. It is also notable that Beijing became more supportive of sanctions against North Korea when Pyongyang carried out nuclear and missile tests in open defiance of UN Security Council resolutions.

With China's attitudes towards economic statecraft changing, it is important for the outside world to better understand the strategic thinking and

---

[1]White Paper on China's Foreign Assistance, full text available at: http://www.gov.cn/gzdt/2011-04/21/content_1849712.htm.

motivations behind Beijing's use of its economic prowess for strategic, political, diplomatic, and security objectives. Many analysts believe that economic power will become more and more important in a world that is becomingly increasingly interdependent. Samuel Huntington, for instance, noted that 'economic activity is probably the most important source of power...in a world in which military conflict between major states is unlikely [and] economic power will be increasingly important in determining the primacy or subordination of states'.[2] Compared to other policy tools, 'economic measures are likely to exert more pressure than either diplomacy or propaganda, and are less likely to evoke a violent response than military instruments'.[3]

This edited volume attempts to investigate the driving forces behind China's economic statecraft and the actual practice of economic statecraft in China's international politics. It seeks to systematically examine how China has used its economic power to co-opt, cooperate with, and coerce other players in international politics. The book includes four parts. The first part, containing three chapters, explores China's economic statecraft in relation to China's core national interests, which according to various official Chinese documents include the political power of the ruling party in China, sovereignty and territorial integrity, national security, and development rights. The second part attempts to analyze China's economic influence in its neighborhood including Northeast Asia, Southeast Asia, and Central Asia. The key question addressed in this part is how successful China has been in using its economic influence for strategic rivalry and national security objectives. The third part investigates Beijing's economic leverages in two bilateral relations, Sino-US relations and Sino-African relations. The last part addresses the impact of China's growing economic presence on two issues, global financial structure and food security.

China has openly declared that the Taiwan issue is a core national interest. Chapter 1 discusses the effectiveness of mainland China's economic policies towards Taiwan for various political purposes. The chapter begins

---

[2] Samuel Huntington, 'Why International Primacy Matters', *International Security*, 17, no. 4 (Spring 1993), pp. 68–83.

[3] David A. Baldwin, *Economic Statecraft* (Princeton, NJ: Princeton University Press, 1985), 110.

by delineating mainland China's strategic thinking and goals in relation to current Cross-Strait relations from historical and political perspectives. It argues that, like his predecessors, Xi Jinping wants to apply a series of economic statecraft to Taiwan for the achievement of national reunification and protection of national security. The section that follows identifies a few internal factors of Taiwan as the main barrier to mainland China's economic thinking and strategy toward Taiwan. Then, an introduction and analysis of mainland China's tangible economic measures toward Taiwan in recent years are examined to understand how Beijing would deal with Cross-Strait relations when politics often trumps the economic benefits derived from Cross-Strait economic interactions.

Human rights issues also concern the core interests of the ruling elites in Beijing. Frequent human rights disputes between China and the European Union (EU) have been a defining characteristic of China–EU relations since the Tiananmen incident in 1989. Wong in Chapter 2 argues that while Chinese human rights diplomacy was defensive until 1997, Beijing has increasingly been skillful in using its growing economic weight to break down common EU positions that target and embarrass China's human rights record in international human rights fora. China does not limit its human rights disputes with the EU to normative and philosophical arguments. It also adopts a tough carrot-and-stick approach using economic tools to defend and advance its position on human rights disputes with the EU and its member states. Wong finds that since the late-1990s, China has changed its strategic doctrine and begun to use economic diplomacy as a coercive tool. What is even more interesting is that China has developed its own human rights diplomacy to counter Western (mainly European and American) attempts to highlight and embarrass its human rights record. Indeed, China has turned from being a *reactive* target of human rights (after the 1989 Tiananmen incident), to being *proactive* in promoting its own vision of human rights, and using diplomatic and economic tools to deflect or attack European attempts to put China in a corner.

Chapter 3 addresses Beijing's economic power in the context of the South China Sea disputes, with a focus on China–Vietnam relations. With its massive economic power, China's trade relations with Vietnam can be aptly applied to the Hirschmanesque analysis where the trade imbalance in favor of the stronger country is conducive to its political dominance toward the weaker. However, Gong finds that China has been reluctant to exert economic coercion to change the stances of Vietnam in the South China Sea dispute. Instead, China has tried to create more economic incentives such as launching the One Belt One Road initiative and establishing the Asia Infrastructure Investment Bank (AIIB). Chinese economic incentives are intended to achieve a variety of goals. By means of economic incentives, China aims to curb the internationalization of the South China Sea issue. Gong argues that although China has had difficulties in transforming Vietnamese policy to its favor in the maritime territorial dispute, China's economic incentives have impacted the unity of Association of Southeast Asian Nations (ASEAN) members, making it more and more difficult for the grouping to present a common stance on the dispute.

China's expanding influence through economic statecraft has created much anxiety in Asia and the world. Through the case studies of China's economic statecraft toward Japan, Chapter 4 identifies some patterns and the limitations of China's behaviors. As two leading economic powers in Asia, China and Japan have a complicated and dedicate relationship. Pu points out that China's economic statecraft has achieved limited success and sometimes success can be counterproductive. In recent years, Japan has displayed a tendency of not changing its policy preferences under Chinese economic pressure. He further argues that even when the Japanese backed down temporally in the case of the rare earth exports control, China's behaviors caused backlashes in the international community. The limitations of China's economic statecraft reflect a dilemma of China's rise in a highly interdependent Asia. The chapter concludes that while economic statecraft does provide China with a relatively low-risk approach to defending its interests, China must maintain a peaceful environment for its domestic development. The pursuit of economic statecraft will continue to be a tricky art for Chinese policy-makers.

How to deal with North Korea's missile and nuclear provocations is one of China's top diplomatic challenges. China endorsed the UN Security Council sanction resolution against North Korea in response to its first nuclear detonation. Given that China's preference for diplomatic persuasion and material incentive could not pull North Korea to the negotiating table, China changed course and publically resorted to economic coercive measures after North Korea's third nuclear test. As North Korea continued to conduct its fourth nuclear test in 2016, China tightened its economic grip on North Korea. Chapter 5 suggests that although it is too early to draw a conclusive assessment of the effectiveness of China's economic coercive policy, its impact on North Korea, psychologically and materially, should be significant. Cheng contends that by applying economic coercion on North Korea, China makes it clear that North Korea's nuclear provocations are not acceptable and that it can use whatever means to pursue denucleariza-tion of the Korean Peninsula. China also recognizes that economic coercion alone cannot force North Korea to give up its nuclear weapons; carrot and stick should be combined. For the time being, as China tightens its grip on North Korea, China struggles to strike a balance in achieving two conflict-ing objectives: on the one hand, it needs to inflict pain on North Korea and intimidate it to comply with the UNSC resolutions; on the other hand, it should avoid choking the North Korea economy lest it results in a regime change in that country.

Chapter 6 suggests that China's influence in Southeast Asia opens the possibility that China would be able to use its economic clout for political ends; in other words, use 'economic statecraft' in order to achieve its politi-cal, diplomatic, or security goals. Although this would seem to be a natural development, the reality is more complex. It is often difficult to determine the extent to which China's deliberate attempts to improve its economic ties with Southeast Asia resulted in China's main political and strategic objec-tive since the mid-1990s, as opposed to other factors such as the balance of power or constructivist norms. After 2012, China's economic statecraft towards Southeast Asia has mainly taken on the form of the Maritime Silk Road (MSR), which aims to counter some of the more negative sentiments arising from the South China Sea, as well as to cement China's geostrategic position in the region. Lim argues that it is too early to tell how effective the Chinese new economic initiatives, such as the 21st Century MSR and the AIIB, will be at advancing China's aims.

Chapter 7 examines the success of China's economic expansion in Central Asia and the strategic consequences for the region. Ever since the collapse of the Soviet Union, China has been marching westward, to and through formerly Soviet Central Asia, in search of resources, markets, and ways to address its skewed internal development that still favors its more dynamic eastern coast. So extensive has its regional economic presence become that Central Asia is now representing China's western leg of economic expansion and development. Muzalevsky argues that increasingly, China views its activities in the region as a way to meet its strategic imperatives of developing its poorer western frontier and mitigate geopolitical risks in Asia-Pacific, where the United States and Japan are perceived as seeking to contain its rise. He contends that China has already displaced Russia as the region's largest economic partner, driving the reconfiguration of the region's geopolitics. The chapter suggests that with time, this reconfiguration is bound to assume a military, rather than just economic, dimension as China will increasingly have to protect its burgeoning economic interests in the region.

Chapter 8 examines China's strategic use of economic statecraft within Sino-American relations. Given the high level of economic interaction between the United States and China and the competitive security dynamics, one might expect to find the relationship rife with instances of economic statecraft. Surprisingly, there are relatively few cases of what political scientists might recognize as 'economic statecraft'. Why? Norris argues that the field's conception of economic statecraft is too narrow. A more accurate understanding of the relationship between international economics and national security offers insight into the strategic dimensions of international economic interaction. The chapter begins by outlining the contours of the puzzle raised by Chinese economic statecraft vis-à-vis the United States. The author then defines economic statecraft before examining how China uses economic statecraft in its relationship with the United States. Norris concludes with a brief discussion of some recent episodes that may be considered cases of Chinese economic statecraft. The analysis in this chapter suggests that as Chinese outward direct investment grows, US policymakers will need to be better able to distinguish when economic interaction may result in security consequences. Without a more rigorous theoretical framework, there is a danger that Chinese investment in the United States will increasingly become politicized. The result will be a drift toward increased US–China tensions and forgone economic benefit to both sides.

Since the turn of the century Chinese infrastructure loans have attracted much attention from scholars, politicians and media alike, mostly because they have been widely used by Beijing as a tool to expand China's economic interests in Africa. These loans have successfully opened the gates for Chinese construction and resources companies to penetrate African markets, while simultaneously expanding China's political capital over a continent that had for decades struggled to attract much needed infrastructure funding. Chapter 9 explores the role of positive economic statecraft tools in Africa since the founding of the PRC in 1949 in pursuing Chinese foreign policy goals, focusing particularly on development financing targeting infrastructure. Alves argues that the use of this kind of economic incentives has been persistent throughout the history of the PRC, has shown remarkable resilience in view of changing contexts and obstacles, and accounts for a reasonable amount of successes in achieving China's tactical and structural goals, in both political and economic realms, on the continent over the past six decades.

How does a rising China engage with global financial governance? To what extent is China able to change the global financial structure in order to protect and promote its national interests? How do other major powers respond to China's challenge? What are the consequences for the global financial structure and its stakeholders as a result of China's impact? Chapter 10 addresses these questions and argues that even though the process of change has been slow and incremental, the challenge posed by China is real and credible. Most countries adopt ways to adjust to the changes brought about by emerging economies in general and China in particular. The result of these changes means that the global financial structure has become more pluralized, polarized, diffused, developmental and problem-solving in nature. The chapter tests these ideas against the backdrop of the revitalization of the US economy in response to the global financial crisis, the difficulties that China faces both internally and externally, and the capabilities of other major states to try to maintain the status quo. Chan concludes that the world is likely to continue to muddle through while China rises in economic influence.

Zhang and Li in Chapter 11 analyze China's expanding presence in the global agricultural sector. China's fast-growing economy has accelerated consumer demand to the point that further aggravates an already alarming food security situation. On the one hand, China's total food consumption is rapidly rising — partly due to the rapid population expansion, and partly due to the growing affluence and resulting demand for better and diversified food. On the other hand, China's industrialization and urbanization continue to exacerbate China's resource shortages and limit its agricultural production capacity. In response to this challenge, China is gradually moving away from a strategy of achieving self-sufficiency to a dual strategy of utilizing both domestic and international resources. Such international resources are obtained through trade, foreign land lease and purchase, and merger and acquisition of foreign agricultural businesses. This chapter argues that given the strategic importance of food resources, and the worsening global food security outlook, food security inevitably plays an increasingly important role in Chinese foreign relations.

A few major conclusions can be drawn from these studies. First of all, the findings of these chapters suggest that China may not have developed a grand and coherent strategic approach to economic statecraft. There seems to be major differences in China's use of economic techniques in response to human rights issues and territorial disputes. On territorial disputes, Beijing seems to be more reluctant to employ its economic power to compel its rivals to make concessions. Second, many chapters in this volume note that there are significant limitations to the efficacy of China's economic statecraft. The limitations may have to do with the lack of a coherent strategy, the Chinese economy's dependence on exports, and poor coordination among the Chinese agencies. Third, it seems that at present decision-makers in China feel more comfortable in practicing economic statecraft in a positive manner. In most cases, Beijing is inclined to use its economic power as a tool for inducement and reward. Fourth, China is gradually becoming more prepared to use its economic power for coercive purposes.

Part One
China's Use of Economic Power for Core Interests

Chapter 1

The Politics of Mainland China's Economic Statecraft in Relation to Current Cross-Strait Relations*

Kwei-Bo Huang

Mainly owing to the rapid growth of economic, political, and military power of mainland China (the People's Republic of China, PRC) and the intensified internal political struggles leading to a more divided society in Taiwan (the Republic of China, ROC), relations across the Taiwan Strait have been further complicated in the past decade. It seems that mainland China has felt more certain about its advantage in Cross-Strait relations, and that Taiwan has become more doubtful about its political and economic space for survival.

For mainland China, its economic, political, and military leverages constitute a strong basis against Taiwan independence. Owing to the decreased emphasis on the application of military capabilities and the gradual reduction in tension in the Taiwan Strait, mainland China has been exercising more economic and political means to woo Taiwan in various ways after May 2008. Such means do not always have to be treated separately in the analysis of Cross-Strait relations. Sometimes mainland China's economic policy toward Taiwan can lead to certain political implications or consequences that shape the political nature of Cross-Strait relations. One of

*The author would like to express his gratitude for the materials and opinions provided by Professor Chung-Chih Chen [陳仲志].

the more obvious cases is mainland China's reception of Taiwan's investment and professionals, mostly in the fields of high-tech and management, under the Economic Cooperation Framework Agreement (ECFA) signed in June 2010 by the Taipei-based Straits Exchange Foundation (SEF) and the Beijing-based Association for Relations Across the Taiwan Straits (ARATS). Both agencies have been authorized by the respective governments to deal with Cross-Strait matters in various dimensions such as economy, culture, technology, and so on. The ECFA's economic and political implications have been the focus of many academic works.[1]

For Taiwan, it has been in an inferior position regardless of the economic, political, or military affairs in relation to mainland China. Despite the fact that Taiwan has performed well on the world economic stage,[2] Taiwan still needs a boost to reinforce its economic power as one of the key pillars for Taiwan's survival and development. Another key pillar is Taiwan's vibrant democracy which has created the pluralist nature in politics and helped Taiwan to be accepted by most of the democracies in the world. Yet the economic and political achievements of Taiwan cannot prevent it from being isolated from the international community. Moreover, Taiwan's and mainland China's respective economic strengths may bring about diplomatic competition between the two governments.

Again, during the presidency of Ma Ying-jeou [馬英九], Cross-Strait relations changed dramatically, basically from confrontation to rapprochement and accommodation. Ma argued that the development of Taiwan–mainland China relations should follow the principles of 'economics first,

---

[1] See, for example, Daniel H. Rosen and Zhi Wang, *The Implications of China–Taiwan Economic Liberalization*, Policy Analyses in International Economics No. 93 (Washington, DC: Peterson Institute for International Economics, 2011), pp. 138–198, 141–142; Da-Nien Liu and Hui-Tzu Shih, *New Economic Development Opportunities for Taiwan in the Post-ECFA Era*, Asie. Vision No. 51 (Paris: IFRI Center for Asian Studies, 2012), pp. 16–29; and Tsai-Lung (Honigmann) Hong, 'The ECFA: a pending trade agreement?', in Peter C. Y. Chow, ed, *National Identity and Economic Interest: Taiwan's Competing Options and the Implications for Regional Stability* (New York: Palgrave Macmillian, 2012), pp. 48–54.

[2] According to the Center for Economics and Business Research (CEBR) in London, by the Gross Domestic Production (GDP) in US dollar, Taiwan ranked 25th in the world and 6th in Asia (after mainland China, Japan, India, South Korea, and Indonesia). See CEBR, 'World Economic League Table 2015', available at: http://www.cebr.com/reports/world-economic-league-table-2015/.

politics later' and of 'easy decisions first, tough calls later'. To respond, mainland China gradually adjusted its attitudes and policies to a relatively softer approach to Taiwan through economic and social exchanges; nevertheless, it has never given up its pursuit of national reunification by attempting to establish an irreversible framework to better control Cross-Strait relations. Regardless of the unpredictable political dynamics between Taipei and Beijing, Cross-Strait economic affairs have been the most tangible indicator of the peaceful development of Cross-Strait relations. Such functional interactions also helped establish concrete institutionalization in Cross-Strait relations, which would foster sustainable peace, stability, and prosperity between Taiwan and mainland China.

The vital meeting between the head of Taiwan's Mainland Affairs Council (MAC) Wang Yu-chi [王郁琦] and the head of mainland China's Taiwan Affairs Office (TAO) Zhang Zhijun [張志軍] in mainland China (Nanjing) on 11 February 2014 denoted the beginning of official political engagement between the two sides of the Taiwan Strait after more than six decades. The so-called 'Wang–Zhang Meeting' has extraordinary significance in Cross-Strait relations. It not only resulted in agreement to establish bilateral communication channels between the MAC and the TAO, but also symbolized the strengthening of mutual trust as the two ministerial-level officials in charge of Cross-Strait affairs met officially for the very first time.

At those meetings of the heads of Cross-Strait affairs, a couple of functional and institutional (or 'quasi-political') issues were touched upon. Examples include Taiwan as a transit stop for mainland travelers, the trade-in-goods agreement, and Taiwan's participation in regional economic cooperation mechanisms in the Asia Pacific. These will be further discussed later in this chapter.

Following this model, the top leader of the two sides of the Taiwan Strait finally met in Singapore on 7 November 2015, a meeting commonly called as 'Ma–Xi Meeting' between Ma and Xi Jinping [習近平]. The fact that the two top leaders were willing to meet on an equal footing and shelve political disagreement over the issues of political status (e.g., no reference to sovereignty and jurisdiction in public meetings and remarks) and title (e.g., calling each other 'Mr.' instead of official titles) — has demonstrated the goodwill and flexibility of both governments to create a precedent if the future top leader of Taiwan does not deviate from the political arrangement or foundation shaped intermittently since the early 1990s, including the 1992 Consensus sometimes described as 'One China, respective interpretations' by Taiwan. Taiwan insists on the ROC, whereas mainland China stands firm on the PRC. Arguably, from these meetings, mainland China wanted a steady political framework and resilient economic cooperation and social exchange mechanisms that can keep Taiwan from drifting away. Ma's leadership wished that from these meetings, Taiwan could ensure a stable process of institutionalizing Cross-Strait relations that could result in equality, dignity, and greater mutual trust across the Strait.

In the past, mainland China used many rhetoric attacks and threats of use of force against Taiwan at critical junctures of Taiwan's political development, in the hope that it could influence the results of Taiwan's major elections and deter the rising wave of Taiwan's independence. Knowing the long-lasting political divergence that has been intertwined with complex domestic politics of Taiwan, political leaders of mainland China have appeared to adjust their strategy toward Taiwan in the context of internal-external linkages. History shows that such a strategy has worked on the external front but not on the internal front. Internally, they have seemed to mix economic and political means to strengthen the 'united-front' work on Taiwan. Still, Taiwan underwent two regime changes: in 2000, the Democratic Progressive Party (DPP) won the presidential election; in 2008, the Kuomintang (KMT) regained power in the central government. Now the DPP is the ruling party again, under the leadership of Tsai Ing-wen [蔡英文] unwilling to recognize the 1992 Consensus or the 'One China, respective interpretations' understanding created by the Lee Teng-hui [李登輝] government and followed by the Ma government. Mainland China has obviously not succeeded in preventing the majority of the people of Taiwan from voting for a pro-independence political party. Externally, they have been able to make good use of mainland China's economic and political influences to oppress Taiwan's international space, denounce the ROC's sovereign status, and illegitimize attempts aimed at claiming an 'ROC sovereignty' or creating a 'Taiwan sovereignty'.

The following sections will begin with an introduction to the strategic thinking and goals of mainland China on the so-called 'Taiwan issue'. Strategic objectives of mainland China in Cross-Strait economic interactions will be explained by analyzing major contacts between the two sides of the Taiwan Strait. Then, Taiwan's dynamic domestic politics will be briefly explained as a main obstacle to mainland China's economic strategy and policy toward Taiwan. Finally, an examination of the economic exchanges between the two sides, mostly between May 2008 and early 2016 will produce some tangible findings to inform future observations on the political factors influencing mainland China's economic policies toward Taiwan.

Strategic Objectives and Thinking

Beyond a doubt, the strategic objectives of mainland China toward the 'Taiwan issue' have remained the same since the separation of the two sides of the Taiwan Strait (i.e., achieving national reunification and enhancing national security).

Mainland China, like the rest of the countries in the world, pursues its goals of national security and interests in the face of internal and external constraints. From Mao Zedong [毛澤東] to Xi Jinping, mainland China has vowed to unify Taiwan under the principle of 'One China'. It sees Taiwan as an inseparable part of 'China' and allows no foreign intervention in national reunification. In dealing with Cross-Strait relations, mainland China has always wished to compel Taiwan to engage in bilateral political negotiations and accept political and legal terms in favor of Beijing; respond to irredentism and patriotism that can mobilize its own people to support the Communist Party of China (CPC) government; catch up with or counter the US hegemony; and deter the possible rearmament of Japan in the West Pacific. In other words, reunification (i.e., territorial integrity) and national security have been perceived and portrayed by the mainland Chinese authorities as the most critical strategic goals in its relations with Taiwan.

Mainland China had often used the 'One China' principle in its interpretation of Cross-Strait relations. Although Taiwan, under the leadership of Lee Teng-hui [李登輝], would like to refer to the political foundation of Cross-Strait engagements as the 'One China, respective interpretations' understanding acquired jointly by both Taipei and Beijing in 1992, mainland Chinese leaders and senior officials still refuse to accept Taiwan's position and claim the 'One China' part only. For instance, in January 1998, the ARATS's top negotiation official of mainland China Tang Shubei [唐樹備], responded to the SEF's request for the resumption of talks on the basis of 'One China, respective interpretations' by arguing that it was unrealistic to contend 'One China, respective interpretations' because the consensus reached by the ARATS and the SEF in 1992 was that, in Cross-Strait consultations, both parties simply needed to recognize that the stance of both sides of the Strait was 'One China' and that they did not have to discuss the political notion of 'One China'.[3]

Yet it seems that Beijing's harsh tone could be moderated by showing some willingness to negotiate with Taipei as long as the latter could embrace a less rigid definition of 'China'.[4] For example, after the term 1992 Consensus — 'One China, respective interpretations' by Taiwan's definition was coined by the then MAC minister Su Chi [蘇起] to replace or supplement the oversimplified 'One China' a few weeks before he stepped down from office in May 2000, the 1992 Consensus was first quoted by the head of the TAO Bureau of Information in April 2001 in memory of the eighth anniversary of the 'Koo–Wang Talk'.[5] Mainland China still emphasized that this consensus was based on the fact that both sides verbally insisted on 'One China' in principle.[6]

Another example is that, in July 2000, Qian Qichen [錢其琛], the then deputy leader of the CPC Central Committee's Leading Group for Taiwan Affairs and PRC vice premier, asserted that

> '[a]s far as Cross-Strait relations are concerned, the "One China" principle means there is only One China, Taiwan is a part of China, and the sovereignty and territorial integrity of China cannot be divided', and 'the "One China" does not necessarily stand for the PRC'.

---

[3] 'Tang Shubei xiwang lianghui jizao zhankai zhengzhi tanpan chengxu xing shangtan' [Tang Shubei hopes the ARATS and the SEF will hold procedural talks for political negotiations as soon as possible], *People's Daily*, overseas edition (27 January 1998), p. 2.

[4] Yunhan Chu, 'Making sense of Beijing's policy toward Taiwan: the prospect of Cross-Strait relations during the Jiang Zemin era', in Hun-mao Tien and Yunhan Chu, eds., *China under Jiang Zemin* (Boulder, Colorado: Lynne Rienner Publishers, 2000), p. 194.

[5] The Koo–Wang Talks were talks held between Straits Exchange Foundation (SEF) chairman Koo Chenfu and ARATS chairman Wang Daohan in Singapore in 1993. The first talk began in Singapore on 27 April 1993. On 29 April, Koo and Wang signed four agreements. See 'Koo–Wang Talks', *Encyclopedia of Taiwan*, available at: http://taiwanpedia.culture.tw/en/content?ID=3906.

[6] 'Zhang Mingqing: xienyou "Jiuer gongshi", houyou "Wangku huitan"' [Zhang Mingqing: The '1992 Consensus' came first, followed by the 'Wang–Koo Talk'], *China News Service* (28 April 2001), available at: http://big5.china.com.cn/chinese/31550.htm.

A few weeks later, Qian adjusted his 'One China' statement by saying that '[t]here is only One China in the world; both mainland and Taiwan belong to China; and the sovereignty and territorial integrity of China brooks no separation'. Ever since Chen Shui-bian won the presidential election in March 2000, mainland China, still maintaining the supremacy of its own 'One China' principle, has compromised, at least technically. It is willing to use the 1992 Consensus and shift its policy priority from reunification to the prevention of formal Taiwan independence, in the hope that Taiwan would not move politically away from China.[7]

In spite of the flexibility in the application of the 'One China', Beijing leaders did not recognize the existence of ROC in Taiwan. In late April 2005, the KMT honorary chairman Lien Chan [連戰] visited mainland China to start the party exchange between the KMT and the CPC on the political foundation of the 1992 Consensus and anti-Taiwan independence. Lien and Hu stressed that the two sides should not fall into a vicious circle of confrontation but instead enter a virtuous circle of cooperation, seek together opportunities for the peaceful and steady development of Cross-Strait ties, trusting and helping each other, as well as creating a new situation of peaceful win–win, in order to bring about brilliant and splendid prospects for the Chinese nation. The two parties reached a consensus of a wide range of issues — the promotion for the early resumption of Cross-Strait dialogue, the signing of a peace accord and the development of a mechanism for military mutual trust.[8] Yet, this party-to-party platform on an equal footing

---

[7]Huang Jiashu, 'Liangnian lai Beijing dui Tai zhengce zhi xinyi' [On the new thinking of Beijing's policy toward Taiwan in the past two years], paper presented at an off-the-record roundtable on the Taiwan Issue, Brookings Institution, Washington, DC, pp. 1–2; and 'Wang Zaixi: zhizhi Taidu shi Zhonghua ernu dangqiande jinpo renwu' [Wang Zaixi: curbing Taiwan Independence is the urgent task facing the Chinese nation for the present], *China News Agency* (3 January 2004). Both are quoted in Jing Huang, 'Hu Jintao's pro-status quo approach in Cross-Strait relations: building up a One-China framework for eventual reunification', in Cal Clark, ed, *The Changing Dynamics of the Relations among China, Taiwan, and the United States* (Newcastle: Cambridge Scholars Publishing), p. 106. Also see Meng-ju Hsieh, 'Qian Qichen: dalu Taiwan tongshu yigezhongguo' [Qian Qichen: Both Mainland and Taiwan Belong to One China], *China Times*, August 26, 2000, p. 4.

[8]'Text of KMT–Beijing agreement', *BBC NEWS* (29 April 2005), available at: http://news.bbc.co.uk/2/hi/asia-pacific/4498791.stm; and Caroline Hong, 'Lien, Hu share "Vision" for peace', *Taipei Times* (30 April 2005), p. 1.

did not mean that leaders in Beijing no longer treated Taiwan as a local government.

Furthermore, mainland China has obviously differentiated between the internal (insiders) and the external (outsiders) when it comes to the principle of 'One China'. For mainland China, so long as Taiwan agreed on this principle, the conditions by which Taiwan and mainland China interact can be flexible, as implied before. But internationally, Taiwan can by no means represent 'China' or act as an independent political entity. In line with the principle of 'One China', mainland China has appeared willing to engage Taiwan as long as such an engagement will not be regarded as a model of 'One China, one Taiwan' or 'two Chinas'.

It is important for mainland China to keep Taiwan in a political framework that is mutually acceptable and neutral or favorable for the former's 'One China' formula. All KMT and DPP governments would like to be treated with equality and dignity via an implicit 'ROC–PRC', 'Taiwan–mainland China', or 'Taiwan–China' arrangement, but the CPC government has often seen the meetings with Taiwan's representatives or officials as 'Chinese domestic affairs' and purposefully given Taiwan a provincial status, or a status of the special autonomous region, in its 'One China' interpretation aimed at the international community.[9] An arguable exception (or controversially, a practice of 'one country, two governments') is the Ma–Xi meeting in Singapore on 7 November 2016, a historic event where the top leaders of the two sides of the Taiwan Strait met on an equal footing in a third party's territory (outside Taiwan and mainland China which includes Hong Kong and Macau).

Generally speaking, mainland China's principal strategic thinking about the resolution of the 'Taiwan issue' has evolved from use of force in the 1950s and the 1960s to both use of force and international political

---

[9]By the same token, for example, in the case of Taiwan's participation in the World Health Organization (WHO), the 2005 Memorandum of Understanding between mainland China and the WHO formally places Taiwan under the reign of the PRC. Furthermore, the 'Procedures concerning an arrangement to facilitate implementation of the International Health Regulation (2005) with respect to Taiwan Province of China' even outlines the way to interact with Taiwan in a stricter way. See Sigrid Winkler, 'Taiwan in international organizations', in Jean-Pierre Cabestan and Jacques deLisle, eds., *Political Changes in Taiwan under Ma Ying-jeou: Partisan Conflict, Policy Choices, External Constraints and Security Challenges* (London and New York: Routledge, 2014), pp. 252–254, 257.

(diplomatic) suffocation between the 1970s and the 1990s, and then to multiple economic and societal exchanges that garner more support of the people of Taiwan nowadays (but Beijing still has not renounced the use of force against Taiwan). It should be noted that such a contemporary strategic thinking has been backed up by mainland China's strong military presence and ability to limit Taiwan's international participation, particularly in the regional and global economic and financial cooperation.

Mainland China has maintained Taiwan as one of its core interests not only by firmly opposing the independence movement of Taiwan but also by refuting any foreign interference in the 'Taiwan issue'. Despite the hawkish attitude toward Taiwan independence, flexibility did not wane in mainland China's Taiwan policy. Just one week before the ROC presidential election in March 2000, mainland Chinese premier Zhu Rongji [朱鎔基] warned that blood will be shed if Taiwan declared itself an independent country.[10] Zhu also alerted Taiwan's voters to make the right choice, or they might have no chance to regret.[11] Once again, Chen Shui-bian [陳水扁] of the DPP won the election, resulting in another critical marker in Taiwan's sour relations with mainland China. Yet some obvious flexibility appeared to occur in mainland China's policy toward Taiwan. Before this election, mainland Chinese leaders made clear that they would regard a victory by the DPP as a move toward Taiwan's independence with potentially serious consequences. Once the result was in, they stated that they would adopt a 'wait-and-see' attitude toward the DPP government in Taiwan.[12]

Never retreating from the goal of national unification, mainland China enacted the Anti-Secession Law in March 2005 to manage the dynamics of Cross-Strait relations in the new millennium.[13] In Article 6, the

---

[10] Rebecca MacKinnon, 'China will be watching new Taiwan leader very carefully', *CNN* (18 March 2000), available at: http://transcripts.cnn.com/TRANSCRIPTS/0003/18/cst.16. html.

[11] 'Analysis: China's nightmare', *BBC News* (20 March 2000), available at: http://news.bbc. co.uk/2/hi/asia-pacific/683860.stm.

[12] Francis Markus, 'Milestone in China–Taiwan ties', *BBC News* (19 March 2000), available at: http://news.bbc.co.uk/2/hi/asia-pacific/682686.stm.

[13] See, for example, Kwei-Bo Huang, 'The anti-secession law and the distributive bargaining across the Taiwan Strait', *Views and Policies* 2(1) (September 2005), pp. 93–112; and Chunjuan Nancy Wei, 'China's anti-secession law and Hu Jintao's Taiwan policy', *Yale Journal of International Affairs* 5(1), (Winter 2010), pp. 112–127.

CPC government vows to adopt measures including economic exchange and cooperation and people-to-people exchange to maintain stability in the Taiwan Strait and develop Cross-Strait relations. Article 8 of the Anti-Secession Law specifies that 'the State Council and the Central Military Commission shall decide on and execute the non-peaceful means and other necessary measures' in case 'the "Taiwan independence" secessionist forces should act under any name or by any means to cause the fact of Taiwan's secession from China'.

In addition to the Anti-Secession Law aimed at the Chen administration, in March 2005, Hu Jintao [胡錦濤] set forth four points regarding mainland China's position toward the 'Taiwan issue'. They are: never sway in adhering to the 'One China' principle, never give up effort to seek peaceful reunification, never change the principle of placing hope on the Taiwan people, and never compromise in opposing the secessionist activities aimed at Taiwan independence.[14] In December 2008, after Chen stepped down, Hu further offered six basic proposals — the so-called Hu's Six Points — for peaceful evolution of Cross-Strait interactions when Cross-Strait relations became more predictable after May 2008. The six points are: first, to firmly abide by the 'One China' principle and enhance political mutual trust; second, to advance economic cooperation and promote common development; third, to promote Chinese culture and strengthen spiritual bonds; fourth, to strengthen two-way visits of people and expand exchanges in various circles; fifth, to safeguard national sovereignty and hold consultations on external affairs; and sixth, to end the state of hostility and reach a peace agreement.[15]

It is evident that Xi's strategic thinking toward Taiwan is very similar to that of Hu; that is, under the 'One China' principle and framework, mainland China and Taiwan can hold equal consultations concerning Cross-Strait political issues and make sensible arrangements to facilitate the gradual

---

[14] 'President Hu sets forth guidelines on Taiwan', *Xinhua News* (4 March 2005), available at: http://news.xinhuanet.com/english/2005-03/04/content_2653447.htm.

[15] Hu Jintao, 'Let us join hands to promote the peaceful development of Cross-Straits relations and strive with a united resolve for the great rejuvenation of the Chinese nation', speech at the Forum Marking the 30th Anniversary of the Issuance of the Message to Compatriots in Taiwan, 31 December 2008, available at: http://www.gwytb.gov.cn/en/Special/Hu/201103/t20110322_1794707.htm.

resolution of Cross-Strait political differences.[16] A similar statement issued by Zhang of the TAO in May 2013 is that the gradual resolution of Cross-Strait political differences could be achieved through dialogues that were based on the basis of 'One China', in pursuit of the common understanding, and to diminish the divergences.[17]

Xi spent 17 years, from 1985 to 2002, in Fujian Province and took up various party and government posts there. In 1999, he was promoted to the deputy secretary of the CPC provincial committee and acting governor of Fujian. He put a lot of emphasis on Fujian–Taiwan economic cooperation. He experienced the 1996 Taiwan Strait crisis, the 'special state-to-state theory' in 1999, and the first regime change in Taiwan. In facing the dramatic changes in Cross-Strait relations and Taiwan domestic politics, not only did he increase investment from Taiwan,[18] he also supervised the local military command. His exposure to the 'Taiwan issue' may have led him to view Cross-Strait relations with flexibility and pragmatism.[19]

The Xi administration, with the unchanged goals already set by its predecessors, appears to aim at establishing an irreversible political and legal framework to regulate Cross-Strait relations. While Beijing agrees with Taipei on the 'economics first, politics later' approach to bilateral issues, in its quest for closer economic ties with Taiwan, it could be losing its patience in seeing Taiwan's refusal to engage in Cross-Strait political dialogue or Taiwan's move away from ultimate reunification.

Even as Cross-Strait relations have improved saliently in recent years, both Hu and Xi have restated the need for reunification between mainland

---

[16]This claim was put forward by Hu in his report at the 18th Party Congress in November 2012.

[17]Tse-hung Lin, 'Zhang Zhijun: Yizhong Kuangjia Jiuer Gongshi jiangou liangan zhengzhi' [Zhang Zhijun: One-China framework and 1992 Consensus to construct Cross-Strait politics], *United Daily News* (23 May 2013), available at: http://udn.com/news/mainland/main1/7915989.shtml.

[18]Pang Li, 'Xi Jinping's 17 years in Fujian', *China.org.cn* (21 November 2012), available at: http://www.china.org.cn/china/2012-11/21/content_27179199.htm.

[19]Edward Wong and Jonathan Ansfield, 'China grooming deft politician as next leader', *The New York Times* (23 January 2011), available at: http://www.nytimes.com/2011/01/24/world/asia/24leader.html.

China and Taiwan. For instance, 'Enriching the Practice of "One Country, Two Systems" and Advancing China's Reunification' was the exact sub-headline in Hu's report at the 18th Party Congress in November 2012, which possibly denoted Hu's desire for a historic legacy in Cross-Strait affairs. Xi has often claimed that national reunification 'is not merely unification in form, but more importantly, a spiritual connection between the two sides'.[20]

Xi has promoted the 'Chinese Dream' unequivocally as the future philosophical (or political) foundation of mainland China's development.[21] In October 2013, he expressed his hope that this 'Chinese dream' would be fulfilled with a peaceful unification with Taiwan. He argued in the meantime that, 'it is the duty of the new CPC leadership to continue promoting the peaceful development of Cross-Strait ties and the peaceful reunification of the two sides of the Taiwan Strait'.[22] He also contended that the 'Chinese Dream' could be closely linked to the future of Taiwan, and should be shared by both sides of the Taiwan Strait — 'No power can separate us' (mainland China and Taiwan).[23] Further, he and other top leaders have advocated the concept of one family on both sides of the Taiwan Strait [liangan yijiaqin] and called for greater cooperation for the rejuvenation of the Chinese nation, which is viewed by Beijing as a positive development in the resolution of mutual differences in the future.[24] To echo this concept, Yu Zhengsheng [余正聲], chairman of the National Committee of Chinese People's Political Consultative Conference (CPPCC), claimed that mainland China would work to enhance political mutual trust and maintain favorable exchanges with Taiwan, on

---

[20] 'Xi steadfast on reunification', Xinhua News (26 September 2014), available at: http://news.xinhuanet.com/english/china/2014-09/26/c_133675240.htm.

[21] 'Xi: China confident of sustainable economic growth', The China Daily (3 November 2013), available at: http://www.chinadaily.com.cn/china/2013-11/03/content_17077146.htm.

[22] 'Xi meets KMT's Lien, stresses Cross-Strait ties', Xinhua News (25 February 2013), available at: http://news.xinhuanet.com/english/china/2013-02/25/c_132191064.htm.

[23] 'Commentary: Xi takes Cross-Strait ties new level', CCTV (22 February 2014), available at: http://english.cntv.cn/20140222/102920.shtml.

[24] 'Xi meets Taiwan politician ahead of APEC gathering', Xinhua News (6 October 2013), available at: http://news.xinhuanet.com/english/china/2013-10/06/c_132775470.htm.

the basis of adherence to the 1992 Consensus and opposing Taiwan's independence.[25]

According to Xi, under the framework of 'One China', Cross-Strait economic cooperation can be boosted jointly by Taiwan and mainland China. Strengthening Cross-Strait high-level dialogues and coordination and improving institutionalization in economic cooperation by picking up the pace in the negotiation over the ECFA thus become significant and necessary. The two sides should expand two-way investment, deepen cooperation in financial services, and accelerate industrial cooperation.[26] Besides, he emphasized that both the economies of the two sides of the Taiwan Strait belong to the Chinese nation. With the new economic development and cooperation in the Asia Pacific, the two sides could better deal with challenges only by cementing cooperation.[27]

In the eyes of Beijing leaders nowadays, economic exchange and cooperation are very essential for improving Cross-Strait relations. For example, Yu has vowed that mainland China would actively seek follow-up talks of the ECFA and adopt more measures to facilitate youth exchanges across the Strait, among others.[28] In May 2015, at the 10th Cross-Strait Economic, Trade and Culture Forum, commonly known as the KMT–CPC Forum [*guogong luntan*], Yu pointed out that the forum should continue its focus on welfare with exchanges of economic policy and industrial plans. He urged joint effort to help ordinary people, small and medium-sized enterprises as well as farmers and fishermen.[29]

At the same time, however, Xi has demonstrated a tough stance in dealing with the reunification issue. Knowing that the Cross-Strait political disputes

---

[25]'Mainland committed to peace, stability across Taiwan Strait', *Xinhua News* (27 January 2015), available at: http://news.xinhuanet.com/english/china/2015-01/27/c_133950749.htm; and 'Mainland committed to peace, stability across Taiwan Strait', *Xinhua News* (2 February 2016), available at: http://news.xinhuanet.com/english/2016-02/02/c_135068763.htm.

[26]'President Xi meets Taiwan politician', *Xinhua News* (8 April 2013), available at: http://news.xinhuanet.com/english/china/2013-04/08/c_132293193.htm.

[27]'Xi meets Taiwan politician ahead of APEC gathering'.

[28]'Mainland committed to peace, stability across Taiwan Strait'.

[29]Guo Yan, 'Cross-Strait economic forum held in Shanghai', *China Radio International* (4 May 2015), available at: http://english.cri.cn/12394/2015/05/04/2702s877127.htm.

can be gradually resolved, Xi has held resolutely in October 2013 that they 'cannot hand those problems down from generation to generation'.[30] In September 2014, for the first time, he openly highlighted the concept of 'One Country, Two Systems' in Beijing.[31] In March 2015, he contended that the 1992 Consensus was the foundation for Cross-Strait political trust, dialogue and consultation, and the development of future ties. According to Xi, mainland China's approach to Cross-Strait relations would be dictated by 'four resolutes' [*sige jianding*]: to resolutely pursue peaceful development; to resolutely adhere to the common political basis; to resolutely bring benefit to the people across the Taiwan Strait; and to resolutely join hands in bringing about national revitalization. Apparently, Xi asserted once again that Beijing would not alter its stance on the 1992 Consensus or the principle of 'One China' for the sake of Cross-Strait talks and cooperation.[32]

In March 2015, Xi maintained that 'the key factor deciding where the Cross-Strait ties goes is the development and progress of the Chinese mainland'. He also affirmed that it would 'trigger an earthquake and topple hills' if the 1992 Consensus — whose core has been based on the recognition that both mainland and Taiwan belong to 'one and the same China' — as the foundation and precondition of Cross-Strait talks was challenged or altered.[33] This has attracted lots of attention because he rarely expresses such an assertive view on Taiwan.

In July 2015, Xi signed the National Security Law which states that 'maintenance of national sovereignty and territorial integrity is a shared obligation of all the Chinese people, including compatriots from Hong

---

[30] 'Xi meets Taiwan politician ahead of APEC gathering'.

[31] 'Xi steadfast on reunification'.

[32] 'Xi's "four resolutes" on Cross-Strait ties: a message to DPP', *Want China Times* (11 March 2015), available at: http://www.wantchinatimes.com/news-subclass-cnt.aspx?id = 20150311000090&cid = 1101.

[33] 'Xi stresses Cross-Strait peaceful development, urges vigilance against Taiwan Independence', *Xinhua News* (4 March 2015), available at: http://news.xinhuanet.com/english/2015-03/04/c_134037908.htm. In the text of the Xinhua News article, the phrase 'trigger an earthquake and topple hills' cannot be found but it was included in CCTV news that day. See Ping-chung Sung and Su-mei Lu, 'Xi budianming xiang Lǜ hanhua: rentong yi Zhong' [Xi speaks loud to the green without identifying names: acknowledge One China], *China Times*, (5 March 2015), available at: http://www.chinatimes.com/newspapers/20150305000881-260301.

Kong, Macao and Taiwan'.[34] This clause did not receive consent from majority of the people in Taiwan.

In fact, beginning from late 2014, mainland China has undertaken some unilateral actions that were believed by Beijing leaders to meet the ultimate goal of national reunification. These unilateral actions will be introduced later. A possible explanation for that is: the CPC government, based on its own subjective understanding, has realized that the KMT government, despite having a steady majority following in the Legislative Yuan (LY) during the presidency of Ma, was incapable of implementing anything substantial for Cross-Strait ties. Its subjective understanding has been manifested by the KMT government's failure in Cross-Strait Trade-in-Services Agreement (TiSA) in spring 2014 and also by surprising yet unsuccessful charges brought against the MAC principal deputy minister Chang Hsien-yao [張顯耀] in August 2014.

What is worth scrutinizing as well is Beijing's political calculation of Taiwan's desire for participating in regional economic cooperation. It is a commonly acceptable argument in the KMT government that Taiwan's regional integration in the Asia Pacific will help Taiwan's economic performance; thus the potential benefits of Cross-Strait economic cooperation can persuade Taiwan's general public to support Cross-Strait economic and trade negotiations.[35] With that, Beijing might be facing a strategic dilemma. Helping Taiwan to become integrated in the region can become a double-edged sword, in the sense that assisting Taiwan can improve Beijing's image in Taiwan's society but reinforce 'Taiwan identity', either directly or indirectly, but in the international arena, the 'Taiwan identity' can be utilized as a useful and powerful tool for promoting Taiwan's independence. The CPC government's caution and reservation in Taiwan's international space are evident signs of this strategic dilemma.

---

[34] 'China adopts new law on national security', *Xinhua News* (1 July 2015), available at: http://news.xinhuanet.com/english/2015-07/01/c_134372812.htm; and 'China "rude" to include Taiwan in national security law: MAC', *Focus Taiwan* (1 July 2015), available at: http://focustaiwan.tw/news/aipl/201507010032.aspx.

[35] '2014 nian Boao Yazhou luntan–Xiao rongyu dongshizhang he Li Keqiang huimian' [The 2014 Boao Forum for Asia–Honorary Chairperson Siew meets with Li Keqiang], *The Cross-Strait Common Market Foundation* (10 April 2014), available at: http://www.crossstrait. org/?p=192.

Main Obstacles: Taiwan's Changing Political Environment

The CPC government's objectives and strategic thinking toward Taiwan are facing some salient resistance due to the complexity of Cross-Strait relations. Mainland China wants to garner the support of Taiwanese people by scores of economic and trade exchanges and agreements, some of which have been described as the 'yielding profits' strategy. Such a strategy is often interpreted as a soft measure to enhance Cross-Taiwan Strait ties toward peaceful unification. As former premier of the PRC Wen Jiabao [溫家寶] once elaborated in 2010, full consideration would be given to the different sizes of the economy and market conditions of the two sides of the Straits, as well as the interests of small and medium-sized businesses, ordinary people, and particularly farmers in Taiwan. He also said that Beijing would let the people of Taiwan benefit more from the ECFA.[36]

Nonetheless, some pro-independence parties and vacillating, or fearful, general public of Taiwan are watching every move taken by mainland China. Therefore, economic and trade exchanges and agreements between Taiwan and mainland China have triggered their concern and worry, particularly when the KMT government pushed the Cross-Strait TiSA full speed ahead at the LY in March 2014.[37]

A key factor shaping such a cautious attitude in Taiwan is the CPC government's unmovable objectives toward ultimate reunification with Taiwan. This is accompanied by the refusal to announce no use of force against Taiwan and by the relentless downgrading of the legal and political status of Taiwan in the international arena. People in Taiwan are not able to use the official title 'ROC' or 'Taiwan' at most major international occasions. They also resent being represented by a sovereign government that has no *de jure* and *de facto* rule over Taiwan. Starting from the last term of Lee, their frustration has been roused and amplified by the growth of 'Taiwan identity', by the independence appeals confronting a rising mainland Chinese regime during Chen's presidency, by the political and economic uncertainties and

---

[36] 'Premier Wen Jiabao meets the press (14 March 2010)', *China US Focus* (14 March 2010), available at: http://www.chinausfocus.com/library/government-resources/chinese-resources/remarks/premier-wen-jiabao-meets-the-press/.

[37] Kwei-Bo Huang, 'Beyond the Cross-Strait trade in services agreement: seeking a "2014 Consensus" for Taiwan', *Brookings Institution* (April 2014), available at: http://www.brookings.edu/research/opinions/2014/04/30-taiwan-economic-consensus-huang.

risks associated with the gradual expansion of Cross-Strait interactions promoted by Ma, as well as by the possible loss of sovereign and independent status that have been enjoyed by the people in Taiwan after the separation of the two sides of the Taiwan Strait. All these have led partially to a critical social protest against the TiSA in spring 2014, and landslide losses of the KMT both in the local elections at the end of 2014 and in the presidential and LY elections in January 2016.

In March 2014, the dubiousness of the negotiations and consequences of the TiSA and the ensuing Cross-Strait agreements resulted in the Sunflower Movement, namely large-scale protests initiated by anti-PRC protesters, prompting a strong awareness of the risks associated with the KMT's rapprochement policy and economic exchanges with mainland China after May 2008.

Despite the fact that DPP used very long legislative boycotts to delay the pass of the TiSA and that some protesters, including undergraduate and graduate students, illegally occupied the LY's chamber from 18 March to 10 April 2014 and broke into the headquarters of the Executive Yuan during 23–24 March of the same year, it was obvious that the appeals presented by the Sunflower Movement gained sympathy of the general public. The series of polls in the post-Sunflower Movement era show the following results: (1) about one-third of the interviewees thought it was fine to occupy the LY, while only less than one-fifth thought it was fine to break into the headquarters of the Executive Yuan; (2) more than half of the interviewees believed the consequence of the Sunflower Movement was positive; (3) the majority of the interviewees felt the voices of the younger generations were taken into consideration to a greater extent; (4) the younger generations tended to view national sovereignty more importantly than economic interests; and (5) the number of adherents to the KMT reduced while the number of DPP supporters increased.[38]

---

[38] See, for example, 'Lienhebao mindiao: shehui geng zhongshi nianqingren shengyin' [United Daily News poll: society thinks more highly of the voice of young people], *United Daily News* (18 March 2015), available at: http://udn.com/news/story/7776/772286; and Chih-Jou Jay Chen, 'Taiyanghua yundong gaibian le minzhong de zhengzhi taidu ma?' [Has the Sunflower Movement altered people's political attitudes?], paper presented at the 2015 Workshop on China's Impact, Institute of Sociology at the Academia Sinica, 16 October 2015.

During the Sunflower Movement, the 'legislate first, review second' approach was endorsed by the DPP. Some of the key protesters demanded the clause-by-clause review of the TiSA. It is evident that the political struggles within the KMT, mainly between Ma and LY speaker Wang Jin-pyng [王金平], a KMT member, weakened the KMT government's capacity to negotiate with the domestic constituencies over the TiSA and ensuing Cross-Strait agreements.

Former ROC vice president Vincent Siew [蕭萬長] discerned three major concerns of the people in Taiwan on the day of the retreat of the protesters as he was meeting PRC premier Li Keqiang [李克強] at the Boao Forum for Asia in 2014. The three major concerns are: first, complementary partnership between Taiwan and mainland China can decline into economic rivalry; second, Taiwan's access to mainland markets is restricted by trade barriers arising from huge differences in institutions and management between the two sides of the Strait; and third, Taiwan urgently needs to join the ongoing process of regional economic integration but is facing obstacles.[39] Li responded that mainland China was willing to offer Taiwan increased access to the former's markets, and even to open up economically for Taiwan before opening further to foreign countries. He added that closer economic ties between mainland China and Taiwan will create better conditions for Taiwan to join other regional trade pacts.[40]

Regardless of the results of Cross-Strait economic cooperation, as mentioned earlier, the KMT suffered greatly from a couple of elections since late 2014. In addition to the KMT government's mediocre domestic governance and political communication, the political configuration of Taiwan has begun to change after the Sunflower Movement. The pan-Blue vs. pan-Green competition in politics has been influenced by the rise of the third force, some of which detest 'China' and vow to struggle for Taiwan independence. Besides, it seems that the Taiwanese society was gradually losing self-confidence to confront mainland China.

---

[39] '2014 nian Boao Yazhou luntan–Siew rongyu dongshizhang he Li Keqiang Huimian' [The 2014 Boao Forum for Asia–Honorary Chairperson Siew met with Li Keqiang].

[40] 'Premier Li promotes Cross-Strait economic cooperation', *Xinhua News* (10 April 2014), available at: http://news.xinhuanet.com/english/china/2014-04/10/c_133253162.htm; and An Baijie and Zhao Yinan, 'Li stresses Cross-Straits harmony', *China Daily* (11 April 2014), available at: http://usa.chinadaily.com.cn/china/2014-04/11/content_17426801.htm.

The link between the gradual loss of self-confidence in Taiwan's society and the support for the Sunflower Movement needs to be examined more carefully. But it is highly possible that some of the people in Taiwan have sensed the rapid progress in mainland China and deeply worry about their own future,[41] thus generating a widespread mood of reluctance to accept the KMT government's policy for closer economic cooperation with mainland China. The TiSA and ensuing agreements to be negotiated between the two sides are sometimes viewed as a means of mainland China's economic statecraft on Taiwan. Then, the rising anti-Beijing sentiment triggered by Beijing's plan to recover Taiwan via military and non-military methods, has been treated as a hindrance to Taiwan's independence by certain political parties and civic groups which are against further Cross-Strait exchanges.

It is also worth noticing that the high participation of the young voters have an effect on those elections as well. The Sunflower Movement has inspired the younger generation to participate in public affairs and to monitor the government. Convincingly, most of them who have a strong Taiwan[ese] identity did not adhere to the KMT's campaign platform which include opening up Taiwan's market to mainland China at a pace the KMT would prefer.[42]

Within Taiwan, such new internal causes are affecting and altering the political structure of Cross-Strait relations, thus adding to the complexity of mainland China's contemporary economic policy toward Taiwan.

---

[41] 'Tai Xin Zhong Gang sidi Huaren huping, sheishi zuijinbu shehui?' [Evaluating one another among the ethnic Chinese in Taiwan, Singapore, China, and Hong Kong: whose society is the most advanced?], *Yuanjian* [Global View] (30 November 2015), available at: http://www.gvm.com.tw/webonly_content_7152.html. In this survey, Taiwan received seven lowest scores out of nine categories, including wealth distribution, administration, and parliamentary efficiency, from the lowest to the third lowest. The *Taipei Times* has the same argument. See 'Editorial: It's the economy, stupid', *Taipei Times* (3 December 2014), p. 8.

[42] In the 2016 elections, for example, nearly half of young voters were for the DPP, while the rest were more supportive of the People's First Party, not the KMT. See Stacy Hsu, 'Strong disapproval of Ma led to KMT's rout: survey', *Taipei Times* (3 December 2014), p. 1; and Christine Chou, 'Election results, polls align on Taiwan's presidential race: pollsters', *The China Post* (18 January 2016), available at: http://www.chinapost.com.tw/taiwan/national/presidential-election/2016/01/18/456374/Election-results.htm.

Actions (Policy Options)

In most cases, a government's action is chosen as a calculated solution to a strategic problem. Having touched upon mainland Chinese leaders' objectives and strategic thinking toward Taiwan and the associated main obstacles, this section delineates the actions of the Xi administration toward economic exchanges with Taiwan, and attempts to explain from a political perspective.

An important assumption that goes with this section is that the economic statecraft of mainland China carries considerable political meaning. In this regard, it is not easy to find direct quotations from the government and party documents of mainland China, but it can be inferred that economic cooperation and concessions made by Beijing have been aimed at performing vital political and united front functions in Taiwan and that mainland China's operatives would continue to build up its resources, and strengthen its capability to influence and shape Taiwan's political process and policy efforts toward peaceful unification without firing a shot.[43] Given the discreet and secretive nature of Beijing's united-front strategy, it is likely that, strictly speaking, lots of economic activities that cross the Taiwan Strait could be part of the CPC government's plan to intervene in Taiwan's internal affairs to achieve reunification. This has reminded some people of Hong Kong's relations with and economic dependence on mainland China after the handover in 1997.[44]

As stated in the '1979 Interim Provisions on Trade Relations with Taiwan of the PRC Ministry of Foreign Trade and Economic Cooperation', trade with Taiwan has been treated by Beijing as a special arrangement targeted at the people of Taiwan in the business and industrial sectors for the purpose

---

[43] Parris H. Chang, 'Beijing's strategy to "buy" Taiwan: coerced unification without firing a shot', *WorldTribune.com* (19 February 2014), available at: http://www.worldtribune.com/10-beijings-strategy-buy-taiwan-coerced-unification-without-firing-shot/.

[44] See, for example, Sonny Lo, 'The mainlandization and regionalization of Hong Kong: a triumph of convergence over divergence with mainland China', in Joseph Y. S. Cheng, ed., *The Hong Kong Special Administrative Region in Its First Decade* (Hong Kong: City University of Hong Kong Press, 2007), pp. 215–219; and Jong Wong, 'CEPT: a gift from Beijing?', in Yongnian Cheng and Chiew Ping Yew, eds., *Hong Kong under Chinese Rule: Economic Integration and Political Gridlock* (Singapore: World Scientific, 2013), pp. 21–34.

of ultimate national unification. In 1979, the Standing Committee of the National People's Congress issued a letter to 'Taiwan compatriots' and developed a range of policies toward Taiwan to boost Cross-Straits relations, promote trade and economic cooperation, encourage visits and enhance mutual trust between the two sides under the basic principle of peaceful reunification and 'One Country, Two Systems'. The PRC State Council enacted 'Regulations Encouraging Compatriots from Taiwan to Invest in the Mainland' in 1983 and passed the 'Provisions concerning the Encouragement of Protection of Investment by Compatriots from Taiwan' in 1988 which offered some preferential arrangements to Taiwan's entrepreneurs, followed by the creation of Taiwan Investment Zones in 1989 in some provinces close to Taiwan.

After both sides of the Taiwan Strait established unofficial ties in the early 1990s, conceivably guided by the same political strategy, the PRC State Council enacted the 'Law of the People's Republic of China on Protection of Investment by Compatriots from Taiwan' (PICT) and passed the 'Rules for the Implementation of the PICT' in 1994 and 1999, respectively. The same thread of thought is that, as instructed by the State Council, Fujian Province invented a Cross-Strait experimental basis for agricultural cooperation in 1996 in Zhangzhou, followed by a Cross-Strait experimental area for agricultural cooperation in 1997 in Fuzhou.

Between 2000 and 2008, there were sporadic actions taken by mainland China and Taiwan — mostly the KMT which was an opposition party and the Taiwan provincial organizations. For instance, the Western Taiwan Straits Economic Zone was proposed by the Fujian Province in 2004 to further integrate Taiwan with mainland China. Five major cities were identified to serve as windows of Cross-Strait exchanges: Zhangzhou, Quanzhou, Xiamen, Wenzhou, and Shantou. Partly due to the slowdown of Cross-Strait relations at that time, this pilot subregional economic project was included in the 11th Five-Year Plan of mainland China but it materialized only in 2011 when the State Council approved.

Looking at the positive side, the Lien–Hu meeting in April 2005 discussed the establishment of some mechanisms to promote economic cooperation and Cross-Strait ties. Examples include the opening of regular commercial flights and direct shipping, and the strengthening of investment and agricultural cooperation. After the meeting, Beijing lifted restrictions on mainland Chinese tourists to Taiwan, removed tariffs on more than 10 kinds of Taiwanese fruit, and allowed imports of six more fruit species, in the hope that a timely boost for Taiwan's economy could be delivered by the KMT–CPC platform. Immediately, the first 'Cross-Strait Agricultural Cooperation Exhibition and Taiwan Agricultural Products Trade Show', in collaboration with the Farmers' Association of Taiwan Province, was held in Shanghai in July 2005, and the pilot areas for Taiwan's peasants entrepreneurship began in 2006, in Zhangpu, Fujian and Qixia, Shandong, respectively. There are at least 29 Taiwan peasants' entrepreneurship parks now.[45]

Mainland China also launched a series of people-to-people exchange programs in such fields as education, religions, ethnic communities, business and industry, agriculture and fishery, and art and culture. These programs are sometimes seen as part of the united-front strategy of the CPC to place the hope of reunification on the people of Taiwan.[46] These people-to-people exchanges, along with economic measures and programs, serve to reinforce the ties between the two sides of the Taiwan Strait and to diminish the confrontational nature of Cross-Strait relations.

Beijing has managed to coax the DPP government and offered unilaterally preferential measures and exchange programs to the people of Taiwan. One of the most significant is the party-to-party exchanges with the KMT. These measures and programs that sometimes produced positive non-political results imposed great pressure on the DPP government, and could be used by Beijing to implement its Taiwan policy and promote propaganda targeted at both Taiwan and the international community.

The aftermath of the slowdown of Cross-Strait relations between 1996 and 2008, saw the conclusion of several economic and trade-related agreements between Taiwan and mainland China. In addition to the ECFA

---

[45] Jiun-Mei Tien, 'Zhongguo dalu "Taiwan nongmin chuangyeyuan" zhi fazhang xiankuan yu dui Taiwan zhi yingxiang' [The development of mainland China's Taiwan peasants' entrepreneurship parks and their impact on Taiwan], *Taiwan Yinhang Jikan* [Bank of Taiwan Quarterly], 62(4) (December 2011), pp. 113–139.

[46] This principle of 'laying the hope of national reunification to the people of Taiwan' was first raised in January 1979 in the 'Message for the Compatriots in Taiwan' by the Standing Committee of the National People's Congress, and has been re-emphasized by some CPC leaders on Taiwan.

(June 2010), the Cross-Strait Bilateral Investment Protection and Promotion Agreement (August 2012), and the TiSA (June 2013), both sides reached agreements on air transportation (November 2008), sea transportation (November 2008), postal service (November 2008), mainland tourists traveling to Taiwan (June 2008), financial cooperation (April 2009), intellectual property rights protection and cooperation (June 2010), bilateral cooperation in the standardization of technologies in the fields of LED lighting, photovoltaics and flat-screen monitors (June 2011), as well as the avoidance of double taxation and improvement in cooperation on tax operations (August 2015). Cross-Strait memorandums of understanding (MOUs) on cooperation related to the supervision of banking, securities, futures, and insurance were also signed in December 2009.

Although these agreements and MOUs address the economic interests and general welfare of people on both sides of the Taiwan Strait without touching on sovereignty issues,[47] the ECFA signed in June 2010 still represents both opportunities and challenges for Taiwan, and can be somewhat political in nature. It can surely boost Taiwan's economic growth and Cross-Strait economic interflows. However, certain facts — such as a huge increase in the approved foreign direct investment from mainland China to Taiwan during 2010–2014, and a high trade dependence rate on mainland China and Hong Kong which reached its peak during the second term of Chen's presidency (a little bit over 40%) — show that the ECFA may enlarge Taiwan's economic overdependence on mainland China and increase the hollowing-out of Taiwan's industries. All these could weaken Taiwan's capacity to act. Beijing seeks national reunification and will use attractive economic policies to woo Taiwan. Future Cross-Strait relations will be problematic if the people of Taiwan do not believe that the ECFA would benefit Taiwan's economy in general. Moreover, the deepening of Cross-Strait economic relations may lead the people of Taiwan to deliberate why mainland China is willing to develop economic cooperation with Taiwan but is reluctant to let Taiwan launch bilateral free trade negotiations

---

[47] 'Cross-strait Relations', *The Republic of China Yearbook 2015* (Taipei: R.O.C. Executive Yuan, 2016), available at: http://www.ey.gov.tw/en/cp.aspx?n=A6407797E00AD99E.

with others.[48] In the eyes of the CPC leaders and officials, as PRC foreign minister Wang Yi [王毅] claimed in September 2013, gradual integration between Taiwan and mainland China 'through two-way interactions and cooperation will lead to ultimate reunification'.[49]

Mainland China appears willing to grant some economic concessions during negotiations with Taiwan under the ECFA, in the hope that all concessions it has made would enhance Cross-Strait ties and pave the way for ultimate peaceful unification. Examples include the application of the 'first among equals' policy to Taiwanese businesses in mainland China since the Jiang Zemin [江澤民] period, as well as the 'yielding profits' strategy on Taiwan in Cross-Strait economic and trade-related agreements. The political scheme of Beijing behind the scene is very clear. Beijing's pursuit of national unification is by tempting the people of Taiwan with economic benefits and also with the slogan 'both sides of one family'. Beijing is also indicating a grave future in Cross-Strait relations ('an earthquake will be triggered and the hills will topple') should the 1992 Consensus no longer exists as the political foundation for the two sides.

In June 2014, two months after the Sunflower Movement, Zhang of the TAO visited Taiwan for the second meeting between the heads of Cross-Strait affairs. He also traveled to the southern part of Taiwan to meet various groups of people to allay the concerns of some people in Taiwan who are opposed to further Cross-Strait economic cooperation. He also met with Chen Chu [陳菊], an important DPP member and mayor of Kaohsiung, who has won every Kaohsiung mayor elections since 2006. Furthermore, an unverified report by *Reuters* on 26 November 2014 revealed how the united-front agencies of the CPC viewed economic exchanges between Taiwan and mainland China as a way to fulfill the 'Chinese dream' and make reunification a reality. By mitigating investment problems and settling legal disputes

[48] Kwei-Bo Huang, 'In pursuit of gradual stabilization and peace dividends: cross-Taiwan Strait relations and their influence on the Asia Pacific', *Maryland Series in Contemporary Asian Studies* 2011(3), pp. 41–43, available at: http://digitalcommons.law.umaryland. edu/mscas/vol2011/iss3/1.

[49] Wang Yi, 'Toward a new model of major country relations between China and the United States', speech at the Brookings Institution, Washington, DC, 20 September 2013, available at: http://www.fmprc.gov.cn/mfa_eng/wjb_663304/wjbz_663308/2461_663310/t1078768. shtml>.

for resident Taiwanese, these agencies can create a more friendly business environment to promote the CPC government's unification policy.[50]

In addition to mainland China's economic united-front strategy, it was often argued that mainland China would like to undertake those measures to court Taiwan's capital because the success of its economic reform and development would reinforce the CPC's legitimacy.[51] By now, this argument has lost some ground largely because mainland China has the capacity to attract a great deal of capital investment from a wide range of countries.

While negotiating with Taiwan over the other pacts, Beijing sometimes raised its tone by reiterating that any delay in the implementation of the TiSA could make it difficult for the two sides to secure a trade-in-goods deal on schedule.[52] Zhang of the TAO held that it was unrealistic to deal only with economic issues while ignoring political ones.[53] Noticeably, mainland China's two-tier policy toward Taiwan — advancing economic ties while pressing more for political contacts and ultimate reunification — has been conducted in a more delicate and concrete way. By being delicate and concrete in dealing with Taiwan, mainland China appears to place the hope of reunification on the people of Taiwan, while strengthening its own comprehensive power in order to undertake unilateral actions that facilitate Cross-Strait exchanges or caution against any possible move of Taiwan.

To better illustrate this point, the following paragraphs will touch upon four issues: mainlanders travelling to Taiwan, mainland Chinese passengers transiting Taiwan, the Cross-Strait trade-in-goods agreement, as well as participation of both sides of the Taiwan Strait in regional economic cooperation and integration.

---

[50]Yimou Lee and Faith Hung, 'Special report: how China's shadowy agency is working to absorb Taiwan', *Reuters* (26 November 2014), available at: http://www.reuters.com/article/us-taiwan-china-special-report-idUSKCN0JB01T20141127.

[51]Yu-shan Wu, 'Mainland China's economic policy toward Taiwan', in Bih-jaw Lin and James T. Myers, eds., *Contemporary China in the Post-Cold War Era* (Columbia, South Carolina: University of South Carolina Press, 1996), pp. 393–412.

[52]'Two Cross-Strait pacts progressing simultaneously: Chinese official', *Focus Taiwan* (27 October 2013), available at: http://focustaiwan.tw/news/aall/201310270018.aspx.

[53]'First Cross-Strait peace forum pools political wisdom', *Xinhua News* (11 October 2013), available at: http://news.xinhuanet.com/english/china/2013-10/11/c_132789521.htm.

There were 4.14 million mainlanders touring in Taiwan in 2015, with a net increase of 196,000 from 2014, accounting for about 40% of visitor arrivals to Taiwan. Meanwhile, foreign visitor arrivals to Taiwan reached 10.43 million. Individual travelers from mainland China accounted for about 30% of the volume of mainland Chinese tourists visiting Taiwan in 2015. These tourists' high spending directly boosted the domestic economy via hotels, restaurants, local tour operators, and souvenir and gift-related businesses. A speculation in Taiwan is that mainland Chinese visitors to Taiwan would drop 30% between 20 March and 30 June 2016 due to emerging political uncertainties in the Taiwan Strait.[54] If the report is true that Beijing has begun to enforce policies that restrict a certain number of mainland Chinese tourists from travelling in Taiwan, revenue in certain sectors will be affected. Such a preemptive policy appears to be a subtle warning against any substantial changes under the new government of the DPP.[55]

The issue regarding mainland Chinese passengers transiting Taiwan was complicated as Beijing insisted on the optimization of Cross-Strait air routes. Taiwan wanted to separate these two issues, but was willing to discuss the air routes specified in the Cross-Strait Agreement on Air Transportation (November 2008) and the Cross-Strait Supplementary Agreement on Air Transportation (April 2009). During negotiations in 2008, both parties decided to open a two-way direct flight route in the northern lane and in the southern lane across the Taiwan Strait respectively, and set up a direct handover procedure between the air traffic control departments on either side across the Strait. During negotiations in 2009, both parties decided to open another two-way direct air route in the northbound lane and in the southbound lane, separately.

For Taiwan, the opening of mainlanders transiting through Taiwan would profit Taiwan-based airline companies and revive Taiwan's major airport,

[54]Claudia Liu and Y.F. Low, 'Drop in tourist arrivals from China a political issue: President Ma', *Focus Taiwan* (19 April 2016), available at: http://focustaiwan.tw/news/acs/201604190011.aspx.
[55]Elizabeth Shim, 'China restricting tourism to Taiwan after elections', *United Press International* (23 February 2016), available at: http://www.upi.com/Top_News/World-News/2016/02/23/China-restricting-tourism-to-Taiwan-after-elections/1471456255035/.

Taoyuan Airport, by an increased number of passengers through Taiwan. At the Ma–Xi meeting in November 2015, when Ma raised this transit issue again, he finally received a small but positive response from the Xi administration in early January 2016; that is, mainland China announced that, as a pilot plan effective on 1 February 2016, mainland Chinese passengers from Chongqing, Nanchang, and Kunming were allowed to make a transit stop. Only hundreds of mainland Chinese tourists stopped over in Taiwan due to the lack of effective publicity and also Beijing's incremental and precautious way of implementing this pilot plan in late April 2016. Although mainland China seems unwilling to make more compromise, Taiwan plans to ask Beijing to adhere to a fully open policy at an upcoming Cross-Strait air transportation meeting.[56]

The Cross-Strait trade-in-goods agreement was scheduled for negotiations right after negotiations over the TiSA ended in 2013. But the pace of negotiations slowed down due to Taiwan's large-scale social protest against the TiSA in spring 2014 and the ensuing promise of the KMT government that nothing would be signed until the LY in Taipei had passed a draft Cross-Strait agreement oversight act.

Taiwan and mainland China completed 12 rounds of negotiations on this agreement (the 12th round was held in November 2015), but the 13th round stalled when Taiwan endeavored to receive the zero-tariff status for its flat panel, machine tool, automobile, and petrochemical sectors — which have been seen as critical ones by mainland China — and turned down mainland China's request to lift Taiwan's ban on 615 categories of mainland Chinese farm produce, including those Taiwan does not grow, or grows little, and those Taiwan has allowed foreign imports under the framework of the World Trade Organization (WTO). A bilateral preparatory meeting was held in January 2016, but some of the issues still remain unresolved, according to Taipei.[57]

---

[56]Pei-fen Zhang, 'Lüke zhongzhuan, Huahang danyue lankeliang jin 200 ming' [Mainland Chinese passengers transiting, China Airlines touts for close to 200 a single month], *China Times* (26 April 2016), available at: http://www.chinatimes.com/newspapers/20160426000155-260204.

[57]'Goods trade agreement talks not concluded: economics minister', *Radio Taiwan International* (7 March 2016), available at: http://english.rti.org.tw/m/news/?recordId=43430.

In mid-March 2016, president of the ARATS Chen Deming [陳德銘] said that both sides could 'take a nap' since the oversight act bill has not been passed by Taiwan's LY. He also maintained that, because both sides of the Strait have recognized the 'One China' principle — not under a 'state-to-state' framework — mainland China would see people of Taiwan as 'one of us' and continue to show goodwill to Taiwan at various Cross-Strait meetings.[58]

Taiwan's and mainland China's participation in regional economic cooperation and integration is politically sensitive for the two sides. Taiwan has always felt highly restrained in this matter, regardless of the ruling parties. During Chen's presidency between May 2000 and May 2008, Taiwan succeeded in joining the WTO in January 2002, under the title of Separate Customs Territory of Taiwan, Penghu, Kinmen, and Matsu (TPKM). This achievement was based mainly on the previous effort of the Lee administration that submitted the accession package in mid-1999. Progress was also made in the Organization for Economic Cooperation and Development (OECD). In December 2001, Taiwan as an official observer was permitted to participate in the Competition Law and Policy Committee of the OECD, under the title of 'Chinese Taipei'. Then, Taiwan was able to participate in two more OECD committees, the Steel Committee (as an official observer) and the Fisheries Committee (as a project observer) in October 2005 and May 2006, respectively.

Under the Asia-Pacific Economic Cooperation (APEC) framework, Taiwan is not allowed to hold any APEC ministerial meetings or summits. Taiwan could simply send to the APEC Leaders' Summits the president of the LY, incumbent or former officials of the ministerial level, or business leaders. Within the DPP government, former Vice President Li Yuan-zu [李元簇] and former vice premier Tsai Ing-wen were some potential candidates who acted as special envoys of Chen Shui-bian. Beijing rejected these candidates but did not identify the reason(s) clearly, probably due to sour Cross-Strait relations and the pro-independence attitude of the DPP government.

---

[58]Li-Chuan Wang and Cheng-Chung Lin, 'Chen Deming: Lu yizhidui Tai shishanyi jingdeng Cainushi huiying' [Chen Deming: Mainland keeps showing goodwill to Taiwan and waits for Madam Tsai's response], *United Daily News* (24 March 2016), available at: http://url-site.com/chendeming_on_tsai.

An official and founding member of the Asian Development Bank (ADB), Taiwan has been forced to change its official title since 1986 from the Republic of China to 'Taipei, China'. The KMT and the DPP governments have protested in vain at each annual meeting.

During Ma's era, from May 2008 to May 2016, even though Taiwan, again under the title of Chinese Taipei, has been able to participate in UN specialized agencies such as the World Health Assembly (WHA, an organ of the World Health Organization) as an observer since May 2009 and in the Assembly of the International Civil Aviation Organization (ICAO) as a guest of the President of the ICAO Council since September 2013, and even though Taiwan secured economic cooperation deals with New Zealand and Singapore respectively in 2013, it is obvious that mainland China has remained ambiguous about Taiwan's economic cooperation agreements with its major trade partners in the Asia-Pacific. Taiwan encountered an insurmountable obstacle and failed to join most emerging bilateral and multilateral economic cooperation and integration in a meaningful way. This insurmountable obstacle comes mainly from the general political and strategic thinking in mainland China that Taiwan's meaningful participation in major international organizations is an internal affair of China, and that such participation may be exploited by major political parties of Taiwan and result in 'two Chinas' (when the KMT is in power) or 'One China, One Taiwan' (when the DPP gains power). Beijing, knowing Taipei's longing for greater international space and Taiwan's fear of being marginalized in regional economic cooperation, would be willing to confront this tough issue as long as its 'One China' principle can remain intact and Taipei gives a heads-up to Beijing before it bids for meaningful participation in international activities. So far, mainland China has been exerting its influence to discourage Taiwan's major trade partners from concluding an economic cooperation agreement with Taiwan.[59]

At the closed-door meeting between Ma and Xi in November 2015, Taiwan expressed its strong interest in applying for Trans-Pacific Partnership

---

[59]Li Jing, 'Beijing meddling in Taiwan bids to forge trade pacts, minister claims', *The South China Morning Post* (6 October 2014), available at: http://www.scmp.com/news/china/article/1610237/beijing-meddling-taiwan-bids-forge-trade-pacts-minister-claims.

(TPP) membership and its wish to participate in the Regional Comprehensive Economic Partnership (RCEP).[60] Moreover, Taiwan emphasized that both parties should participate in regional economic cooperation in a way that strengthens Cross-Strait economic and trade ties.[61] Without news of Xi's reply at this meeting, one can simply speculate that mainland China would insist that Chinese people on both sides of the Taiwan Strait deepen the mutually beneficial exchange and cooperation by upholding the 'One China' principle as the political foundation. The meetings (between the heads of Cross-Strait affairs in Taiwan and mainland China) which began in February 2014 continued on a regular basis, with a few dialogues on Taiwan's participation in regional economic cooperation and integration. It seems that Taiwan has the urgency to discuss this issue, particularly when the TPP has concluded its negotiations in early 2016. At the fourth meeting in October 2015, the most recent statement that was mutually agreeable to both sides of the Taiwan Strait is that Cross-Strait economic and trade cooperation and participation in regional economic integration should be complementary and promoted continuously.[62]

To date, how to use the ECFA as a bridge for Taiwan's participation in the RCEP is still indefinite because mainland China's official stance is not indicated. Despite Taiwan's high level of interest, there has been no concrete deed on the mainland Chinese side to foster both parties' participation in the RCEP.

In addition to the RCEP, the China factor also accounts for Taiwan's strong interest in membership of the TPP. Neither Taiwan nor mainland China has joined TPP negotiations before the initial agreement was reached

---

[60]The TPP with 12 members is now led by the United States, but the United States has not participated in the RCEP.

[61]'Full text of ROC President Ma Ying-jeou's remarks in meeting with mainland Chinese leader Xi Jinping', *Mainland Affairs Council of the Executive Yuan New Release* (9 November 2015), available at: http://www.mac.gov.tw/ct.asp?xItem=113323&ctNode=6337&mp=3&xq_xCat=2015.

[62]'The fourth meeting between heads of Cross-Strait competent authorities held in Guangzhou; both sides adhere to consolidating "institutionalized Cross-Strait negotiations" and "official interaction" mechanisms based on the "1992 Consensus" to advance towards truly stable Cross-Strait relations', *Mainland Affairs Council of the Executive Yuan New Release* no. 54 (14 October 2015), available at: http://www.mac.gov.tw/ct.asp?xItem=113156&ctNode=6337&mp=3&xq_xCat=2015.

among the current 12 parties in February 2016. Regardless of mainland China's intent regarding TPP membership in the future, it will not wish to see Taiwan join the TPP while it has not participated. It is very possible that Taiwan's hope to participate in the TPP will hinge partially on the political attitude of mainland China. Despite the fact that Kin Moy, the United States deputy assistant Secretary of State, clearly stated in March 2014 that the United States welcomed Taiwan's interest in the TPP,[63] and that Daniel R. Russel, the United States assistant Secretary of State, affirmed in April 2014 that the United States supported Taiwan 'to participate in the international community in a manner befitting a large economy and modern society with a great deal to contribute',[64] the 'China factor' obviously remains if mainland China refers to the 'One China' principle that excludes Taiwan from an equal status with mainland China and tries to sway some of the original TPP members that have good relations with it.

Recently, Taiwan's bid for the Beijing-led Asian Infrastructure Investment Bank (AIIB) has manifested that Cross-Strait financial cooperation has been built on sand. Not only did Beijing, along with its allies in the AIIB, reject Taiwan's bid submitted in late March 2015 to become a founding member, it also changed its tone about this issue. Mainland China welcomed Taiwan to participate in the AIIB under an appropriate name at the onset of Taiwan's bid.[65] The Ma administration was willing to join the AIIB in the capacity of an ADB member, as promulgated in the Article 3, Paragraph 2 of the AIIB's 'Articles of Agreement'. After the landslide loss of the KMT in the presidential and legislative elections in January 2016, nevertheless, mainland China has toughened its position and declared in April 2016 that Taiwan is 'not sovereign or not responsible for the conduct of its

---

[63]Kin Moy, 'The promise of the Taiwan Relations Act', testimony before the US House Foreign Affairs Committee, Washington, DC, 14 March 2014, available at: http://www.state.gov/p/eap/rls/rm/2014/03/223461.htm.

[64]Daniel R. Russel, 'Evaluating US policy on Taiwan on the 35th anniversary of the Taiwan Relations Act', testimony before the Subcommittee on East Asian and Pacific Affairs of the US Senate Committee on Foreign Relations, Washington, DC, 3 April 2014, available at: http://www.state.gov/p/eap/rls/rm/2014/04/224350.htm.

[65]Austin Ramzy, 'Taiwan's bid to join China-led development bank hits early snags', *The New York Times* (1 April 2015), available at: http://sinosphere.blogs.nytimes.com/2015/04/01/taiwans-bid-to-join-china-led-development-bank-hits-early-snags/.

international relations' and is supposed to follow the case of Hong Kong whose request was sent to the Ministry of Finance in Beijing. As always, mainland China wants to cause no problems with the appearance of 'Two Chinas' or 'One China, One Taiwan' in this case.[66] Besides, mainland China does not want to make Taiwan's accession to the AIIB as a gift to Tsai and her DPP government.

Conclusion

The nature of Cross-Strait economic interactions is both economic and political. The strategic thinking of mainland China has always centered on 'One China', regardless of various interpretations provided by concerned parties. The goals of mainland China include the maintenance of legitimacy and ruling basis, the prevention of the United States' hegemonic dominance and the revival of Japanese militarism, as well as the ultimate reunification of China. The more feasible policy options range from a threat of the use of force to a profit-yielding approach that could garner more support of the people in Taiwan. Between both lies political rhetoric pressure either on Taiwan's economic interactions with mainland China or on Taiwan's very limited international space.

Through ups and downs in Cross-Strait relations, both sides have exercised obvious self-restraint to minimize the outbreak of armed conflicts in the Taiwan Strait. In addition, for mainland China, since the late 1970s, it has tried to use various economic means, such as the ECFA, to draw Taiwan to its side. The pursuit of national reunification has appeared to receive overwhelming consideration. Economically, Taiwan has become much more dependent on mainland China than it had been in the past. Politically, Taiwan has not moved closer to mainland China. Some non-political Cross-Strait differences may be resolved gradually and peacefully, but problems will

---

[66]Beijing wants to refer to Article 3, Paragraph 3 of the AIIB's 'Articles of Agreement' to define Taiwan as a non-sovereign applicant. For details, see Yuan-ming Chiao, 'AIIB membership not a "domestic issue": MAC', *The China Post* (23 October 2015), available at: http://www.chinapost.com.tw/taiwan/china-taiwan-relations/2015/10/23/449047/AIIB-membership.htm, and Yuan-ming Chiao, 'Taiwan AIIB member bid must go through PRC ministry: China', *The China Post* (10 April 2016), available at: http://www.chinapost.com.tw/taiwan/national/national-news/2016/04/10/463044/Taiwan-AIIB.htm.

arise once the notion of 'One China' or 'One China, respective interpretations' as the foundation for bilateral communication is specified further. The current state of ambiguity has helped both sides of the Strait to achieve something and avoid many unsurmountable political barriers.

Mainland China's ulterior motives in its two-tier policy toward Taiwan to achieve national reunification through soft approaches are becoming more evident. Taiwan understands why mainland China willingly applies political ambiguity in Cross-Strait contacts while working eagerly on economic means to keep Taiwan within its reach. Taiwan's internal constraints: rising domestic opposition against closer economic ties with mainland China and growing Taiwanese frustration stemming from failure to expand international space have prevented mainland China from realizing national unification at a pace it has preferred. In the near future, whether mainland China can be patient enough to maneuver well in a complicated relationship with Taiwan, both economically–politically and internally–externally driven, remains to be seen.

Chapter 2

China's Use of Economic Tools in Its Human Rights Disputes with the EU

Reuben Wong

Economic diplomacy can be defined, following David Baldwin, as 'the use of economic means by a state to achieve its interests and goals'.[1] It is state-craft that uses a range of economic tools to achieve foreign policy ends. By this definition, China's economic diplomacy and use of economic tools since its opening in 1978 and especially after the EU–China Partnership and Cooperation Agreement (PCA) was signed with the EU's predecessor, the European Communities (EC) in 1985, has conventionally been viewed in Europe as mercantilist, highly strategic, and very effective at breaking down EU unity through 'divide-and-rule' tactics.[2] Bonnie Glaser has suggested that China's use of economic diplomacy has become increasingly

---

[1]David A. Baldwin, *Economic Statecraft* (Princeton, NJ: Princeton University Press, 1985), p. 8.

[2]John Fox and François Godement, *A Power Audit of EU–China Relations* (London: European Council on Foreign Relations, 2009); Reuben Wong, 'Towards a common European policy on China?: Economic, diplomatic and human rights trends since 1985', *Current Politics and Economics of Asia* 17(1), (2008), pp. 155–182; Katinka Barysch, Charles Grant, and Mark Leonard, *Embracing the Dragon: The EU's Partnership with China* (London: Centre for European Reform, 2005); Richard Grant, ed., *The European Union and China: A European Strategy for the Twenty-First Century* (London: Routledge/RIIA, 1995); Michelle Leskovska, '*The Politics of Chinese Investments in the European Union during the Financial Crisis*', Master's thesis, National University of Singapore, 2013.

sophisticated and worrying.[3] There is evidence of this in the September 2010 incident when China blocked shipments of rare earth minerals to Japan.

Human rights monitoring is a sensitive and highly visible component of the political dialogue between China and the EU.[4] The EU, which is primarily dominated by liberal democracies like France and Germany, has found it important to propound human rights as 'an appealing way to legitimize power' primarily in the field of individual political and civil rights and as a contribution to human dignity.[5] Nevertheless, 'human rights' monitoring has been a major theme of China–EU relations only since the Tiananmen Square crackdown in June 1989.[6] Until the end of the Cold War, few member states made human rights a major plank in their bilateral relations with China apart from the Netherlands, Denmark, and Sweden.[7] The Tiananmen incident subsequently politicized the EU's approach to economic relations with China and signaled the convergence of economic and human rights diplomacy.[8] The imposition of sanctions in light of China's human rights violations and United Nations Commission on Human Rights (UNCHR) issues in EC–China relations shifted much of the discussions related to China to the European Council and Common Foreign and Security Policy (CFSP) structures.

In the field of human rights, Chinese diplomacy has undergone a steep learning curve to a situation today where it uses its economic heft and political influence to silence, reduce, or fend off criticisms of its human rights record by European actors — the European Parliament (EP), member states,

---

[3]Bonnie Glaser, 'China's coercive economic diplomacy: A new and worrying trend', *Center for Strategic and International Studies* (6 August 2012), available at: http://csis.org/publication/chinas-coercive-economic-diplomacy-new-and-worrying-trend.

[4]D. Forsythe, *Human Rights in International Relations* (Cambridge: Cambridge University Press, 2012), p. 10.

[5]*Ibid.*

[6]Commission of the European Communities (2004). *The EU's China Policy*, 22 June.

[7]Rosemary Foot, *Rights Beyond Borders: The Global Community and the Struggle over Human Rights in China* (Oxford: Oxford University Press, 2000), p. 48.

[8]For example, the Commission which had hitherto refrained from political comments, issued a statement expressing 'consternation' and 'shock' at the 'brutal suppression' in Beijing, and cancelled foreign trade minister Zheng Tuobin's scheduled visit to Brussels. See D. Shambaugh, *China and Europe 1949–1995* (London: Contemporary China Institute, SOAS, 1996), p. 11.

the European Commission, civil society, non-governmental organizations (NGOs) among others. I would argue that China adopts a positive form of economic diplomacy that offers commercial incentives.[9] It focuses on politically significant nations to help prevent a unified Western front, and rallies developing countries to defeat Western censure of Chinese human rights abuses.[10] Since the late-1990s, China has changed its strategic doctrine and begun to use economic diplomacy as a coercive tool. After 10 years or so of a policy based primarily on economic carrots, China has begun to show a willingness to use economic diplomacy for coercive means.

What is even more interesting is that China has developed its own human rights diplomacy to counter Western (mainly European and American) attempts to highlight and embarrass its human rights record. Indeed, China has turned from being a *reactive* target of human rights (after the 1989 Tiananmen incident), to being *proactive* in promoting its own vision of human rights, and using diplomatic and economic tools to deflect or attack European attempts to put China in a corner. At the same time, the EU — both as a whole and as individual member states — has found itself faced with the 'classic dilemma in soft law decisions', namely the extent to which human rights issues should be pushed for when physical and economic security are direct trade-offs.[11]

The second section traces the evolution of China's reactions to human rights diplomacy from the EU and its member states; the third section analyses the rise of Beijing's own human rights diplomacy in its relations with the EU.

China as Reactive Target to EU Human Rights Hectoring (1989 to 1997)

The years immediately before 1989 were promising, both politically and economically, for China and the European Communities (the precursor to

---

[9]Michael Mastanduno, 'Economic statecraft, interdependence, and national security: Agendas for research', *Security Studies* 9, no. 1–2 (1999), pp. 288–316.

[10]Ming Wan, *Human Rights in Chinese Foreign Relations: Defining and Defending National Interests* (Pennsylvania: University of Pennsylvania Press, 2001), available at: http://www.upenn.edu/pennpress/book/13504.html.

[11]D. Forsythe, *Human Rights in International Relations.*

the EU). First, diplomatic relations had been established in 1975. This was followed by the first bilateral trade agreement in 1978 and a Trade and Cooperation Agreement in 1985 (still in force). Additionally, an EC Delegation was established in Beijing in 1988.

However, the political goodwill (albeit not the economic interactions) was derailed after the EC imposed common political and economic sanctions following the Tiananmen massacre in Beijing on 4 June 1989. In the initial years following Tiananmen, China found itself in both a defensive and reactive position in relation to Europe. Many of the student leaders had sought exile in Western Europe; the June 1989 Madrid summit had imposed 10 sanctions on China (including an arms embargo, which is still in place), and the picture of China as a major abuser of human rights was etched firmly in the international community's imagination.[12]

China attempted to take the initiative to change these negative perceptions. For example, Beijing hosted the World Women's Rights Conference in 1995. The conference was the largest event which the United Nations had ever organized at that point in time and saw 189 UN member states unanimously agree on the Beijing Platform for Action (BPFA). But most of the decade saw Chinese leaders and officials trying very hard to shake off the stigma of Tiananmen. Most high-level visits to Europe were marked by demonstrations organized by Chinese dissidents and European human rights NGOs. These groups constantly reminded the European general public and leaders of the lives lost in Tiananmen, ongoing human rights issues in Tibet, and problems in Chinese society over freedom of speech and expression. This period was also marked by serious conceptual differences between Chinese and European definitions and perspectives on human rights, in terms of cultural and historical applicability and relevance to non-Western and Chinese contexts.[13] Forsythe has posited that international relations can be viewed as a clash of civilizations in this context — dominant

---

[12]Some student exiles were even given a 'starring' place in the 1989 Bastille Day parade and celebrations in Paris on 14 July 1989. See Rosemary Foot, *Rights Beyond Borders*, p. 117

[13]Wai Ting, '*Human Rights and EU–China Relations*', in Roland Vogt, ed., *Europe and China: Strategic Partners or Rivals?* (Hong Kong: Hong Kong University Press, 2012), p. 124.

international norms propounded by international organizations 'reflect to a large extent the values of the most powerful members of the international community'.[14]

Indeed, China joined in the 'Asian values' debate led by Singapore and Malaysia in the 1990s, when Asian countries contested the universality of human rights and suggested that development should take precedence over civil and political rights. From their perspective, Asia was simply being 'faithful to its own system of philosophical and political priorities'.[15] The high-water mark in this debate was the 1993 Bangkok Declaration, released ahead of the 1993 Vienna Declaration, in which the Asian states laid claim to cultural relativity and developmental priorities.[16] Singapore's then-foreign minister Wong Kan Seng had warned that 'universal recognition of the ideal of human rights can be harmful if universalism is used to deny or mask the reality of diversity'.[17] Similarly, China emphasized the need to take into account regional diversity in the human rights propositions, even asserting that 'individuals must put the states' rights before their own'.[18]

Substantively, the 'Asian' conception of human rights and privileges promotes economic and social rights, rather than political and civil rights. In contrast, the 1950 European Convention of Human Rights and Fundamental Freedoms, had focused on 'fundamental civil and political rights', with the former including property rights and rights to education.[19] The subsequent European Social Charter addressing social and economic rights were negotiated almost as an addendum rather than an essential, yet notwithstanding this — coupled with the 1986 Convention for the Prevention of Torture and the 1995 Framework Convention for the Protection of National Minorities — the 1950 Convention remains the 'principal achievement of

---

[14]Forsythe, *Human Rights in International Relations*, p. 9.

[15]Amartya Sen, 'Human rights and Asian values', *New Republic* (14 July 1997), pp. 33–40.

[16]Jack Donnelly, 'Cultural relativism and universal human rights'. *Human Rights Quarterly*, 6(4), (1984): pp. 400–419; Bilahari Kausikan, 'Asia's different standard'. *Foreign Policy*, 92, (1993): pp. 24–41; Fareed Zakaria, 'A Conversation with Lee Kuan Yew'. *Foreign Affairs*, 73(2), (1994): pp. 109–126.

[17]Amartya Sen, 'Human rights and Asian values'.

[18]*Ibid.*

[19]Forsythe, *Human Rights in International Relations*, p. 122.

the CE [Council of Europe]'.[20] These normative and substantive differences between Chinese and European conceptions of human rights have led most people in China to believe that the term 'human rights' was 'merely a Western notion created to serve as an instrument to intervene in China's internal affairs'.[21] The different understandings of 'human rights' were politicized to resist perceived Western notions and implicit policy demands on what should or should not characterize Chinese society. At the heart of this were the conflicting perspectives of 'state sovereignty' as opposed to the 'responsibility to protect'; international human rights diplomacy continues to play a role in shaping and reshaping the meaning and scope of the social construct that is state sovereignty. Only towards the end of the 1990s did the term 'human rights' gain gradual acceptance and official recognition in China. The State Council Information Office published many white papers on human rights, and the clause 'the state respects and safeguards human rights' was added to the 33rd article of the Chinese Constitution in 2004.[22] This was, nevertheless, more likely in line with the emerging international consensus on the meaning and significance of human rights, rather than the result of a consensus with the EU. As Forsythe articulates, the 'primary issue about human rights in international relations is not whether they should be acknowledged as fundamental norms. Rather, the primary issue is when and how to implement human rights in particular situations'.[23]

Furthermore, China and the EU's respective human rights diplomacy can be seen as external, relational representations of their internal, normative identities. A constructivist approach to understanding identity studies is useful in addressing human rights diplomacy: diplomacy involves speech and actions critical to the performative aspect of identity construction and consolidation. Indeed, these involve 'verbal practises or substantial narratives that cumulate and influence identities',[24] rather than human rights

---

[20]*Ibid.*

[21]Chi Zhang, 'Conceptual Gap on Human Rights', in Pan Zhongqi, ed., *Conceptual Gaps in China–EU Relations: Global Governance, Human Rights and Strategic Partnerships* (New York and Houndsmills: Palgrave Macmillan, 2012), p. 84.

[22]*Ibid.*

[23]Forsythe, *Human Rights in International Relations*, p. 14.

[24]H. R. Nau, *Perspectives on International Relations: Power, Institutions and Ideas* (3rd edn.) (Washington, DC: CQ Press, 2007), p. 31.

diplomacy being guided solely by interests and norms, *a priori*. On the one hand, China's human rights diplomacy has been guided by its hyphenated identity as a developing-emerging power — one defensively committed to the principle of non-interference in other states' affairs, and one which simultaneously hopes to 'claim its rightful place in international governance with a view to influencing its structures'.[25]

On the other hand, the EU has an established identity as a normative power, one which not only wishes to uphold European norms and values within individual member countries, but also to actively promote these values outside of Europe. What is apparent is, contrary to China's inward-looking posture, an EU strategic culture of activism — enshrined in Article 2 of the Treaty of the European Union — reinforces the EU's identity as a region committed to the values of respect for freedom, democracy, equality, the rule of law, and human rights. A clear divergence between China's indignant resistance to external intervention and the EU's commitment to liberal expansionism thus emerges.

Given the seemingly irreconcilable differences in European and Chinese conceptions of human rights on the one hand, and the convergence of economic interests on the other, a 'satisficing' model of *laissez-vivre* pervaded wherein the EU and its member states were content to bend over backward on human rights in order to compete with the United States and Japan (and with each other) for lucrative contracts and business opportunities in the China market. However, the EU acknowledged that the purpose of its human-rights regime was in maintaining a 'political front of dominance' over China, without risking EU–China economic ties. Ironically, while the EU had placed comparatively less emphasis on economic and social *rights*, these *benefits* were eventually prioritized over the political and civil imperatives of human rights.

Further EU inconsistencies have also been apparent. Although the EU had established an important human-rights dialogue with China, it has suffered from conflicting interests and coordination problems between the

---

[25]T. Stiegler, *Accommodating an Emerging Human Rights Player? Recent Trends in EU–China Human Rights Diplomacy and the (Re-)construction of External Identities*, EU Academic Program Working Paper (14 April 2014), p. 10.

General Affairs Council (GAC), the member states, the European Commission, and the EP.[26] As the shock of Tiananmen faded away, the GAC and larger member states have tended to pay lip service to human rights in order to cultivate good political and economic relations with Beijing. As detailed below, China has been quick to exploit these differences.

Firefighting and Divide-and-Rule

The issue of human rights rattled China's relations with specific EU actors (Member States and EU institutions) negatively after Tiananmen. China was stretched to fight fires on several fronts over issues complicated by human-rights disagreements.[27] For example, Beijing–London relations were dominated by contentious negotiations over the return of Hong Kong to Chinese sovereignty. Although both sides had signed a Joint Declaration (1984) on the terms for the handover on 1 July 1997, the Tiananmen incident in 1989 had raised anxieties about the future of Hong Kong and the protection of its residents' freedoms and human rights. Diplomatic tensions rose farther over suspicions of British intentions following the 1992 appointment of activist governor Chris Patten.[28] Issues of contention included the new 10 billion Euros airport at Chek Lap Kok (Beijing approved this in 1991 only after tortuous negotiations), the right of abode for Hong Kong residents in Britain, and Patten's moves to introduce political freedom in a more democratic Legislative Council than what Beijing had envisaged in 1984.[29]

From 1989 to 1997, the Chinese government aimed to: (a) use economic tools to put Tiananmen behind it and continue 'business as usual' with the EU despite the EU sanctions; (b) isolate and penalize EU member states which tried to embarrass China for its appalling human rights

---

[26] *EU Strategy towards China: Implementation of the 1998 Communication and Future Steps for a More Effective EU Policy*, Commission of the European Communities, COM (2001) 265 final (15 May 2001), p. 11.

[27] Reuben Wong, 'Towards a common European policy on China?'

[28] R. Wong, 'Towards a common European policy on China?', p. 164.

[29] Eberhard Sandschneider, 'China's diplomatic relations with the states of Europe', *China Quarterly* 169 (2002), pp. 35–36; M. B. Yahuda, 'Sino-British negotiations: perceptions, organization and political culture', *International Affairs* 69(2), (April 1993), pp. 245–266.

record; and (c) defeat concerted EU–US effort to hold China accountable in multilateral fora, in particular the UNCHR, where the EU annually co-sponsored with the United States a resolution criticizing China's human rights record.[30] The EC–12 held together in supporting most of these sanctions from June 1989 to October 1990, the period when most of the sanctions were lifted (except the ban on military sales). The Committee on Human Rights (CHR) approach was adhered to each year from 1990 to 1996 (except 1991 when the United States, Britain, and France sought China's vote in the Security Council to endorse allied action against Iraq in the Gulf War). Although the resolution was always defeated by a no-action motion (except in 1995), the move was politically symbolic and significant in underlining the EU's commitment each spring to improvements in China's human rights record.

The British, conscious that their influence in the Asian region could never be more than marginal since the military pull out from Singapore in 1971, found it prudent to 'soft-pedal their interest in human rights and democratic principles' in order to maintain a working relationship with China.[31] When the Chinese government threatened in 1994 to discriminate against British trade because of governor Chris Patten's 'unilateral actions' on constitutional reform in Hong Kong, the EU trade commissioner Sir Leon Brittan warned that the EU would not condone a member state being singled out in this way. Brittan's warning staved off Chinese action against the United Kingdom.[32]

The French under a Socialist president, François Mitterrand, initially took a high-profile principled position on human rights after Tiananmen, but piped down considerably after the Beijing–Paris spat over Taiwan

---

[30]R. Wong, 'Towards a common European policy on China?', p. 170.

[31]Lawrence Martin and John Garnett, *British Foreign Policy: Challenges and Choices for the 21st Century* (London: Royal Institute of International Affairs, 1997), p. 38.

[32]H. Maull, G. Segal and J. Wanandi, eds., *Europe and the Asia Pacific* (London: Routledge, 1998), p. 185. A retired senior official of the Foreign and Commonwealth Office (FCO) Percy Craddock, however, estimated British losses in trade with China at EUR 1–2 billion on account of wrangling over Hong Kong in 1992–1996. See Percy Craddock, *Experiences of China*, new edition (London: John Murray, 1999), p. 281. France in 1991–1992 (over Taiwan) and Denmark in 1997 (over human rights) were, however, singled out for retaliation.

arms sales. French Socialist leaders reacted more emotionally and with less restraint than those of other Western democracies in their support for the Chinese student demonstrators.[33] Paris gave them a special place in the bicentennial Bastille Day parade, and even allowed them to set up the Federation for Democracy in China.[34] Bilateral ties became even more rancorous with the 1990 sale of six French Lafayette frigates to Taiwan (worth US$4.8 billion)[35]; and Taipei's 1992 purchase of 60 Mirage 2000-5 fighter jets. The Mirage sale plunged bilateral relations into a sharp and long-drawn dispute. Beijing retaliated by closing the new office of the French Consulate-General and Economic Expansion Office in Guangzhou, and canceled several large French contracts in China.[36]

Chinese punitive measures against France included passing over French tenders in the award of large contracts for infrastructure building or purchases. The economic consequences of Chinese reprisals contributed to a shrinking French share of the Chinese market. The French share of EU exports to China fell from 16% to 12%.[37] After full diplomatic relations were restored in 1994, Prime Minister Balladur made a fence-mending visit to Beijing. President Jiang's visit to France in September 1994 finally turned the corner when trade agreements worth US$2.5 billion were signed.[38]

---

[33] Peyrefitte criticized Mitterrand's post-Tiananmen policy as based on the '*émotion du moment*'. See Alain Peyrefitte, *La Chine s'est éveillée* (Paris: Fayard, 1997), p. 296.

[34] Rosemary Foot, *Rights Beyond Borders*, p. 117; Françoise Mengin, 'Relations France–Chine, quel anniversaires' agit-il de célébrer? *Rélations Internationales et Stratégiques 14*, (été 1994), pp. 51–52.

[35] Françoise Mengin, 'The prospects for France–Taiwan relations', *Issues and Studies 28*(3), (1992), p. 46; Patricia Wellons, 'Sino-French relations: historical alliance vs. economic reality', *The Pacific Review* 7(3), (1994), p. 345.

[36] The Balladur government estimated at FF 3 billion the value of contracts lost during the 'freeze' in relations. The French employers' association put it at twice that value. See R. Wong, *The Europeanization of French foreign policy*, p. 214, n. 27.

[37] According to Alain Peyrefitte, the French share of China's total trade shrank from 4% to 1.5% while the West German share rose from 3% to 5% between 1981 and 1990. See Alain Peyrefitte, *La Chine s'est éveillée*, p. 301.

[38] Rosemary Foot, *Rights Beyond Borders*, p. 159; René Dorient, 'Un septennat de politique asiatique: quel bilan pour la France?' *Politique Etrangère* 1 (Spring, 2002), pp. 173–188.

1997 Turning Point

Under President Chirac, Paris made a dramatic volte-face shielding China's human rights record from EU and international scrutiny (notably at the 1997 CHR in Geneva). In 1997, foreign minister Hervé de Charette remarked that it was 'preposterous for the West, which invaded and humiliated China in modern times, to 'lecture' China, a country with a 5,000-year old civilization, on the Human Rights Declaration and the US Constitution, which are merely 200 years old'.[39] The new French position was brought to bear at the 53rd UNCHR debate in April 1997 in Geneva. Unable to persuade its EU partners and the Dutch EU Presidency to drop the resolution criticizing China, France decided to withdraw its support from the ritual EU sponsorship of the resolution. Instead France led the 'Airbus group' (France, Germany, Italy, and Spain) in defecting from the common position. It was left to Denmark to draft the resolution, and the United States and 14 other Western countries to co-sponsor it. With the split in EU ranks, the vote was 27 in favor of China's no-action motion, 17 against and 9 abstentions, the most stunning repudiation of the UNCHR mechanism condemning China since the campaign started in 1990.[40] The UNCHR débâcle was celebrated as a spectacular victory by Chinese diplomacy.

Meanwhile, France was heavily criticized by many Western governments for 'kowtowing to Chinese pressure', putting short-term national economic interests over collective long-term EU interests and hence undermining the EU's credibility and its own credentials as the birthplace of human rights.[41] The stage was then set for Chirac's state visit to China in May 1997, where a France–China joint declaration was issued. On human rights, it declared that both parties would 'respect diversity' and take into account the 'particularities of all sides'.[42]

After the French-led defection in 1997, a new European approach to human rights in China was decided by the GAC and codified in the Commission's March 1998 strategy paper 'Building a Comprehensive Partnership

---

[39] R. Wong, 'Towards a common European policy on China?', p. 171.

[40] *Ibid.*

[41] Reuben Wong, *The Europeanization of French Foreign Policy*, p. 95.

[42] Reuben Wong, 'Towards a common European policy on China?', p. 171.

with China'. The 14 March 1998 GAC meeting agreed that at the upcoming 1998 UNCHR session, the EU would 'neither propose nor endorse, either by the organization as a whole or by individual members' any resolution criticizing China. In effect, the French position had won the day and the 'hardliners' found themselves tied to an EU position projected by France. With this '*not* to co-sponsor' European position (albeit with reservations expressed by the 'hardliners'), the UNCHR resolution with the United States has been reached at the Council each March since 1998. The Council has typically agreed that the EU should adopt the following approach at the UNCHR on China.[43]

A Proactive Chinese Human Rights Diplomacy (1997 onwards)

China's human rights diplomacy saw early beginnings in 1997. At first, it was aimed at breaking the ritual and annual EU–US cooperation in the UNCHR, which saw the major Western states co-sponsoring a resolution condemning China's human rights record. The literature has focused on Chinese human rights diplomacy centered on EU member states and international organizations. This was obvious in very public disputes surrounding symbolic actions such as the heckling of the Olympic torch as it wound its way through the streets of Paris and London in 2008. But it was also evident with Beijing showing displeasure and cancelling summits with the EU and France after French president Nicolas Sarkozy met with the Dalai Lama.

This more self-confident and sophisticated human rights diplomacy can be subdivided into two phases: (i) 1998 to 2009 and (ii) 2009 onwards. In the first phase (1998 to 2009), Chinese diplomacy focused on the EU member states and intergovernmental structures such as the GAC. This decade opened with the 50th anniversary of the UDHR (Universal Declaration of Human Rights) and the February 1998 decision by the GAC to abstain from sponsoring a resolution at the UNCHR (a decision which the EP criticized). To justify its position, the Council listed a number of improvements in China's human rights. These included the release of the

---

[43]*Ibid.*, p. 172.

Sakharov prize recipient Wei Jingsheng, China's signature and proposed ratification of the International Covenant on Economic, Social, and Cultural Rights (ICESR), China's invitation to the High Commissioner on Human Rights Mary Robinson, and the visit of the UN Working Group on Arbitrary Detention to China in 1997.[44]

1998 to 2009: Courting the Commission and EU Member States

Chinese diplomacy at first concentrated on wooing the Member States and the European Commission, in a bid to appeal to the Europeans' material interests to downplay human rights. Kohl's Germany was the preferred partner and relations with Germany, the role model. Germany's policy of 'silent diplomacy' emphasized trade with China.[45] Although it supported the Madrid sanctions on post-Tiananmen China, Germany under Kohl continued 'business as usual' half a year later, breaking away from the economic sanctions before they were officially lifted in September 1990. Germany was the first EU country to define a national policy toward the Asia-Pacific region and it made China the center of its Asia policy. Among the large EU countries, Germany is probably the most sensitive to China's sense of 'face', and thus it studiously avoided situations or actions that might be construed as high-handed by the leadership in Beijing. No wonder that the Germany–China relationship is often looked upon as a 'special' one.[46] Except for the British and French problems over Hong Kong or Taiwan, Germany usually backed down on issues involving Beijing's sense of sovereignty and national pride. For example, Kohl refused to approve the sale of 10 submarines and 10 frigates to Taiwan in January 1993 and reaffirmed Germany's 'One China' stance.[47]

---

[44] *Ibid.*; Wenwen Shen, '*EU–China Relations on Human Rights in Competing Paradigms: Continuity and Change*', in T. Christiansen, E. Kircher, and P. Murray, eds., *The Palgrave Handbook of EU–Asia Relations* (New York: Palgrave, 2013), p. 170.

[45] Eberhard Sandschneider, 'China's diplomatic relations', pp. 38–39; Christoph Nesshöver, 'Bonn et Paris face à Pékin (1989–1997): vers une stratégie commune?', *Politique Etrangère* no. 1 (1999), pp. 91–106.

[46] Jean-Pierre Cabestan, 'Sino-Western European relations: Distant neighbours or distant rivals?', *China Review* (Autumn/Winter 1995), pp. 42–44; Kay Möller 'Germany and China: A continental temptation', *The China Quarterly*, no. 147 (September 1996), pp. 706–725.

[47] *Ibid.*, pp. 720–723.

Chancellor Gerhard Schröder continued to concentrate on promoting economic relations with China while paying nominal lip service to German foreign policy interests in areas such as human rights and environmental protection. In 2000, the German government canceled an export license for a German-made satellite to Taiwan following official protests during Schröder's visit to Beijing.[48] Germany has been active in promoting cultural exchanges with China. In 2000, there were more students from China (10,000) studying in Germany than there were from Poland or France, making them the largest group in Germany. The German Foreign Ministry's 2002 policy paper on East Asia admitted that while predictions in the 1990s of an 'Asian century' had been premature, the sum of the Asia-Pacific nations' economic, political, and market potential rendered it a more prominent feature in German foreign policy, 'though also as a rival and source of critical developments with possible worldwide consequences'. It also recognized that regional realignments and power shifts after the 1997 Asian crisis and September 11 attacks made it more incumbent on Germany to work through the EU and other organizations, to exercise German influence in countries such as China.[49] Angela Merkel's first visit to China in May 2006 continued her predecessors' pattern of cozy relations with China and downplaying human rights, even though she distanced herself from Schröder's controversial attempt to lift the China arms embargo.[50]

Unlike Britain and France, the Commission has enjoyed a less problematic relationship with China. Since an EC Delegation was established in Beijing in 1988, which was followed by a political dialogue in 1994 and an annual summit with China in 1998 (regular ministerial level meetings began in 1995), the Commission as an actor has begun to challenge the traditional dominance of London, Berlin, and Paris in Europe's relations with China. The Commission's activism in China has grown in line with its rising profile in Asia. The Commission's March 1998 'Comprehensive

---

[48]R. Wong, 'Towards a common European policy on China?', p. 166.

[49]*East Asia: Tasks of German Foreign Policy at the Beginning of the 21st century, Auswärtiges Amt* (Berlin), (2002), p. 14, available at: http: //www.auswärtiges-amt.de/www/en (accessed 25 May 2004).

[50]Jonathan Eyal, 'Merkel shows China it's not business as usual', *The Straits Times* (25 May 2006).

Partnership with China' initiative which envisaged a comprehensive partnership between the European Union and China, aimed to upgrade political consultation to annual summits, dialogue on human rights, support for China's accession to the World Trade Organization (WTO), as well as the promotion of bilateral trade and investment and the first EU–China summit — held in London immediately after second Asia–Europe summit (ASEM II).

China also entered into 'strategic' cooperation with the EU, especially in aerospace and satellites. A joint Sino–European satellite navigation cooperation center was opened in Beijing in February 2003 — the same year in which China became the third nation to send a man into space. Besides, an agreement was reached in September for China to finance up to 230 million Euros or one-fifth of Galileo, the EU's 1.1 billion Euros satellite positioning system which is seen as an alternative to the US Global Positioning System. The announcement of the Galileo decision made a positive prelude to the sixth EU–China summit the following month in Beijing, though human rights, market access, and the EU's growing trade deficit with China continued to be niggling issues.[51]

Evidence that China had begun to take the EU seriously as an actor can also be found in the publication of the Chinese Foreign Ministry's first-ever 'EU policy paper' in October 2003. The paper noted that the EU was an important international player in the trend toward multipolarity, and that the euro and the EU's expansion to 25 members in 2004 served to augment the EU's weight in international affairs. Although there were 'twists and turns' in China's relations with the EU, both were not security threats to each other, but shared fundamentally similar views and interests on trade and world order.[52]

Notwithstanding the progress in EU–China relations in 2003 to 2004, Taiwan, Tibet, trade, and human rights issues continue to be frequent bones of contention. In 2003, the EP's Liberal, Democrats, and Reform (ELDR) Group attempted to invite Chen Shui-bian, Taiwan's president, to address the EP in Brussels (France had refused to issue a visa for the address at

---

[51] R. Wong, "Towards a common European policy on China?", p. 168.
[52] *China's EU Policy Paper* (Beijing: Chinese Foreign Ministry, 13 October 2003).

the EP's building in Strasbourg).[53] However, Belgium caved in to Beijing's demands when the Chinese embassy threatened that Belgium–Chinese relations could be 'set back 10 years' if the Belgian government proceeded to issue the visa to Chen. The decision to refuse the visa was then presented as a veto by the GAC, despite support from the foreign ministers of Belgium, Sweden, and Denmark.[54]

In 2004 to 2005, China found out that there were clear limits to how far it could develop a strategic partnership with the EU when US interests were at stake. The EU found itself under a lot of pressure from the United States when Paris and Berlin prematurely announced that the EU arms embargo on China — in place since 1989 — would soon be lifted. Although the US sells more weapons to China than all the EU member states combined (416 million Euros in 2003), the EU's response on this issue was construed as a litmus test of loyalty by Washington. The resulting dissensions within the EU scuttled the lifting of the embargo, and instead intensified US–EU joint consultations and intelligence sharing on China.[55]

While relations with France improved under the presidency of Jacques Chirac from 1995, political problems related to Taiwan continued to hinder their bilateral relations. After Paris approved the sale of an observation satellite by the French–British company Matra Marconi to Taiwan in 1999 over Chinese protests, French companies were excluded from the public tender to construct a gas terminal in southern China. The Chinese were also

---

[53]The EU acknowledges Taiwan as a 'Separate Customs Union'. This *de facto* 'economic recognition' is based on the latter being among the EU's most important trade partners (larger than Australia or Canada). The Tibetan government-in-exile opened an office in Brussels in April 2001, and the Dalai Lama campaigns actively in Europe (Finland, Sweden, and others). Taiwan's accession to the WTO in January 2002 has also helped its external relations. See Georg E. Wiessala, *The European Union and Asian Countries* (London: Sheffield Academic Press/UACES, 2002), pp. 102–105.

[54]Reuben Wong, 'Towards a common European policy on China?', p. 50.

[55]Katinka Barysch, *et al.*, *Embracing the Dragon*, pp. 62–64; D. C. Gompert, François Godement, Evan S. Madeiros, and James C. Mulvenon, *China on the Move: A Franco-American Analysis of Emerging Chinese Strategic Policies and Their Consequences for Transatlantic Relations* (Washington DC: RAND, 2005); François Godement, 'Europe's second thoughts on China embargo: Trouble over planned arms sales may eventually result in closer US–European coordination', *YaleGlobal* (25 March 2005).

unhappy with the high profile accorded to the Dalai Lama's visit to France in September 2000.[56]

The first decade of the 21st century ended with an extended list of human rights incidents and issues culminating in the 2008 Beijing Olympics. Following the Chinese state's crackdown on riots that erupted in Lhasa, Tibet in March 2008, the EP focused on China in debates on external policy. The EP then awarded the 2008 Sakharov Prize to Chinese dissident Hu Jia in 2008, 'acknowledging the daily struggle for freedom of all Chinese human rights defenders'.[57] At the member state level, there were major street protests in Paris and other cities during the Olympic torch relay, highlighting the strong public concerns about human rights problems in China, especially in Tibet. Sarkozy added fuel to the fire by suggesting that a boycott of the Olympic opening ceremony was possible. France was then singled out for retaliation.[58]

2009 onwards: Soft Power Diplomacy

The very public rituals of condemnations, demonstrations, threats of boycotts, and limited sanctions followed by counter-condemnations and then a gradual return to normalcy, are well-known and often in the news and academic analysis. But at the same time, the development of a nuanced and more sophisticated Chinese diplomacy has been taking place. This new human rights diplomacy is characterized by a more proactive slew of measures and public diplomacy from Beijing; a willingness to engage with the most powerful and consistent centers of human rights activism in Europe (NGOs and EP); and a strategic cultivation of European commercial interests that might help act as Beijing's 'internal' lobby against human rights actions against China.

First, a more proactive public diplomacy from Beijing is taking shape. China's recent proactive public diplomacy seems to align with its consolidating identity as an 'instrumental "emerging power"'.[59] This needs to be reconciled with its more entrenched identity as a developing country

---

[56]R, Wong, *The Europeanization of French Foreign Policy*, p. 72 and p. 213, n. 12.

[57]Wenwen Shen, 'EU–China relations on human rights', p. 171.

[58]*Ibid.*, p. 172.

[59]T. Stiegler, 'Accommodating an emerging human rights player?', p. 2.

committed to the principles of 'mutual respect for each other's territorial integrity and sovereignty' and 'non-interference in each other's internal affairs', as 'basic norms' governing Chinese foreign policy and diplomacy.[60] Instead of relying on reactive, defensive measures in response to EU human rights diplomacy, Beijing has made proactive attempts to also *adapt* (as opposed to simply *adopt*), international normative standards for human rights. The transition from being a norm-taker to a norm entrepreneur is evident from Chinese emphasis on the cultural particularity rather than universality of human rights. Chinese president Xi Jinping emphasized in Belgium at the College of Europe in 2014 'the unique value system in the Chinese outlook of the world', 'harmony without uniformity', as well as the 'need to respect each other's path of reform'.[61]

China's human rights diplomacy has also further developed in the arena of the United Nations, noticeably symbolized by its election into the UN Human Rights Council (UNHRC) in 2013. While this election was met with objections by many human rights actors critical of China's domestic human rights records, China's successful candidacy signals greater Chinese normative power 'to protect state sovereignty from what it considers undue interference in domestic affairs through overly critical resolutions'.[62] This newly assertive normative power is manifested in characteristically Chinese vetoes of resolutions to address human rights violations in Iran, Sudan, and North Korea between 2010 and 2011.

Furthermore, while China typically eschews leadership in the UNHRC, the beginnings of proactive diplomacy can be seen in actions such as its advocacy for a General Assembly Resolution on a 'Declaration of Human Social Responsibilities'. Indeed, China took the lead in presenting 'draft decisions on this topic at the 60th and 61st sessions of the Commission in 2004 and 2005'.[63] China has also leveraged the potential of the platform of

---

[60] *China's EU Policy Paper.*

[61] 'Speech at the College of Europe', Ministry of Foreign Affairs of the People's Republic of China (2014), available at: http://www.fmprc.gov.cn/mfa_eng/wjdt_665385/zyjh_665391/t1144230.shtml.

[62] 'Keeping the momentum: one year in the life of the Human Rights Council', *Human Rights Watch* (2011), available at: http://www.hrw.org/sites/default/files/reports/hrc0911ForWeb.pdf.

[63] S. Sceats and S. Breslin, *China and the International Human Rights System* (London: The Royal Institute of International Affairs, Chatham House, 2012), p. 9.

the Human Rights Council to promote its own interpretation of human rights, including the key tenets of the prioritization of socio-economic rights, the pursuit of human rights according to a state's stage of development, a focus on the rights of many, as well as stability as a precondition to the enjoyment of human rights.[64] Accordingly, China supported the 10th special session of the Human Rights Council addressing the 'impact of the global economic and financial crises on the universal realization and effective enjoyment of human rights', and also co-sponsored the resultant resolution.[65]

Furthermore, China adapted its use of economic tools in human rights diplomacy, from a reactive, defensive use of economic tools to uphold the principle of non-interference, to proactive, aggressive measures allowing a more flexible interpretation of what was once a 'basic norm'. China has deployed economic tools — primarily direct economic aid, but also in some cases, through the sale of arms in Sri Lanka, Zimbabwe, and Burma, countries deemed by the West to have highly questionable human rights records. In offering foreign aid premised on the non-imposition of political conditions on recipient countries, China has created a 'model with its own characteristics',[66] one discernibly preferable to the EU model of aid being contingent on human rights improvements. Indirectly through economic diplomacy in developing countries, China has tactically also resisted the emerging Western norm of humanitarian intervention which justifies interference in other states' domestic affairs in the name of protecting human rights.

Nobel Peace Prize Controversy in Sino–Norwegian Relations (2010 to 2104)

A prominent example of China's evolving nature of economic diplomacy would entail the hard-line response of Chinese authorities toward the award of the 2010 Nobel Peace Prize to human rights activist Liu Xiaobo. The award of the prize to Liu by a five-member Norwegian Nobel Prize

---

[64] *Ibid.*, pp. 7–8.

[65] *Ibid.*, p. 23.

[66] 'China's Foreign Aid', Information Office of the State Council (China), *Xinhua News* (21 April 2011), available at: http://news.xinhuanet.com/english2010/china/2011-04/21/c_13839683.htm.

committee incurred the wrath of Hu Jintao's government and was viewed as flagrant interference in China's internal affairs. This subsequently culminated in an immediate statement from the Chinese Ministry of Foreign Affairs (MFA) who unequivocally criticized both the Norwegian government and the Norwegian Nobel Prize Committee by stating that 'giving the Peace Prize to such a person (Liu Xiaobo) was completely contrary to the purpose of the award and a blasphemy of the Peace Prize'.[67]

As a member of the WTO, the Chinese government was cognizant that it was unable to issue a decree or law that explicitly restricted exports of Norwegian salmon because such a policy would have been in blatant violation of WTO non-discrimination principles and could easily be challenged by Norway. Instead, China's State Administration of Quality Supervision, Inspection, and Quarantine issued an order: 'Public Notice on Strengthening Inspection and Quarantine of Imported salmon', also known as Document 9 [*guanyu jiaqiang jinkou sanwenyu jianyan jianyi de gonggao* 关于加强进口三文鱼检验简易的公告] which had called for quality control checks on all salmon exports.

Norwegian salmon exports had been at the forefront of Chinese punitive measures when China had announced an extensive ban on Norwegian salmon infected with Infectious Salmon Anemia (ILA) — a virus that is harmless to humans but prevalent in European waters. Ironically, while other Nordic countries had encountered similar ILA concerns, the heavy-handed degree in which Norway's salmon exports had been singled out compared to these countries with similar ILA problems seemed to carry political overtones.[68] From 2010 to 2014, Norway's share of the Chinese salmon market declined significantly, from 90% to 30% as Chinese consumers turned to Scottish salmon as a viable substitute.[69] More importantly, Oslo's attempts to become the first European country to negotiate a free-trade agreement with China reached a standstill because Beijing stated that

[67]Austin Ramzy, 'Chinese dissident Liu Xiaobo wins Nobel Peace Prize', *Time Magazine* (8 October 2010).

[68]Sarah Karacs, 'Norway running short of options as it tries to improve ties with China', *South China Morning Post* (29 September 2014).

[69]Bjoen H. Amland, 'Norway feels sting of China's anger after Liu Xiaobo Nobel Prize win', *The World Post* (6 May 2011).

it needed 'more time for consultations' after Liu was conferred the Nobel peace prize.

The Norwegian government tried numerous conciliatory attempts to outline that the Norwegian Nobel Peace Prize Committee was an independent, separate entity from the government; to placate the Chinese government, it recommended that China be a permanent member on the Arctic Council. But these attempts were dismissed by the Chinese government which had underscored that Norway could only repair Sino–Norwegian ties by undertaking measures such as the removal of the award that had previously been accorded to Liu Xiaobo or the issuance of a public apology. These demands left Norwegian politicians with few options to break the impasse as the issuance of a public apology would have been akin to political suicide — a significant majority of the Norwegian public was of the perception that Liu was fighting for a just cause. At the same time, Norwegian politicians had faced pressure from salmon exporters who argued that a prolonged hard-line stance against China was hurting their long-term economic interests.[70]

Throughout 2010 to 2014, it was evident that China attempted to make an example out of Norway for challenging and embarrassing China's human rights record. Although Norway had not suffered excessively primarily because of its enviable gas reserves and a large budget surplus, it had undeniably missed out on a lucrative market in China's growing seafood industry. It was only in 2015 that China made several partial concessions to Norway by consenting to a new certificate formula which meant that exports of salmon to China could be maintained even though bans persisted in Sor-Trondelag, Nordland, and Troms.[71]

While there had been no explicit reaction by EU nations on China's imposition of economic penalties against Norway (which is not an EU member state), it is clear that China's new-found economic diplomacy raises pertinent questions for specific EU countries — Netherlands, Sweden, and Denmark — which have traditionally been key proponents of human rights but have seen bilateral trade with China increasing exponentially over the

---

[70] *Ibid.*
[71] 'Norway and China agree on salmon exports — Norway govt', *Reuters* (17 April 2015), available at: http://af.reuters.com/article/commoditiesNews/idAFO9N0SQ02220150417.

past decade.[72] The year 2011 marked another significant turning point when Britain's attempts to engage China on the issue of human rights met with swift resistance from premier Wen Jiabao. Premier Wen had forewarned British Prime Minister David Cameron about 'finger-pointing' at China's human rights record if Britain wanted to pursue further economic cooperation with China.[73]

Against the backdrop of China's growing economic prowess and the gradual diminution of US economic clout relative to China's, it is evident that China is in a position of increasing strength. With China being the EU's second largest trading partner, this is particularly evident. The participation of key EU states (Britain, France, Germany, and Italy) in the Chinese-led initiative of the Asian Infrastructure Investment Bank (AIIB), officially launched in 2015, is perhaps another indication that it would be an uphill task for some EU countries to concurrently maintain an intricate balance between an outspoken critic of China's human rights record and safeguarding one's national economic interests.

Engaging EU Human Rights Actors

Perhaps a clearer example of Beijing's new soft power diplomacy on human rights issues is its turn toward proactively *engaging* (instead of clashing) with NGOs and the EP. Due to its critical approach to China, the EP has been described by Chinese media or netizens as the 'anti-China base' and 'trouble-maker' by the Chinese media or netizens.[74]

The EP has been showing an increasing interest in China, primarily due to China's rising power and the growing importance of EU–China relations.

[72]For more statistical information on the growing bilateral relationship between China, Netherlands and Sweden, see 'Trade and Investment Relations between the Netherlands and China 2013', *Ministry of Foreign Trade and Development Cooperation*, available at: http://china.nlambassade.org/binaries/content/assets/postenweb/c/china/zaken-doen-in-china/trade-relations-nl-and-cn-may-2013.pdf and 'Trade between Sweden and China', *Embassy of Sweden (Beijing)*, available at: http://www.swedenabroad.com/en-GB/Embassies/Beijing/Business/Trade-between-Sweden–China/.

[73]James Blitz and George Parker, 'Wen rebukes UK human rights focus', *Financial Times* (27 June 2011).

[74]I am grateful to Yan Shaohua for highlighting Chinese perceptions of the EP to me.

In comparison to other EU institutions or most of the Members States, which are more concerned with the tangible commercial interests in their relations with China, the EP has traditionally taken a much more strident approach, focusing on the political and normative issues. The EP was opposed to the lifting of arms embargo and granting of Market Economy Status to China. In December 2003, shortly after the European Council decided to re-examine the embargo, the EP expressed its strong opposition to the lifting until China had made significant progress on human rights.[75] Since 1987, the EP has also been continuously passing resolutions criticizing China on human rights, Tibet and Taiwan issues. One example of this was a resolution in April 2005, in which the EP claimed that 'strategic partnerships' with third countries must be based on the sharing and promotion of common values. It regretted that relations with China had made progress only in the trade and economic fields, without any substantial achievement in human rights and democracy.

Many of the thorny issues between the EU and China are closely connected with the EP. With the Lisbon Treaty granting the EP the veto power in international agreements, it is argued that the EU and China (while both are in the process of negotiating the PCA) might have to develop their relations in the shadow of the EP. It was for this reason that Song Zhe, the former head of the Chinese Mission to the EU, took the EP as an important stakeholder and believed that the European Parliament will play an increasingly stronger role in the EU's external policies and participate more actively in Europe's relations with China.[76] The Chinese government has also come to realize the importance of better engaging the body. In its first EU Policy Paper in 2003, China expressed its desire to enhance mutual understanding between Chinese and European legislative organs, stating that the relations between the National People's Congress of China and the parliaments of

---

[75]European Parliament Resolution on removal of EU embargo on arms sales to China, P5_TA (2003) 0599.

[76]Ambassador Song Zhe, interview by *Parliament Magazine* (21 April 2010), available at: http://www.chinamission.be/eng/sthd/t684155.htm (accessed 6 October 2013) and Song Zhe, address at the dinner reception organized by the EP (25 January 2011), available at: http://www.chinamission.be/eng/sthd/t684155.htm (accessed 6 October 2013).

EU member countries and the European Parliament are an important link in EU–China ties.

Franco Algieri treats the EP as one of the main actors concerning the formulation and implementation of European foreign policy toward China.[77] Unlike the assumption of traditional analysis that the EU is a unitary actor in European foreign policy, Algieri notes the diversified levels and actors within the EU policy-making system and elaborates how different actors were directly or indirectly involved in EU's China policy process on different issues at stake. Special attention was given to the inter-parliamentarian meetings between the EP and the NPC which produces additional effects to the EU–China political dialogue. Stumbaum analyzes the EP's role in the decision-making of EU foreign and security policy towards China with two case studies.[78] Fraser Cameron examines the views of the EP on issues such as human rights or arms sales to China.[79] He further suggested a dialogue to be promoted between the NPC and the EP for better understanding of the functioning of the parliament system on both sides. In an interesting contrast, Chinese scholars seem to pay special attention to the EP. Lan Yuchun studied the EP's contribution to China–Taiwan relations by examining the performance of the EP towards Taiwan and the implications of the EP's activism for Taiwan.[80] There are some other Chinese scholars who focus on the EP resolutions regarding human rights, Tibet, and the Taiwan issue, but they have not yet fully understood the EP's growing powers and interest in China.

China–EU Trade Disputes

To get around the vacillations in China–EU relations over human rights and the attendant effects on bilateral trade, the Chinese government has

---

[77]F. Algieri, 'It's the System that Matters: Institutionalization and Making of EU Policy Toward China.' In David Shambaugh, Eberhard Sandschneider, and Zhou Hong, eds., *China–Europe Relations: Perceptions, Policies and Prospects* (London: Routledge, 2008).

[78]M. B. Stumbaum, *The European Union and China: Decision Making in EU foreign and Security Policy towards the People's Republic of China* (Baden-Baden: Nomos, 2009).

[79]F. Cameron, 'The Development of EU–China Relations', In Georg Wiessala, John Wilson and Pradeep Taneja (eds.), *The European Union and China: Interests and Dilemmas* (New York: Rodopi, 2009).

[80]Yuchun Lan (2004), 'The European parliament and the China–Taiwan issue: an empirical approach', *European Foreign Affairs Review*, 9(1) (2004), pp. 115–140.

been cultivating commercial interests in Europe that might act as China's internal (i.e., intra-EU) lobby against trade or human rights actions against itself. The strategic cultivation of European commercial interests by China can perhaps be best epitomized by two prominent cases: the 2004 to 2005 'Bra Wars' and 2013 solar panel dispute. The 2004 to 2005 'Bra Wars' saw an estimated 48 million shirts and 4 million bras languish in warehouses after evidence surfaced in July 2005 that China had drastically exceeded the restrictions set in the Shanghai Agreement reached on 10 June 2005 on its textile exports to Europe. While retailers complained that they were unable to obtain the textile goods which they had ordered in good faith from China, representatives from EU textile industries wanted then EU trade commissioner Peter Mandelson to undertake a strong stance against China for having reneged on the Shanghai agreement.

EU trade commissioner Pete Mandelson was subsequently at the forefront of heavy criticism from both (store retailers and representatives of EU textile industries when he was perceived to have adopted a 'piecemeal approach'. Unsurprisingly, countries with large clothing industries such as France, Spain, and Italy subsequently became involved in the dispute when these countries wanted Mandelson to resist pressure to dilute the Shanghai Agreement. On the other hand, countries such as Sweden, Finland, Denmark, and the Netherlands warned of severe job losses in the retail sector and had called for the immediate release of the textiles. The dispute only ended with a compromise made between Mandelson and Bo Xilai which saw the eventual release of the textiles and a concession by China that it would not export any further textiles in 2005 and would count half of the blocked items for its 2006 quota.

The 2004 to 2005 'Bra Wars' were significant in revealing how China had been increasingly adept in exploiting differing trade interests between the panoply of EU domestic producers, retailers, EU national governments, and the supranational EU Trade Commission to fulfill its own agendas. This placed then EU trade commissioner Peter Mandelson in a difficult conundrum and his initial attempts to resolve the impasse saw little success.

The year 2013 was the onset of another major trade dispute between EU member states and China. Against the backdrop of widespread accusations by European solar panel producers that China had engaged in excessive dumping of state-subsidized solar panels (worth 21 billion Euros) in EU countries, an internal investigation was conducted by then EU trade commissioner Karel De Gucht. Although the investigation subsequently found China to have engaged in unlawful dumping practices, there were internal disagreements between various EU countries (national level) and the EU Trade Commission (supranational level) on the level of trade tariffs that would be levied on China.

While countries such as France, Italy, and Spain unequivocally called for the imposition of hefty tariffs as a strong deterrent against future dumping practices, the vast majority of EU countries (led by Germany and the United Kingdom) vehemently opposed the plan for fear of tit-for-tat protectionism by Chinese leaders and losing out on lucrative future trade opportunities. In an attempt to resolve the protracted impasse, De Gucht decided to act in accordance with the legislative rules set forth by the EU Trade Commission and proceeded with the initial decision to impose hefty tariffs on China. Unsurprisingly, this resulted in a swift response by China — the imposition of retaliatory tariffs on the wine industries of the 'troublemakers' (France, Italy, and Spain). China's heavy-handed response had caught French president Francois Hollande off-guard; Hollande then called for an emergency EU summit between all EU member states for urgent negotiations on China's trade practices. Despite repeated calls by Hollande and De Gucht for other EU states to prioritize long-term collective interests over short-term national interests, the ambivalent stance undertaken by Germany, the United Kingdom, and other EU countries eventually saw France, Italy, and Spain retract their former decision to impose heavy trade tariffs on China's solar panels and come to a humiliating compromise. In a short span of six weeks, De Gucht stated that an amicable solution was reached even though in reality, the final agreed price for one solar panel was 0.56 Euro per watt, near the initial price for Chinese solar panels in July.[81]

In a similar vein to the 2004 to 2005 'Bra Wars', the 2013 solar panel dispute was a strategic victory for China and revealed an interesting trend. While it had been of little surprise that Germany would be reluctant to

---

[81] Robin Emmott and Ben Blanchard, 'EU, China resolve solar dispute — their biggest trade row by far', *Reuters* (27 July 2013).

undertake a firm stance against China (as epitomized by their longstanding stance of prioritizing national interests during Chancellor Kohl's and Chancellor Schroder's time in office), it is pertinent to note that other EU countries have gradually began to follow Germany's example and have been hesitant to deploy hard-line protectionist measures for fear of retaliatory measures by China. When one extrapolates on this trend, one might go so far as to posit that the twin examples of the 2004 to 2005 'Bra Wars' and 2013 solar panel dispute can potentially underscore how China might potentially utilize similar 'divide-and-rule' tactics in targeting specific EU countries that criticize its human rights record in the foreseeable future.

Conclusion

The shadow of Tiananmen still hangs over China's relations with the EU. Frequent human rights disputes between China and the EU continue to be a defining characteristic of China–EU relations. But the defensiveness of Chinese human rights diplomacy is gradually giving way to a growing self-confidence in Beijing's economic and political clout to break down common EU positions that target and embarrass China's human rights record in international fora. Chinese officials are increasingly using the language, if not the liberal spirit, of human rights to showcase China's success in achieving second-generation economic, social and cultural rights, while downplaying its shortfalls in first-generation civil and political rights.

But China does not limit its human rights disputes with the EU to normative and philosophical arguments. It remains extremely sensitive to human rights criticisms or acts which are perceived as threats to China's sovereignty. Hence, human rights issues related to Taiwan and Tibet invite robust responses or even punitive actions, usually in the form of economic and political sanctions, from Beijing. Actions construed as interfering in China's domestic politics, such as awarding a Nobel peace prize to a Chinese dissident — which are perceived in the West as honoring *bona fide* human rights activists — are viewed very negatively by Beijing.

China's use of economic tools takes a tough carrot-and-stick approach to defend and advance its position on human rights disputes with the EU and its member states. Since the late-1990s, China has changed its strategic doctrine and begun to use economic diplomacy as a coercive tool. After a decade of a policy based primarily on economic carrots, China has begun to show a willingness to use economic diplomacy for coercive means. What is even more interesting is that China has developed its own human rights diplomacy to counter Western (mainly European and American) attempts to highlight and embarrass its human rights record. Indeed China has turned from being a *reactive* target of human rights (after the 1989 Tiananmen incident), to being *proactive* in promoting its own vision of human rights, and using diplomatic and economic tools to deflect or attack European attempts to put China in a corner. As China transits from a developing, yet emerging power to a normative power, it has embarked on more proactive soft-power diplomacy on human rights engagement and dialogue with the EU, but on its own terms.

Chapter 3

China's Economic Inducement towards Vietnam: What Lies Ahead?

Xue Gong

Economic policy is now an integral part of China's strategy in addressing regional as well as international issues. Trade, investment, and financial policies have been formulated with the primary purpose of supporting China's economic transition from export-led to import-led growth. While China's active economic statecraft advances its commercial interests, it is also used as a tool to expand its influences, especially towards its neighbors. Conceived as a strategy, China hopes its economic statecraft will be able to serve its foreign policy goals in two main ways: to improve the image and goodwill of the target countries, especially its Southern neighbors who are apprehensive of its rise and to achieve favorable outcomes in addressing the South China Sea disputes on a bilateral basis.

Among the members of Associations of Southeast Asian Nations (ASEAN), no other Southeast Asian nation is so dependent on trade with China like Vietnam. China has been enjoying persistent surplus over Vietnam over the past two decades; thus, an asymmetrical economic relationship has emerged between the two countries. According to Hirschman, the trade imbalance in favor of a country is conducive to its political dominance over the vulnerable trading partner.[1] Based on an analysis of Vietnam

---

[1]Albert O. Hirschman, *National Power and the Structure of Foreign Trade* (Berkeley, LA: California University of California Press, 1980).

and China trade patterns later in this chapter, China is found to be in a better position to impose trade leverage over Vietnam. However, China's economic advantage is limited to advancing its geopolitical security interests in the South China Sea disputes. China is seen as reluctant to deploy economic pressure over conflicts amid territorial disputes. Although China has been reported to set tighter measures on the Philippine's banana exports in 2012 after the Scarborough Shoal/Huangyan Island dispute, China has not been seen openly imposing similar barriers to Vietnam's exports.[2] Given China's history of economic sanctions against Vietnam during the period 1975 to 1978, and the asymmetrical relations between the two, it could have signaled its frustration towards Vietnam amid incidents and the outcome is believed to be favorable to China.

Surprisingly, China overreacted to the 2010 Nobel Prize incident by suddenly reducing Norway's salmon export to China. Similar short-term economic threats happened with the rare earth exports to Japan over the Senkaku/Diaoyu Islands issue, the airbus order from France to China over the Dalai Lama issue and the US stance on Taiwan's arms sale issue. On the contrary, China is promoting more economic incentives in the hope of attaining bilateral negotiations on the territorial disputes in South China Sea. For example, China signed new joint development agreements with Brunei and Vietnam for joint exploration and exploitation of fossil fuels in the contested waters in 2013.[3] By offering mutual economic benefits to cooperative countries, China wishes to keep international intervention off the disputes.

This chapter asks why China is limited in translating its economic prowess into influence towards Vietnam. Or more precisely, why does China refrain from imposing trade sanctions for foreign policy purposes? From the perspective of the Chinese government, sanctions are considered as 'an immoral punishment of innocent and vulnerable populations'.[4]

---

[2]Although it has been reported that China successfully threatened and persuaded BP to stop developing gas fields with Vietnam in 2007, China has not been seen as imposing sanctions directly on Vietnam.

[3]Brendan O'Reilly, 'China–Vietnam: More Carrot, Less Stick', *Asia Times* (22 October 2013).

[4]James Reilly, 'China's Unilateral Sanctions', *The Washington Quarterly 35*, no. 4 (Fall 2012): p. 121–133.

Other explanations include questioning the efficiency of economic sanctions, energy-oriented economic outreach, the influences of the United States, the new domestic foreign policy actors in China, and short-term sacrifices for long-term benefits.[5]

This chapter acknowledges the current literature and considers two factors: China's willingness to utilize economic independence as a tool of punishment or inducement and the availability of an effective control mechanism for China's overseas business performance. This chapter argues that though China has the potential of political dominance over Vietnam, China has refrained from doing so intentionally. From the economic perspective, Vietnam has served China's 'going out' strategy that aims to maximize its overseas market share, transfer low-end industry, and upgrade its domestic industry. In addition, due to the geographical proximity, border trade with Vietnam consists of a significant part of China's Great Western Development (*xi bu da kai fa*) project. As supply chains spread across borders, China is benefiting more as a center of Asia's manufacturing. If China adopts trade coercion when political incidents occur, it will likely weaken its stance in its good neighborhood diplomacy and spoil the chances of reaping benefits from the benign regional and international trade. From the political perspective, Vietnam is not an easy case for China to exploit economic relations for political purposes. On the one hand, Vietnam is a gateway for China to export its soft power to ASEAN. On the other hand, the influences of the United States and Japan have limited China's use of economic statecraft, especially economic coercions.

---

[5] Gary Clyde Hufbauer, Jeffrey J. Schott, Kimberly Ann Elliot, and Barbara Oegg, *Economic Sanctions Reconsidered*, 3rd edn., (Washington, DC: Peterson Institute for International Economics, 2007); Adam Segal, *Chinese Economic Statecraft and the Political Economy of Asian Security*, in William W. Keller and Thomas G. Rawski, eds., *China's Rise and the Balance of Influence in Asia* (University of Pittsburgh Press, 2007), p. 242; Linda Jakobson, and Dean Knox. 'New Foreign Policy Actors in China' in *SIPRI Policy Paper* (Stockholm International Peace Research Institute, September 2010); James Reilly, 'China's Economic Statecraft: Turning Wealth into Power' *Lowy Institute for International Policy* (November 2013); Evelyn Goh, 'Limits of Chinese Power in Southeast Asia', East Asia Forum 10 May 2011. Available at: http://www.eastasiaforum.org/2011/05/10/the-limits-of-chinese-power-in-southeast-asia/.

The following discussion consists of four sections. The first section provides an examination of China–Vietnam relations, followed by a discussion on trade relations between the two countries. The second section focuses on the discussion of China's position in regional and global economy and the importance of Vietnam to China by assessing China's investment in Vietnam. The third section is concerned with the strategic willingness of China to politicize economic asymmetry into potential leverage in the context of the South China Sea dispute. In the final section, the conclusion is that economic incentives will likely still be the predominant consideration in shaping China's economic statecraft towards Vietnam, especially in competition for influence with the United States and Japan. Knowing smaller countries like Vietnam are apprehensive of China's prowess, China is expected to curb the tendency to impose political leverage inherent in economic asymmetry.

China's Economic Relationship with Vietnam

The relationship between China and Vietnam since more than 2,000 years ago can be identified as asymmetrical. Historically, Vietnam had struggled through the pre-Imperial tributary system in exchange for sovereignty and independence for centuries. Because of this, the collective memory of China's asymmetrical power has played an important part in shaping Vietnam's foreign policy today.

Before the Sino–Soviet Union split, China and Vietnam enjoyed a revolutionary comradeship as both leaderships shared an intimate relationship, aptly described by a Chinese saying, 'as close as lips and teeth'. Sharing the same revolutionary ideology, China showed great sympathy towards Vietnam during the Indo-china wars for independence and the Vietnam War against the United States by providing a great amount of financial assistance, weaponry equipment, and advisors. However, after the ideological split between Soviet Union and China in the 1960s, Vietnam chose to stand with the former against China. Meanwhile, the Vietnamese government mistreated Chinese descendants residing in Vietnam through a series of economic and social reforms amid the escalating border conflicts. Mistrust peaked between the two countries after China started rapprochement with the United States in the early 1970s. The tensions ultimately led to China's use of economic sanctions and deployment of military support to defend the

Cambodian Khmer Rouge against Vietnam's invasion, in the 1979 border war and skirmishes over islands in the South China Sea. The hostility did not end until the normalization of bilateral relationships in 1991 after Vietnam signed the peace agreements. Not surprisingly, the relationship before the normalcy has been labeled as 'zero-sum confrontation'.

Despite historical mistrust, China has set an example for Vietnam on how to tackle economic reforms and political challenges as a socialist country. As China gears its domestic and foreign policy to economic growth, Vietnam also looks north for economic experiences and opportunities. In 1999, the 16-word guideline, translated as 'long-term, stable, future-oriented, good neighborly, and all-around cooperative relations', defined a new relationship between China and Vietnam. Followed by the Joint Statement for Comprehensive Cooperation in 2000, trade volume and investment began to increase after the conclusion of the land border treaty and cooperation on the Exclusive Economic Zones (EEZ) and relevant negotiations such as fishing in the Beibu Gulf. Since then, the asymmetry between the two countries has been reflected in trade relations.

China–Vietnam trade

The trade between Vietnam and China is very imbalanced. A rapid increase in bilateral trade volumes between China and Vietnam can be seen after the diplomatic normalization in 1991, from only US$32 million to US$50.4 billion. So far, China is Vietnam's largest trading partner and both countries aim to increase bilateral trade to over US$60 billion by 2015.[6] According to the World Trade Organization (WTO), China has become the largest provider for Vietnam's imports that are critical for industrial development and the third largest country (excluding European Union) for Vietnam's exports (see Fig. 3.1). The figures are just part of the official calculation: the informal border trade thrives as part of subregional economic integration and also plays an important part for economic growth in Vietnam's localities.[7]

---

[6]'China Remains Vietnam's Biggest Trade Partner in 2013' (29 January 2014), (accessed 29 January 2014), available at: http://www.chinadaily.com.cn/ business/chinadata/2014-01/29/content_17264283.htm.
[7]The border trade reached US$1,300 million in 2011 (Lao Cai Government, Vietnam, 2012). Chan Yuk Wah, *Vietnamese-Chinese Relationships at the Borderlands* (New York: Routledge, 2013), p. 16.

Export Main Destination	Value in US$ Million	Partner Share
1. European Union (28)	$20,272.00	17.70%
2. United States	$19,681.00	17.18%
3. Japan	$13,064.00	11.41%
4. China	$12,836.00	11.21%
5. South Korea	$5,581.00	4.87%
6. Other	$43,095.00	37.63%
Total	$114,529.00	100.00%

Import Main Origin	Value in US Million	Partner Share
1. China	$29,035.00	25.52%
2. South Korea	$15,535.00	13.65%
3. Japan	$11,602.00	10.20%
4. European Union (28)	$8,761.06	7.70%
5. Chinese Taipei	$8,533.50	7.50%
6. Other	$40,313.44	35.43%
Total	$113,780.00	100.00%

Figure 3.1. Vietnam's top five trading partners by year 2013.

Source: Consolidated from World Bank, the World Trade Centre by 2013.[8]

Serious trade imbalance in favor of China has been increasing (see Fig. 3.2). In 2013, trade with China as a percentage of Vietnam's GDP accounts for over 24.5%, while total trade with Vietnam as a percentage of China is less than 0.5%.[9] The trade deficit against China has increased from US$33 million to more than US$31,714 million, about 18.5% of Vietnam's GDP in the year 2013.[10]

In order to understand the vulnerability of Vietnam's imbalanced trade, it is important to note the unique structure of Vietnam–China trade relations.

---

[8]Vietnam trade profile, Statistics database, *World Trade Center* (September 2013), available at: http://stat.wto.org/CountryProfile/WSDBCountryPFView.aspx?Language=E&Country =VN%2cCN (accessed 12 April 2014), http://wits.worldbank.org/CountryProfile/Country/ VNM/StartYear/2009/EndYear/2013/TradeFlow/Export/Indicator/XPRT-TRD-VL/Partner/ All/Product/Total#; also see Salidjanova, Nargiza, Iacob Koch-Weser, and Jason Klander-man, '*China's Economic Ties with ASEAN: A Country-by-Country Analysis*' In *US–China Economic and Security Review Commission*, Staff Research Report (17 March 2015).

[9]Vietnam's GDP in 2013 was US$171.4 billion while China's was US$9,240.27 billion. The percentage is calculated based on the official data from the World Trade Centre, and the World Bank.

[10]Accessed on 12 April 2015, available at:http://data.worldbank.org/country/vietnam.

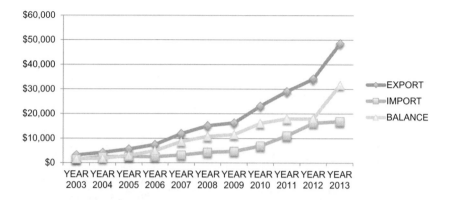

Figure 3.2. Vietnam's trade balance against China.

Source: CEIC database.[11]

Vietnam's exports to China can be categorized into four major groups:

- raw materials such as crude oil, coal, rubber, metal and minerals like bauxite;
- agricultural products such as rice, fruits, vegetables and coffee;
- consumer goods such as handicraft furniture and footwear; and
- fishing products like aquaculture products, fish, and other seafood.

Vietnam runs a trade deficit because China is able to export higher-value commodities that can be divided into four categories:

- industrial equipment and machinery such as cement plants, textiles and transport vehicles;
- energy materials like refined oil, fertilizers, steel and iron, construction materials, chemical products and garment manufacturing;
- agricultural products such as fruits, vegetables and temperate climate seeds; and
- consumer goods and pharmaceutical products, telecommunications, motorbikes, electronics and clothes.

According to Fig. 3.3, it is obvious that China's supplies of electric devices, machinery and refined chemicals are critical to Vietnam's industries

---

[11]Accessed on 12 April 2015, available at: https://www.ceicdata.com/en/countries/china.

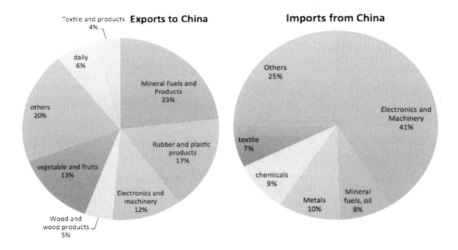

Figure 3.3.   Components of Vietnam's trade with China, 2013.

Source: International Trade Centre.[12]

and economic growth. Conversely, Vietnam's export of raw materials and agriculture products seems less important to China's economy. Although China is considered as energy-driven in its economic foreign policy, the traditional energy suppliers such as the Middle East and Central Asia are still China's main energy providers. As China expands its energy business to Latin America, the import from Vietnam seems relatively insignificant because China has diversified its suppliers.[13] In areas such as garment manufacture and agriculture, Vietnam has to compete with other ASEAN members, as well as face competition from China. Take textile for example, even though China has been moving upmarket to pursue higher-value activities, its share of global textile has actually risen from 42.6% in 2011 to 43.1% in 2013.[14] Where Vietnam has favorable productivity, in agriculture for

---

[12]Accessed on 20 April 2015, available at: http://www.intracen.org.

[13]Kim Dung, Nguyen Thi, Nguyen Manh Hai, and Tran Trung Hieu, '*Impacts of China on Poverty Reduction in Vietnam*', in *Assessing China's Impact on Poverty in the Greater Mekong Subregion*, Hossein Jalilian (ISEAS Publishing, 2013), pp. 162–163.

[14]'Made in China? Asia's Dominance in Manufacturing Will Endure', *The Economist* (14 March 2015), available at: http://www.economist.com/news/leaders/21646204-asias-dominance-manufacturing-will-endure-will-make-development-harder-others-made.

example, it has to import three times more fruits and vegetables from China than it exports, as was the case in 2010.[15]

In terms of raw materials, Vietnam appears to be earning revenue to pay for its imports from China. The truth is that Vietnam has to import more products that have been processed and refined in China. For example, Vietnam exports around 70% of its rubber to China; however, it purchases two-thirds more rubber products from China than it sells.[16] Even in oil sales, Vietnam has to buy refined petroleum from China. In 2012, Vietnam exported US$1,032 million worth of crude oil; however, it imported US$2,499 million of petroleum oil.[17]

China's relatively advanced industrial capabilities contribute to its increasing trade surplus over Vietnam yearly. China's more mature industrialization and financial system enable itself to export higher value-added products to Vietnam, such as industrial equipment and machinery, refined oil and consumer products. This implies that Vietnam's trade-driven economy is heavily dependent on China. This can potentially create leverage for China to apply as economic tools to exert pressure on Vietnam.

According to Hirschman, the differences in trade structure can affect bargaining power in the international political economy. He suggests that possible asymmetrical power can subsequently evolve between trading countries if there is a disequilibrium in favor of one country by introducing two effects of foreign trade:

> *'...a country trying to make the most of its strategic position of its own trade will try precisely to create the conditions that make the interruption of trade of much graver concern to its trading partners than to itself...'*[18]

---

[15] Brantly Womack, 'China and Vietnam: managing an asymmetric relationship in an Era of economic uncertainty', *Asian Politics & Policy* 2, no. 4 (2010), p. 583–600.

[16] *Ibid.*

[17] Calculated based on data provided by CEIC Database, Vietnam trade profile (accessed 20 May 2015).

[18] Albert O. Hirschman, *National Power and the Structure of Foreign Trade* (Berkeley, Los Angeles, California University of California Press, 1980), p. 16.

In this strategic position, *supply effects* and *influence effects* are produced to create the asymmetrical power. Supply effects mean military power accumulated from economic growth while influence effects can produce economic pressure that stems from overdependence in foreign trade, especially the suspension of suppliers that are crucial to the vulnerable countries. Influence effects underscore the fact that large states prefer non-military influence compared to the high costs of military threats. As states become increasingly economically interdependent, economic levers of power have been the option for realizing foreign policy objectives, such as consecutive sanctions on North Korea's trade and assets.[19]

In this scenario, the Hirschmanesque analysis of the imbalanced economic trade relations can be aptly applied to Vietnam–China relations. The different sectors of Vietnam's exports and imports with China illustrate the vulnerability of Vietnam's economic dependence on China. The concerns over China's potential leverage upon Vietnam's vulnerability for its political and security purposes rise in tandem with the South China Sea tensions.[20]

In order to assuage the anxiety and fear of China's economic clout, China has sacrificed some economic benefits in exchange for the trust from ASEAN countries by initiating the China–ASEAN FTA Early Harvest Program (EHP). This program included favorable treatment to the ASEAN states in terms of the partial lifting of trade barriers on certain goods at the expense of China's southwestern provinces.[21] This program has enabled some ASEAN agriculture products to enter China with reduced tariffs while ASEAN members could impose tariffs on China's products until 2010.

However, as the trade deficit continued to grow, so did Vietnam's anxiety about the unhealthy trade relationship with China. Therefore, Vietnam

---

[19] Robert Gilpin, *War and Change in World Politics* (Cambridge: Cambridge University, 1981), p. 218.

[20] D. T. Tran, 'Economic Integration of Vietnam and ASEAN in the context of China's emergence', in *China's Development and Prospect of ASEAN–China Relations*, Center for ASEAN and China Studies (Ha Noi: The Gioi Publisher, 2006), p. 119–128.

[21] Evelyn Goh, *The Limits of Chinese Power in Southeast Asia*, 10 May 2011, available at: http://www.eastasiaforum.org/2011/05/10/the-limits-of-chinese-power-in-southeast-asia/.

Year	US	Japan	China	TPP	World
2009	$8,396,188	−$1,132,490	−$11,270,298	$5,970,915	−$12,852,536
2010	$10,471,014	−$1,288,426	−$12,460,693	$7,541,419	−$12,601,888
2011	$12,415,162	$691,047	−$13,253,068	$8,702,124	−$9,844,180
2012	$14,839,199	$1,462,469	−$16,198,990	$14,782,828	−$748,740
2013	$18,627,473	$1,985,945	−$23,708,784	$20,540,924	$323

Figure 3.4. Vietnam's trade balance in thousand US$ by partners from 2009 to 2013. *Source*: Consolidated from International Trade Center.[22]

began to proactively diversify its trade partners. Although not explicitly stated, China became the inevitable factor to drive Vietnam's decision to participate in the Trans-Pacific Pact (TPP). In 2013, during the Shangri-La Dialogue, Vietnam's president Truong Tan Sang reaffirmed Vietnam's interest in joining the US-led TPP that excludes China.

While Vietnam suffered from increasing trade deficit with China, trade surplus with the United States and Japan helped to balance the situation (see Fig. 3.4). At the same time, trade balance with the TPP will make Vietnam the largest beneficiary of the eliminated tariffs. Therefore, Vietnam's decision to join the TPP is considered an important move to balance China's economic and political clout. Vietnam has become more pragmatic in integrating with the region and the global society as it has reaped benefits from regionalism. Vietnam's decision to join TPP was largely because its trade structure needed a more balanced market for its exports, especially in facing the high degree of protectionism in North America. By the same token, Vietnam's support of China-led economic initiatives such as the Asian Infrastructure Investment Bank (AIIB) has more bearing on its domestic economic demand.

The Primacy of Economic Inducement Concerns

This chapter defines economic statecraft as the application of economic tools (resources and capitals) such as the promotion of trade, and foreign investment as potential economic leverage for political and security

---

[22]Accessed on 15 April 2015, available at http://www.intracen.org.

purposes. Economic statecraft appears less coercive than military statecraft in advancing national interests.[23] This chapter applies Baldwin's dividing economic statecraft into positive and negative aspects, which are also known as both economic inducements and sanctions. In his definition, economic inducements are offered by a country in order to obtain the recipient's compliance. Economic sanctions are punishments to coerce the target by interfering in its economic activities in order to attain a desired change from the target. In short, these target countries can either be rewarded for compliance or penalized as a result of non-compliance. Notwithstanding, Baldwin acknowledges it is not easy to specify if incentives are used to achieve political or economic gains. The clear identification of foreign policy objectives is crucial in assessing a strategy's success in achieving its objectives.

The official Chinese White Paper released in 2011 included the definition of China's core interests as 'state sovereignty, national security, territorial integrity and national unification...for ensuring sustainable economic and social development'.[24] This chapter has outlined China's economic inducement toward Vietnam as follows:

- To ensure a friendly and benign neighborly environment conducive to China's rise. Chinese leadership initiates the image improvement by encouraging more trade, investment and aid packages to mitigate the negative perception of China's military threat. To achieve this, it has actively engaged in multilateralism such as the Greater Mekong Subregion (GMS) economic cooperation, ASEAN +3, and CAFTA (China–ASEAN Foreign Trade Agreement).
- To reduce the influences from the United States and Japan in their competition for power and influence. Rather than transforming Southeast Asia into its backyard, China needs a supportive Southeast Asia to check the power of the United States and Japan.

---

[23]David A. Baldwin, *Economic Statecraft*, (Princeton, NJ: Princeton University Press, 1985).

[24]Zhong Guo De He Ping Fa Zhan [China's Peaceful Development] Zhong Guo Zheng Fu Bai Pi Shu [the White Paper of Chinese Government] Zhong Hua Ren Min Gong He Guo Guo Wu Yuan Xin Wen Ban Gong Shi [The State Council Information Office of the People's Republic of China], September 2011, Beijing, http://www.scio.gov.cn/zfbps/ndhf/2011/201109/t1000032.htm.

- To bolster economic development, especially 'Develop the West', in southwestern provinces adjacent to Southeast Asia and gain greater access to Southeast Asian natural resources such as oil, gas, bauxite, and large export for agriculture and fishery products.
- To manage highly sensitive territory disputes with economic 'divide and influence' by reducing the likelihood of military conflict with conflicting claimants and other big powers at stake. China attempts to consolidate its claims of South China Sea disputes by deterring any internationalization of the issue and by delaying resolution.

As suggested by Baldwin, trade can be used to indicate intentions, signal commitments or project overall foreign policy orientations. China's economy is significantly larger than its counterpart. It enjoys the advantage of an asymmetrical economic relationship with Vietnam. However, China has not exploited this to its own advantage. It seems to prefer incentives to coercion even in sensitive issues or territorial conflict. So why has China refrained from using economic coercions against Vietnam in the South China Sea disputes? The following discussion may give a clue.

ASEAN in China's economic statecraft calculation

The history of the relationship between China and ASEAN member states is marred by perceptions of China as a threat.[25] The end of the Cold War and the 1989 Tiananmen incident forced China to look South for support. Believing in the old Chinese proverb, 'Close neighbors are better than distant relatives', China's good neighbor policy was introduced to build peaceful regional relations so as to surround itself with friendly states.[26] Initial confidence-building attempts on mainly political and security issues were bolstered by economic cooperation in the 1990s.

---

[25]Amitav Acharya, '*Seeking Security in the Dragon's Shadow: China and Southeast Asia in the Emerging Asian order*', in *China and Southeast Asia*, Geoff Wade, ed., Volume VI (Routledge, 2009), p. 273. Also see Richard L. Grant, *China and Southeast Asia: Into the Twenty-first Century* (Honolulu: Pacific Forum/CSIS; Washington, DC Center for Strategic and international Studies, 1993).

[26]Alice Ba, '*Between China and America: ASEAN's Great Power Dilemmas*', in *China, the United States and Southeast Asia: Contending Perspectives on Politics, Security and Economics*, Evelyn Goh and Sheldon W. Simon, eds. (London: Routledge, 2008).

Before joining ASEAN, Vietnam used to be a troublemaker, destabilizing regional peace, and exporting communism. After the 13th National Congress of the Vietnam Communist Party, it adopted a resolution to create a neighborly environment (more friends and fewer enemies). The decision to join ASEAN ramifies the crucial political, economic, and security implications for Vietnam. It improves Vietnam's image and creates more cooperation mechanisms for Vietnam's economic development. After Vietnam's participation, ASEAN became an inevitable factor for China and other countries to consider.

In a changing security environment, China changed its approach to deal with its southern neighbors by cultivating economic inducements. Take the 1997 to 1998 Asian financial crisis for example. China generously refrained from devaluating the Chinese yuan and provided financial aid to several Southeast Asia states. In contrast to the indifference of the United States and Japan, China gained credibility as a responsible player, thereby strengthening closer ties with the Southeast Asian countries. Contrary to the ideology exported, China has realized that an economic offensive better serves its foreign policy goals of improving relations with ASEAN and expanding its influences in Southeast Asia.

At the same time, Chinese attempts to cultivate closer ties through the economy are particularly welcome by most Southeast Asian countries. This is because developing Southeast Asian countries undergoing industrialization and urbanization would place economic development as their first priority. Vietnam is one of them. Realizing this, China has become proactive in reaching free trade agreement. China also favors direct investment in regional and subregional economics within ASEAN. Such an approach has not only economic but also strategic intents.[27] China's active economic presence helps defuse the 'China Threat' perception and the influence of the United States, while securing key markets and resources overseas.[28]

---

[27]Adam Segal, *Chinese Economic Statecraft and the Political Economy of Asian Security*, in William Keller and Thomas Rawski, eds., *China's Rise and the Balance of Influence in Asia* (University of Pittsburgh Press, 2007). p. 242.

[28]Vincent Wang Wei-cheng, '*The Logic of China–Asean Free Trade Agreement: Economic Statecraft of "Peaceful Rise"*'. In *China in the World, the World in China International Conference 'Implications of a Transforming China: Domestic, Regional and Global Impacts'*. Institute of China Studies, University of Malaya, 5–6 August 2007.

In response to ASEAN's concerns over the potential adverse impact on China's entry into the WTO, China's proposal of CAFTA was made. The EHP made within the ASEAN framework is a typical example of China's attempts to express goodwill to its neighbors. Proposed by the previous premier Zhu Rongji at the ASEAN–China Summit, it is considered more political than economic for China because it is carried out at the expense of the local agriculture and plantation product sectors. China's active approach in integrating with its neighbors has increased the latter's appreciation and understanding of China's rise.[29]

As ASEAN increases its pace of integration,[30] any clashes with a single member state may affect China's relationship with other ASEAN members. The 1988 Sino–Vietnamese clash over the Spratly Islands has shown China's determination to protect its claims over the South China Sea. This incident had not only raised concerns from ASEAN members but also changed the security dynamics as the South China Sea dispute has inevitably gained prominence in the context of Sino–ASEAN relations.

Given the complicated history between China and Vietnam, the world is watching how China builds benign relations with the Southeast Asia community. Economically, Vietnam is important in the ASEAN integration program because it is one of the fastest-growing economies among the members. It also serves as the gateway for China to export and import goods within the regional community. Politically, any military action between China and Vietnam will inevitably bring instability into the region. Any miscalculation in the South China Sea disputes may drive its southern neighbors closer to the United States for security reasons, and this is the last scenario China wishes to see. Although the Declaration on the Conduct of Parties in the South China Sea (DOC) was signed among claimants in 2002, the claiming parties, especially China, Vietnam, and the Philippines' recent rush to build facilities and even land around the islands only worsened the situation.

---

[29]Wang Yuzhu, and Sarah Y. Tong, 'China–Asean FTA changes Asean's perspective on China'. *EAI Background Brief*, no. 518 (April 2010).

[30]The integration consists of ASEAN Political-Security Community, Economic Community, Socio-Cultural Community, available at: http://www.asean.org/media-gallery/video/item/the-asean-community-2015.

So far, China has been successful in cultivating a peaceful neighborhood through intraregional trade and participation in regional institutions, such as the ASEAN Regional Forum (ARF).[31] Yet peace does not necessarily equate absolute security, despite the remarkable diminution in the frequency and intensity of military conflict and crises.[32] This perspective is strongly echoed by some Chinese scholars, especially amid great power rivalry.[33]

Great power rivalry and the South China Sea

Despite common interests in economics, conventional geopolitical concerns still exist. Relations between China and Southeast Asian countries have always been marked by historical confrontation and disagreement over the level of US involvement in Asia Pacific.[34] Historical grievances still linger in parts of Asia, despite close economic relations. There is a group which thinks Asia's future may be likened to Europe's bloody past.[35] East Asia is still entangled with competing territorial claims while China's tremendous economic progress has inevitably changed the power balance and even challenged the authority of the United States. The aggressive stance on the maritime disputes in the South China Sea is emblematic of this trend. Inevitably, the United States has reacted towards China's assertiveness and declared that the United States has national interests in freedom of navigation and open assess to Asia's maritime commons.[36]

---

[31]ARF is motivated by economic interests that led to increased tensions and security concerns among some of the key regional players.

[32]Goldstein and Mansfield, *The Nexus of Economics*, p. 10.

[33]Zhou Meng and Zhu Zhen Jiang, 'Zhuang xiang you huan yi shi de jing zhong', [Alarm the bell of awareness of unexpected eventualities] interview with Meng Xiang Qing, deputy head of Strategic Studies Institute from National Defense University of China, Liberation Army Daily [Jie Fang Jun Bao], available at: http://news.mod.gov.cn/pla/2013-09/20/content_4467004.htm.

[34]Amitav Acharya, '*Seeking Security in the Dragon's Shadow: China and Southeast Asia in the Emerging Asian Order*', in *China and Southeast Asia*, Geoff Wade, ed., Vol. VI of *The People's Republic of China and Southeast Asia* (New York: Routledge, 2009), p. 273; also see Richard L. Grant, *China and Southeast Asia: Into the Twenty-first Century* (Honolulu: Pacific Forum/CSIS; Washington, DC Centre for Strategic and international Studies 1993.

[35]Aaron Friedberg, 'Will Europe's past be Asia's future?' *Survival* 42, no. 3 (Autumn 2000): p. 147–160.

[36]Hillary Clinton, Statement made in the 17th ARF Meeting, Hanoi, (23 July 2010).

As China's rise continues, encounters with resistance from other major powers will only persist, especially when China's evolving national interests shift from regional to global scales. To counter these obstacles, China is keen on changing the status quo by leveraging on its economic prowess to form new strategic ties while nudging existing ones in its favor. It also involves the delicate balancing of its own economic dependency as well as its neighbors' on other major powers such as the United States and Japan. According to Ravenhill and Yang, the Chinese government is glad to see the ASEAN economic dependence on Japan, Europe, and the United States gradually shifting to China.[37] With this changing regional trade pattern, China gains the advantage of seeking cooperation with the two powers (the United States and Japan) while at the same time, trying to drive them apart and eventually seeking openings, particularly in Southeast Asia, to broaden China's own base of influence.[38]

The situation in the South China Sea has come to the status of 'a sense of anarchy', a term coined by Indonesian foreign minister Marty Natalegawa.[39] China is among the seven claimants that have competing territorial claims over the continental shelves, reefs, and EEZs in the South China Sea. China's motivation in the South China Sea is very clear: to consolidate its claims among other competitors; deter internationalization of the disputes; prevent conflict escalation; prefer bilateral negotiation; and strengthen claims through military presence, resources drilling, and infrastructure establishment.

According to Fravel, China has pursued a strategy that aims to prevent the escalation of the conflict while delaying the resolution of the dispute. China hopes to consolidate its claims but not at the expense of its economic development.[40] China continues its offensive charms to 'divide and influence' to compete with the United States. China's approach paid off in

---

[37] John Ravenhill, and Yang Jiang, 'China's move to preferential trading: a new direction in China's diplomacy', *Journal of Contemporary China* 18, no. 58 (2009): p. 27–46.

[38] Gilbert Rozman, *Chinese Strategic Thought toward Asia* (New York: Palgrave MacMillan, 2010).

[39] Ian Storey, '*South China Sea: Glacial Progress Amid On-Going Tensions*', in *CSCAP Regional Security Outlook*, Council For Security Cooperation in the Asia Pacific, 2014.

[40] M. Taylor Fravel, 'China's strategy in the South China Sea', *Contemporary Southeast Asia* 33, no. 3 (2011), pp. 292–319.

deterring internationalization of the South China Sea issue and delaying resolution. During the summit of foreign ministers of the ASEAN in Cambodia in 2012, members could not agree on how to counter pressure from Chinese claims in the South China Sea. It was the first time that ASEAN failed to release a joint communiqué. Even Thailand, the ally of the United States, was considered to favor China; it objected to the inclusion of South China disputes to safeguard ASEAN–China cooperation.[41]

To reduce the influence of the United States and ease the anxiety of ASEAN members, China sought to keep maritime cooperation within Asia by initiating the ASEAN–China Maritime Cooperation Fund. China launched a 3 billion Yuan (US$474 million) maritime cooperation fund to ease the concerns of Vietnam and the Philippines. Such an offer acts as a reminder that integrating with China will yield benefits that cannot be easily reaped from other economic powers, especially from the stagnating Japanese and declining US economies.[42] Despite territorial disputes, China is pushing for an even more regionally integrated economic blueprint to expand its influences. Such ambitions are embedded in China's recent Belt and Road Initiative and the AIIB.

Except for the carrot China is offering to Southeast Asia, it is repeatedly manipulating its economic potential to influence the policies of other states.[43] This stance is particularly evident in issues such as the US arm sales to Taiwan, reduced exports of rare earth to Japan and the Senkaku/Diaoyu Islands issue. More recently, China tried to utilize its economic leverage by canceling tourist groups, and slowing down fruit imports to deter the Philippines from challenging its claims after the 2012 standoff around Scarborough Shoal/Huangyan Island. It is uncertain to what extent China's economic manipulation has changed the policy of the Philippines. However, the Philippines government has been seeking stronger security commitment from the United States, and even extended its naval exercise with Japan in

---

[41] 'Thailand says South China territorial dispute should not be allowed to harm ASEAN cooperation', *The Nation* (12 July 2012).

[42] Song Guoyou and Wen Jin Yuan, 'China's free trade agreement strategies', *The Washington Quarterly* 35, no. 4 (Fall 2012): pp. 107–119.

[43] James Reilly, 'China's unilateral sanctions', *The Washington Quarterly* 35, no. 4 (Fall 2012), p. 121.

May 2015. The joint naval exercise is believed to counter China's aggressive maritime behavior.

Compared to the Philippines, Vietnam is more sensitive to China's actions. Vietnam has a collective memory of China in the past. Historical dominance and borderland skirmishes have fueled resentment in the South China Sea conflict. As discussed previously, should Vietnam, as a more vulnerable middle power, worry about the threat of this imbalanced trade relations?

Like the rest of the ASEAN members, the Vietnamese leadership favors a pragmatic approach to connect with the big powers in the region. It has benefited from hedging between a powerful United States present and a prosperous rising China.[44] Despite suspicion between Vietnam and the United States, China has become an inevitable factor that has driven the two countries closer, through non-combat exercises between the two militaries in 2014 and the impending US-led TPP to promote closer economic ties. Although it is hard to foresee Vietnam siding with the United States against China, domestic nationalism has pushed Vietnam to forge closer ties with the United States. This foreign policy shift is not due to trust in the United States; rather, it is a response to check China's power.[45]

Investment

China has been investing in Southeast Asia to bolster its regional influence and advance its strategic interests. Although this investment, together with financial aid, has improved relations with Vietnam and other Southeast Asian countries, its economic charms have proven less effective in this regard.

---

[44]Evelyn Goh, 'Understanding "Hedging" in Asia-Pacific security', *PacNet Newsletter* 43 (31 August 2006); Alice Ba, '*Between China and America: ASEAN's Great Power Dilemmas*', in *China, the United States, and Southeast Asia: Contending Perspectives on Politics, Security and Economics*, Evelyn Goh and Sheldon W. Simon, eds. (London: Routledge, 2008); Ian Storey, *Southeast Asia and the Rise of China: The Search for Security* (London Routledge, 2010), p. 221.

[45]Brantly Womack, '*Identity in Motion: Vietnam since 1976*', in *Asia's Middle Powers? The Identity and Regional Policy of South Korea and Vietnam*, Gi-Wook Shin, Joon-Woo Park and Donald Keyser, eds. (The Walter H. Shorenstein Asia-Pacific Research Center, 2013).

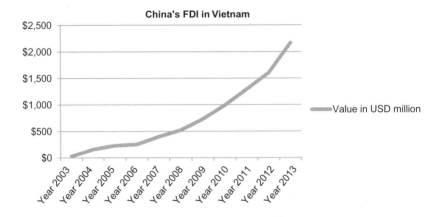

Figure 3.5.   China's FDI in Vietnam in million US$.

Source: CEIC datadase.[46]

Chinese investment in Vietnam has increased dramatically, especially after the previous president Hu Jingtao pursued the 'Going Out' policy (see Fig. 3.5). Resource and infrastructure are the leading aspects of investment. So far, compared with other counterparts, such as South Korea and British Virgin Islands, China is not the largest investor in Vietnam. Its FDI is even smaller with US$42.89 million compared to Thailand's US$51.29 million (see Fig. 3.6). However, it does not mean that China's investment is insignificant. China is said to utilize offshore financial centers such as the British Virgin Islands and Cayman Islands to invest overseas. What is more, a major amount of China's FDI to Hong Kong for capital flight or round-tripping before investing overseas is increasing as well.[47] Due to overcapacity of the domestic market, China's outbound investment is growing dramatically, especially in contrast to the staggering Western investment.

Vietnam is slowly shifting the rudimentary economy to an industrialized economy owing to its lack of necessary capital, human resources, and technology. Therefore, FDI plays a very important role in providing the capital and technology to develop the domestic economy and human resources to

---

[46]Accessed on 12 April 2015, available at: http:// www.ceicdata.com/en/countries/ china.

[47]Maximilian Ernst, 'Sino-Vietnamese relations and cross border economic cooperation-the socioeconomic determinants to Chinese OFDI in Vietnam' BA Thesis. Johannes Gutenberg University, 2013.

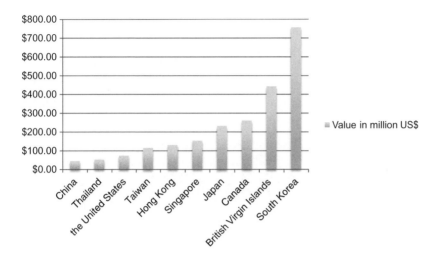

Figure 3.6. Major FDI sources in Vietnam by May 2015

Source: CEIC datadase.[48]

improve the skills of the locals. To assess the impact of China's FDI, it is important to study the industrial sector with the highest Chinese investment.

Generally, China usually invests heavily in sectors such as power, energy, heavy industry, and infrastructure construction in developing countries such as Africa, Latin America, and Southeast Asia. Meanwhile, China merges and acquires technology and services in more developed countries like Western Europe and North America. According to Fig. 3.7, the access to energy plays a more important role for China's investment in Vietnam, followed by transportation and metals production. It is not difficult to find that China's FDI is mostly concentrated in the low-skilled and labor-intensive areas.

The impact of China's investment on Vietnam's socioeconomic development is comparatively insignificant. First, China is transferring its low-cost manufacturing sector to its neighboring countries due to rising wages and production costs, and Vietnam is one of the top destinations. Chinese companies in Vietnam tend to pay lower wages to the Vietnamese than the Chinese, and provide a much lower level of training. In areas such as construction, the Chinese contractors often bring Chinese migrant workers to Vietnam

---

[48]*Ibid.* (accessed 30 May 2015).

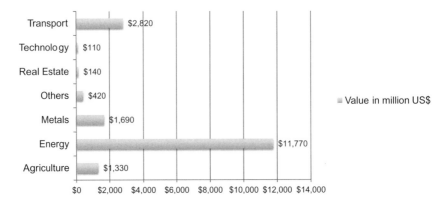

Figure 3.7.   Major Chinese FDI sector in Vietnam 2005–2015.

Source: American Enterprise Institute.[49]

because they have the necessary skills to operate and repair heavy machines, skills lacking among the locals. Among the workers, some are unskilled while others are illegal. Such practices do not improve the employment opportunities for the locals. It is believed that some of the illegal migrant workers have caused social security concerns within the Vietnamese civil society.[50]

Second, China's investments have been widely considered as exploitive and have often alienated local citizens. Vietnam is concerned about China's vast but low-quality investment in resources and energy. For example, Vietnam boasts of the third largest reserves of mineral ores, prominently bauxite. The contracts leased to the Chinese companies sparked furious opposition from a variety of Vietnamese groups. At the same time, most illegal exports of mineral ores are also believed to be bound for China.

It is reported that some technologies used by mines operated by the Chinese companies are prohibited in China. However, due to the lack of technology and expertise in mining, many Vietnamese companies choose to

---

[49] Chinese Investments & Contracts in Vietnam 2005–2015, available at: http://www.aei.org/ china-global-investment-tracker/?gclid=Cj0KEQjw4qqrBRDE2K_z7Pbvjo8BEiQA39AI mf-EaPcbmg11g9Baz_zBQHg0eDMjAKWY4BA5mVj0vz4aAlLr8P8HAQ.

[50] Jason Morris-Jung, 'An ethnographic glimpse: on the trail of Chinese-Vietnamese mining cooperation', *ISEAS perspective* 25 (25 May 2015).

partner with China.[51] To the disappointment of the Vietnamese, the Chinese contractors usually import equipment and machinery from China rather than purchase from the local suppliers. Even if equipment from China is not the most advanced, it fits in with Vietnam's much less advanced mining operations. And due to geographic proximity, it is easier for the companies to seek maintenance from China than from Japan or Europe.

However, the development of advanced production and organizational management approach as well as the awareness of Corporate Social Responsibility (CSR) has enabled experienced investors from Western Europe and the United States to expand their international influences. On the contrary, China's intention of spreading soft power and building a benign image has incurred sharp criticism and even resistance in Vietnam. Meanwhile, relations with Vietnam are increasingly coming under strain owing to China's nationalistic rhetoric over the South China Sea and infrastructural development activities around the disputed area. For example, in 2014, the HD-981 oil rig activities, together with collision between the Chinese coast guard and Vietnamese fishing vessels caused anti-China protests, leading to riots and attacks against mainly Chinese businesses and nationals.

China's Willingness to Transform Economic Asymmetry into Potential Leverage

Being in an asymmetrical relationship with Vietnam, China is in a position that benefits from economic interdependence with Vietnam when it meets the prerequisites for exerting economic coercions. However, China has refrained from applying such tools against Vietnam. To understand this, one can refer to previous literature on economic coercion focusing on the involvement of third parties; the nationalism of the target country offset the effectiveness of economic coercion, as well as the pressure from domestic interest groups investing overseas.[52]

---

[51] *Ibid.*

[52] Such as Jean-Marc F. Blanchard, Edward D. Mansfield, and Norrin M. Ripsman, 'The political economy of national security: economic statecraft, interdependence, and international conflict', *Security Studies* 9, no. 1–2 (1999), pp. 1–14; Daniel W. Drezner, 'The trouble with carrots: transaction costs, conflict expectations, and economic inducements',

China's case is unique because it attempts to separate business from politics. Unlike the United States whose economic statecraft mainly target international issues such as human rights or non-proliferation of massive weapons, China often utilizes economic statecraft to advance its own national interests with caution.[53] After its admission to the WTO, China has reaped the benefits of a more open global market by abiding by the rules. On the one hand, the nature of WTO prohibits arbitrary trade sanctions for political manipulation. At the same time, the CAFTA rule is that parties shall endeavor to refrain from increasing restrictions or limitations that would affect the application of the Agreement.[54] On the other hand, economic sanctions in China have less legal, moral, ideological, and practical grounds to manipulate.[55] Accordingly, China is not ready to exploit the favorable asymmetrical relations even if it has potential to do so.

Furthermore, economic coercion is a blunt tool for China even if it fits the situation of Hirschmanesque effects of dominating bargaining position over Vietnam. Keohane and Nye point out that asymmetrical economic interdependence can generate political influence in foreign relations but it does not always work to the advantage of larger states. China's economic coercion is likely to bring about the suspension of trade that may hurt certain domestic interests groups such as local government dependent on border trade and cross-border investment. By the same token, the use of this punishment may discourage economic regionalism and harm China's

---

Security Studies 9, nos. 1–2 (1999), pp. 188–218; Timothy C. Lehmann, 'Keeping friends close and enemies closer: classical realist statecraft and economic exchange in U.S. interwar strategy', *Security Studies* 18, no. 1 (2009), pp. 115–147; David A. Baldwin, and Robert A. Pape, 'Evaluating economic sanctions', *International Security* 23, no. 2 (Autumn, 1998), pp. 189–198; Gary Clyde Hufbauer, Jeffrey J. Schott, Kimberly Ann Elliott, and Barbara Oegg, *Economic Sanctions Reconsidered.* (3rd edn.). (Washington, DC: Peterson Institute for International Economics, 2007).

[53]James Reilly, 'China's unilateral sanctions', *The Washington Quarterly* 35, no. 4 (Fall 2012).

[54]Article 13, 'ASEAN China free trade agreement 2002 framework agreement', ASEAN Briefing (4 November 2002).

[55]James Reilly, 'China's unilateral sanctions', *The Washington Quarterly* 35, no. 4 (Fall 2012).

own economy in the end, especially its backward western provinces which have close economic relations with Vietnam and other Southeast Asian countries.

As mentioned earlier, the continuous forging of economic relations with Vietnam is conducive to China's economic development. Trade relations with Vietnam provide a gateway for the development of China's Guangxi and Yunnan provinces. These impoverished provinces are thirsty for more economic cooperation and open markets. Li points out that local liberalism serves as a driving force to influence the central government for further economic cooperation.[56] Therefore, the two provinces have spared no effort in lobbying the central government to support provincial interests including the Myanmar–Yun Nan pipelines and the annual China–ASEAN Expo in Guangxi. In 2007, China proposed a Beibu Gulf Economic Rim (BGER), an idea first mentioned in the China–ASEAN agreement on a framework for concluding a regional free trade agreement. This proposal was part of China's Great Western Development, which aims to improve the competency of its less-developed southwestern provinces. BGER has emerged as a new highlight for China–ASEAN cooperation, especially for Vietnam. It also boosts the cross-border trade by serving as two corridors linking Yunnan and Guangxi with Vietnam along the Tonkin Gulf in areas such as trade, agriculture, industry, and transportation.[57] At the same time, entry into Vietnam will serve as a launch pad to link up with other Southeast Asian countries.

Vietnam is important for China's regional diplomacy and its domestic growth, especially the southwestern provinces, and it is also not an easy target for China to wield economic coercion for political purposes. Vietnam is currently upgrading its manufacturing and supply chain facilities. Vietnam's participation in the US-led TPP agreement is expected to increase Vietnam's competency against China's in the textile industry

---

[56]Li, Mingjiang, 'Local liberalism: China's provincial approaches to relations with Southeast Asia', *Journal of Contemporary China* 23, no. 86 (2014), pp. 275–293.

[57]'President Luong holds talks with Hu Jintao', Ministry of Foreign Affairs of Vietnam, available at: http://www.mofa.gov.vn/en/nr040807104143/nr040807105001/ns050719102537.

because Vietnam believes that through the TPP, its companies can gain access to technology and manufacturing skills to upgrade production.[58] Vietnam foresees that it may be able to compete with China and even compensate for its trade deficit with China through a trade surplus with TPP members, especially with the United States. Even though the process has been sluggish, TPP has become an inevitable factor to unnerve China. In response, China has been quick in initiating the AIIB to expand Chinese investment and influence in Asia. In this regard, China may continue to use economic incentives unless there are other better alternatives to project its influence.

In addition to TPP, the quality and reputation of China's investment has faced a backlash in some developing countries, such as Myanmar, Sri Lanka, Indonesia, and Vietnam. Vietnam's public outcry and protest over China's mining investment suggests that China's investment has limited effectiveness in spreading its goodwill. Nevertheless, Vietnamese nationalistic sentiments over the heightened South China Sea disputes after the oil-rig incident pushed Vietnam to diversify its investment sources. Do Thang Hai, the deputy trade and industry minister, acknowledged that 'the recent political issues in relations with China are promoting us to diversify'.[59] Therefore, investment from Japan to Vietnam flourished with a wide range of projects that cover areas such as value-added automation and pharmaceutical manufacturing.

Although the complications arising from the South China Sea make none of the claimants back off from their claims, China skillfully applies 'divide and influence' to reduce the unity of ASEAN on this matter while strengthening its claim by building facilities and lands. Economic incentives may not be able to change the stances of the claimants, but the spillover effect on the indirect stakeholders can influence the unity of ASEAN. ASEAN does not have a unified stance on the South China Sea conflict. There are different reasons for this. Thriving trade relations with China is one of

---

[58]Dezan Shira, 'China set to lose out to Vietnam as U.S. TPP deal looms', *China Briefing* (6 February 2013).

[59]Tom Wright, and Mitsuru Obe, 'Vietnam plays key role in China–Japan aid battle' (27 March 2015), available at: http://www.wsj.com/articles/vietnam-plays-key-role-in-china-japan-aid-battle-1427431451.

the most important factors that prevent the other countries from pressuring China.[60]

So far, China has not officially and explicitly declared the South China Sea as one of its 'national core interests' equal to the Taiwan issue.[61] It means that there is space for negotiation and cooperation in this matter. Nowadays, Vietnam is able to deal with global powers without taking sides, as most Southeast Asian countries do. From a position of independence and geopolitical calculation, Vietnam is able to enjoy economic opportunities while keeping superpowers in check by balancing interests. As long as China and Vietnam can manage their relations over the disputes in a way that does not threaten both the sovereign rights of China and Vietnam, economic cooperation can provide incentives for bilateral negotiation.

Conclusion

This chapter argues that even though China has the potential to exert political dominance over Vietnam, it has refrained from doing so because of China's consideration of economic inducement toward Vietnam. Inducement consists of several key elements. Economically, it is based on China's domestic economic growth demand, especially in boosting China's 'Develop the West' project in southwestern provinces. Vietnam has served as China's gateway to Southeast Asia and China has benefited from an open and integrated regional economy where it is able to maximize its overseas market share, transfer low-end industry and upgrade its domestic industry. Should China persist in trade coercion for political reasons, it will likely weaken its good neighborhood diplomatic stance and lose out on the benefits from engaging in regional and international trade. Moreover, China's low-quality

---

[60]Ho Khai Leong and Samuel C. Y. Ku, *China and Southeast Asia: Global Changes and Regional Challenges*. (Singapore: Institute of Southeast Asian Studies, 2005); Luke Hunt, 'Can ASEAN unite on South China Sea?' The *Diplomat* (17 November 2012), (accessed 2 February 2014), available at: http://thediplomat.com/2012/11/can-asean-unite-on-south-china-sea/.

[61] 'China's Declaration of Key Interests Misinterpreted', *Beijing Review* (26 August 2013), (accessed 12 January 2014), available at: http://www.china.org.cn/world/2013-08/26/content_29824049.htm.

FDI and unhealthy trade balance with Vietnam has pressured the latter to diversify its economic partners so as to reduce the reliance and negative impact of China's economic activities.

Legally, China has been bound by the agreements of WTO and CAFTA that prohibit arbitrary trade sanctions for political purposes. China is not ready for unilateral sanctions as it has less legal and moral grounds for doing so. China remains cautious of the effectiveness of economic coercion because it can be a blunt sword hurting itself. It is, therefore, likely that China will continue to use economic incentives to reduce containment from its competitors and maritime dispute claimants, like it did before by isolating the international status of Taiwan.

From a political perspective, Vietnam is not an easy case for China to exploit bilateral economic relations for political purposes. On the one hand, the Vietnamese have collective memories over China's historical dominance so nationalistic sentiments still affect the foreign policy of Vietnam. On the other hand, the alluring TPP and other economic and security assistance from the United States and Japan can limit the effectiveness of China's economic statecraft, especially economic coercions.

China's economic inducement is designed for the long run and ASEAN is the main reason for China to do so. By means of economic inducements, China attempts to deter the internationalization of the South China Sea issue through the strategy of 'divide and influence'. The unity of ASEAN over the maritime disputes has been tested and will continue to be tested. While China is actively playing its charm offensive toward Southeast Asia, it is difficult to foresee economic statecraft guaranteeing China's success in influencing Southeast Asian states to do what they could otherwise not have done.[62] Conditions such as the projection of maritime power, domestic nationalism, and great power rivalry in the South China Sea have made it a trickier situation than the land border conflicts that occurred almost four decades ago. Yet there is no better way other than economic inducements for China to appease its southern neighbors. However, whether China changes its course of economic incentives hinges on the response from the United States and its alliance.

---

[62]David A. Baldwin, *Economic Statecraft*, p. 20.

After the Third Plenum of the 18th CPC Central Committee, it has become quite clear that China will continue to consolidate its neighborhood diplomacy. In the foreign minister's words, the new government has attached greater importance to neighborhood diplomacy in its overall diplomatic agenda.[63] With so many factors at play, economic inducement is not an easy approach for states to realize their foreign policy goals, but China will continue to utilize it as long as it serves its interests.

---

[63] Wang Yi, Foreign Minister, 'Embark on a New Journey of China's Diplomacy', Last modified by Ministry of Foreign Affairs of the People's Republic of China at the symposium 'New Starting Point, New Thinking and New Practices 2013: China and the World', (16 December 2013), (accessed 5 January 2014), available at: http://www.chinaembassy.org.sg/eng/xwdt/t1109943.htm.

Part Two

China's Economic Influence in Its Neighborhood

Chapter 4

Interdependent Rivals: China's Economic Statecraft towards Japan

Xiaoyu Pu

In April 2015, 57 nations became founding members of the Chinese-led Asian Infrastructure Investment Bank (AIIB), which was designed to satisfy Asia's expanding need for infrastructure. The United States and its allies struggled to put together a response. Among international observers, some applauded China for wielding soft power to aid Asia's growth, while others viewed China's move as undermining the US-led economic order and using aid as a tool to advance China's strategic agenda.[1] AIIB is one of many examples of China's attempts to transform its economic power into diplomatic influence. Since China pursued its opening and reform in 1978, China has transformed itself from a marginalized actor in the world economy into one of the leading economic powers in the world. Eager to deploy its economic might for strategic benefits, China is using economic statecraft more frequently and more assertively. China's economic statecraft creates opportunities but also causes anxiety in Asia and around the world.

In the East Asian context, how does China use its economic power to pursue foreign policy goals toward Japan? This chapter begins with a review

---

[1] 'Who is Afraid of AIIB?' *Foreign Affairs*, 7 May 2015, available at: https://www.foreignaffairs.com/articles/china/2015-05-07/whos-afraid-aiib.

of the key features of China's economic statecraft, followed by a discussion of the context of Sino–Japanese relations. The following three sections contain three case analyses of China's economic statecraft toward Japan: rare-earth control, boycott of Japanese goods, and contested leadership in regional cooperation. These case analyses suggest that China and Japan have an interdependent relationship, and the Sino–Japanese relationship is composed of both cooperative and competitive elements. The ambivalent nature of the relationship has shaped China's economic statecraft. The conclusion summarizes key findings.

China's Economic Statecraft

In international relations, statecraft refers to the selection of means for the pursuit of foreign policy goals, and economic statecraft refers to the use of economic tools to advance strategic and security interests.[2] As China's interests are expanding, Chinese leaders have turned to a range of economic tools to shape the attitudes and policies of other countries. China's use of economic means to advance its diplomatic objectives is neither unique nor new. All great powers have sought to deploy economic tools for strategic advantage.[3] During the Cold War, Chinese leaders provided foreign aid to many developing countries in support of their diplomatic and ideological struggles.[4]

Regarding the purpose of economic statecraft, some scholars argue that 'security externalities' should be the focus of economic statecraft. Examples of security externalities include transfer of sensitive technology, loss of

---

[2] David Baldwin's seminal work defines economic statecraft as 'governmental influence attempts relying primarily on resources that have a reasonable semblance of a market price in terms of money'. See David Baldwin, *Economic Statecraft* (Princeton, NJ: Princeton University Press), p. 19. Although Baldwin's analytical framework has been influential, his definition is widely regarded as too narrow. This chapter takes a broader definition of economic statecraft.

[3] Daniel W. Drezner, *The Sanctions Paradox: Economic Statecraft and International Relations*, No. 65 (Cambridge: Cambridge University Press, 1999).

[4] Shuguang Zhang, *Beijing's Economic Statecraft During the Cold War, 1949–1991* (Baltimore, MD: Johns Hopkins University Press, 2014).

strategic industries, concentrated supply or demand dependence and so on.[5] Other scholars conceptualize the goals of China's economic statecraft more broadly, including strengthening resource security, enhancing political relationships and soft power, and boosting commercial opportunities for national firms.[6] The specific strategies of economic statecraft might include foreign aid, direct investment, preferential trade agreements or state procurements, sanctions, embargo, and so on. These tools of economic statecraft can be deployed either as positive incentives or as punitive measures.

As China's economic power rises, Chinese leaders are reconsidering ways to transform China's wealth into diplomatic influence. China's economic statecraft is based on its expanding economic power. China's economy is the world's second largest economy in terms of nominal GDP, and the world's largest economy in terms of purchasing power parity, according to the International Monetary Fund (IMF). China is the largest manufacturing economy in the world as well as the largest exporter of goods in the world. China is also the world's fastest growing consumer market. China is the largest trading partner for over 100 countries, and it is the largest trading partner of most of its neighboring countries. China's trade surplus has enabled it to run up the world's largest current account surplus and amass huge foreign exchange reserves. China's state-led development model has left Chinese leaders with enormous control over its economy. Chinese leaders pursue their goals through government agencies such as the Ministry of Commerce, the Ministry of Finance, the National Development and Reform Commission as well as the People's Bank of China. Capital for China's economic statecraft comes primarily from the banking sector.[7]

---

[5]William J. Norris, 'Economic statecraft with Chinese characteristics: The use of commercial actors in China's grand strategy'. PhD diss., Massachusetts Institute of Technology, 2010, 19; William J. Norris, *Chinese Economic Statecraft: Commercial Actors, Grand Strategy, and State Control* (Ithaca and London: Cornell University Press, 2016), pp. 13–14.

[6]Deborah Bräutigam and Tang Xiaoyang, 'Economic statecraft in China's new overseas special economic zones: soft power, business or resource security?' *International Affairs*, 88, no. 4 (2012), pp. 799–816.

[7]For a summary of Beijing's economic resources and governmental agencies for economic statecraft, see James Reilly, 'China's economic statecraft: Turning wealth into power', *Lowy Institute for International Policy* (2013), pp. 2–4.

Generally speaking, Chinese leaders prefer economic carrots to sticks as a means of exercising diplomatic influence. Incentives offer mutual economic benefits and build closer political ties. Beijing's calculation is that economic engagement will eventually produce desirable changes in targeted countries. Typical examples of incentives include foreign aid, state purchases, generous trade agreements, and infrastructural projects. Foreign aid is a primary resource for China's economic statecraft. According to the White Paper on Chinese foreign aid, the scale of China's foreign aid has been expanding. During the period 2010–2012, China appropriated 89.34 billion yuan (US$14.41 billion) of foreign aid in the following forms: grant (aid gratis), interest-free loan, and concessional loan.[8] China's aid is used to help bolster diplomatic relationships, and the largest part of China's aid goes to Asia and Africa. China's leaders rely on the lure of China's domestic market and the potential of Chinese investment to sway reluctant leaders in wealthier industrialized nations such as the United Kingdom and Japan. China hopes that the benefits of trade and investment will empower commercial interest groups within the target country to accommodate China's preferences. The consensus of Chinese leaders, since the late 1990s is that China should try to create favorable international conditions for continuing China's domestic growth while reducing risks stemming from the China threat image.[9] Through economic statecraft, China has tried to reassure its neighbors that China is not an emergent threat but an opportunity. Many scholars conceptualize China's policy toward Asian neighbors as 'charm offensive' diplomacy.[10] The first wave of the charm offensive was launched in 1997 when Beijing declared that it would not devalue the Renminbi (RMB) during the Asian financial crisis and China reinforced it a few years later with a proposed China–ASEAN free trade agreement (FTA). President Xi Jinping's proactive regional diplomacy could be viewed as the second

---

[8]Information Office of the State Council, PRC, 'China's Foreign Aid', 2014, available at http://news.xinhuanet.com/english/china/2014-07/10/c_133474011.htm.

[9]Avery Goldstein, *Rising to the Challenge: China's Grand Strategy and International Security* (Stanford, Stanford University Press, 2005).

[10]Joshua Kurlantzick, *Charm Offensive: How China's Soft Power is Transforming the World* (New Haven, CT: Yale University Press, 2007).

wave of charm offensive.[11] Beijing held a major conference on peripheral diplomacy (*zhoubian waijiao*) on 24 to 25 October 2013. Participants included all of the standing members of the Chinese Communist Party (CCP) Politburo. The focus on China's regional diplomacy at such a high-level meeting was unprecedented. The meeting laid out some long-term goals of China's regional diplomacy. Xi's speech catalogued the tools of economic aid, trade, scientific, security, and public diplomacy for China's regional strategy. According to Xi, 'We [China] must strive to make our neighbors more friendly in politics, economically more closely tied to us, and we must have deeper security cooperation and closer people-to-people ties'.[12] At this meeting, Xi identified a four-part philosophy to guide diplomacy toward such nations, centering on efforts to convey or realize *amity, sincerity, mutual benefit,* and *inclusiveness.* These are all positive features generally resonant with earlier approaches to regional diplomacy. Regarding economic diplomacy, China proposed to build 'One Belt and One Road' (*yidaiyilu*), which refers to the 'Silk Road Economic Belt' and 'Twenty-first Century Maritime Silk Road'. These concepts were put forward by President Xi during his visit to Central Asia and Southeast Asia respectively in 2013.[13]

Despite the emphasis on positive incentives, China remains willing to deploy punitive economic measures in defense of its national interests. In recent years, China has been flexing its economic muscle more frequently.[14] China tries to exert influence through reciprocity, whereby desired behavior is rewarded while undesired behavior is punished. China's coercive diplomacy is not new. In the history of Chinese foreign policy, China has tried to use coercive diplomacy to pressure countries like Vietnam and Philippines. In many instances, Beijing implemented a calculus of signals. China would first deter an adversary from taking actions contrary to Chinese interests by threatening the use of military force; if deterrence failed, China justified

---

[11] Bonnie S. Glaser and Deep Pal, 'Is China's Charm Offensive Dead?' *The Jamestown Foundation*, available at: http://www.jamestown.org/programs/chinabrief/single/?tx_ttnews%5Btt_news%5D=4269 (accessed 8 June 2015).

[12] Xinhua, 'Xi Jinping: China to further friendly relations with neighboring countries', available at: http://news.xinhuanet.com/english/china/2013-10/26/c_125601680.htm.

[13] http://english.peopledaily.com.cn/n/2014/0605/c90883-8737468.html.

[14] James Reilly, 'China's unilateral sanctions', *The Washington Quarterly* 35(4), (Fall 2012), pp. 121–133.

its use of military force on the basis of self-defense.[15] Compared with the traditional coercive diplomacy through military threat, economic sanctions as a form of statecraft offer a low-risk way to signal China's dissatisfaction and also appease the nationalistic domestic audience.

While China's diplomatic influence is expanding, its economic statecraft has important limitations. China's economic statecraft is not guided by a coherent grand strategy.[16] At the domestic level, the diverging preferences among different actors within China result in incoherent and contradictory approaches to economic statecraft.[17] At the international level, the degree of influence that China can wield over particular countries varies depending on the size of the targeted economy. Given China's economic power, a minor shift in China's trade can have a massive effect on smaller economies such as Laos or Cambodia. However, Chinese influence on larger economies is much more limited. For instance, even though China is the largest creditor of US government debt, China cannot coerce the United States into changing its policies.[18] Similarly, China's influence toward Japan is much more limited compared with China's influence on Philippines or Thailand. China's economic statecraft could also be counterproductive in diplomacy as China's coercion could exacerbate anxiety among its Asian neighbors, generating backlashes, and balancing responses across the region.

Sino-Japanese Relations: History, Power, and Complex Interdependence

Scholars often point out the perplexing deterioration of Sino-Japanese relations, despite the deepening economic interdependence between the two

---

[15]For the study of these regularities, see Paul H. B. Godwin and Alice L. Miller, 'China's Forbearance has Limits: Chinese Threat and Retaliation Signaling and Its implications for a Sino-American Military Confrontation', *China Strategic Perspectives*, No. 6 (National Defense University, 2013).

[16]James Reilly, 'China's Economic Statecraft: Turning Wealth into Power', p. 4.

[17]For the analysis of the incoherence of China's economic statecraft, see William J. Norris, *Chinese Economic Statecraft: Commercial Actors, Grand Strategy, and State Control*, pp. 48–51.

[18]Daniel W. Drezner, 'Bad debts: Assessing China's financial influence in great power politics', *International Security*, 34, no. 2 (2009), pp. 7–45.

countries. Although China and Japan have been deepening economic inter-dependence over the last three decades, their relationship has been increas-ingly tense. This runs contrary to the liberal theory of international relations that posits that economic interactions should bring peace to a bilateral rela-tionship.[19] For many Chinese and Japanese, the reason for the rising tension is self-evident. The most prominent sources of tension include territorial disputes, the Japanese prime minister's visits to Yasukuni Shrine, contested memories of the Nanjing Massacre, the anti-Japanese demonstrations in China, and the decade-long reparation litigation against Japan.

The Sino–Japanese relationship reveals a complex mix of cooperation and competition elements. China's economic statecraft reflects this ambiva-lent attitude. An important concept to understand the Sino–Japanese rela-tionship is complex interdependence, which was put forth by international relations theorists Robert Keohane and Joseph Nye[20] to show how interna-tional relations are transformed by interdependence. The theorists recognize that the complex transnational connections and interdependencies between states and societies are increasing while the use of military force and power balancing are decreasing.[21] In essence, complex interdependence poses a challenge for one country to pursue economic statecraft toward another country. In a highly interdependent context, the political and economic effects of economic statecraft are often complicated and delicate. In Sino–Japanese relations, complex interdependence would suggest that Beijing is motivated to enhance international cooperation and manipulate economic interaction.

The Sino–Japanese relationship in the post-World War II era could be divided into different periods. Even before China and Japan established a formal diplomatic relationship in 1972, some initial economic ties were established between the two countries. In December 1971, the Chinese and Japanese trade liaison offices began to discuss the possibility of restoring diplomatic trade relations, and in July 1972, Kakuei Tanaka became the

---

[19]John R. Oneal and Bruce Russett, 'Assessing the liberal peace with alternative specifica-tions: Trade still reduces conflict', *Journal of Peace Research*, 36, no. 4 (1999), pp. 423–442.
[20]Robert Owen Keohane and Joseph S. Nye, *Power and Interdependence: World Politics in Transition* 2nd edn. (Boston: Little, Brown, 1977).
[21]*Ibid.*

new Japanese prime minister. The 1972 Nixon visit to China encouraged the Sino-Japanese normalization process, and Tanaka's visit to Beijing culminated in signing a joint statement on 29 September 1972. It established diplomatic relations between Japan and China. Subsequently, the bilateral economic relationship grew rapidly. The development of complementary interests flourished from the 1980s to the mid-1990s, and this period could be viewed as a golden age in contemporary Sino–Japanese relations. The two sides had deepened their economic cooperation despite controversial historical issues.[22]

From late 1990s to 2010, Sino–Japanese relationship entered into an era of cold politics and hot economics.[23] Economic ties were deepened, and China became the biggest destination for Japanese exports in 2009. During this period, Sino–Japanese relations were still troubled by territorial disputes and historical controversies. Top leaders of both countries tried to protect the economic relationship from being strained by political tensions. Sino–Japanese relations appeared to reach a turning point after Shinzo Abe became the prime minister of Japan in September 2006. In the absence of high-level visits over several years of tense relations, Prime Minister Abe tried to 'break ice' with China by his official visit to China. His visit was well received in China, generating a new momentum in the bilateral relationship.

However, the recovery of the bilateral relationship was transient. In the early 2010s, Sino–Japanese relations deteriorated further due to new diplomatic and political crises. The Senkaku/Diaoyu Islands dispute resulted in hostility: some aggressive encounters in the East China Sea, heated rhetoric, and anti-Japan protests in China. From 2010, China and Japan entered into a period of strategic competition characterized by cold politics and cold economics. Rising political tensions have threatened interdependent economic ties. Although top leaders of the two sides have decided to build a mutually beneficial strategic relationship, it is hard to know if this goal can be achieved in the short term. Meanwhile, within the societies of both countries, perception between the Japanese people and Chinese people is

---

[22]Allen S. Whiting, *China Eyes Japan* (Berkeley: University of California Press, 1989).

[23]Min Gyo Koo, 'The Senkaku/Diaoyu dispute and Sino–Japanese political-economic relations: Cold politics and hot economics?' *The Pacific Review*, 22, no. 2 (2009), pp. 205–232.

increasingly negative. According to a 2014 BBC World Service Poll, 3% of Japanese people view China's influence positively, with 73% expressing a negative view. Meanwhile, 5% of Chinese people view Japanese influence positively and 90% express a negative view.[24]

The deeper causes of political tensions are the shifting balance of power and the changing strategic environment. In the 1970s and 1980s, Japan was willing to support China's economic modernization for several reasons. First, the Soviet Union was regarded as the primary geopolitical challenge for the United States, China, and Japan, so there was a strategic foundation for Sino–Japanese cooperation. Second, China was still far from being perceived as a threat for Japan as there was a large power gap between the two countries. Japan was one of the most advanced economies in the world while China was still a poor and fragile developing country. Third, top leaders had established some tacit agreements to build a better relationship. For instance, China would give up its formal rights for Japanese war compensation while Japan would provide economic aid to China.[25] In the current decade, China's rapid economic rise and military power expansion signal a significant transition of geopolitical power. The anticipation of a much stronger China increasingly worsened Japanese perception of their relationship with Beijing.[26] On the Chinese side, China has gradually abandoned its low-profile approach in diplomacy to pursue a much more assertive regional diplomacy strategy.[27] China's rising power and assertive approach have pushed Japan to strengthen its security cooperation with the United States, and the strengthening of US–Japan alliance has made

---

[24] BBC World Service Poll, 2014, p. 21 and p. 37.

[25] While the Chinese government gave up the rights to ask for war compensation, the Chinese people and society did not give up. There are many war reparation movements in Chinese society. See Bin Xu and Xiaoyu Pu, 'Dynamic statism and memory politics: A case analysis of the Chinese war reparations movement', *The China Quarterly*, 201 (2010), pp. 156–175.

[26] For a detailed analysis of how Japan responds to the rise of China, see Sheila A. Smith, *Intimate Rivals: Japanese Domestic Politics and a Rising China* (New York: Columbia University Press, 2015).

[27] For the analysis of China's assertiveness, see Alastair Iain Johnston, 'How new and assertive is China's new assertiveness?' *International Security*, 37, no. 4 (2013), pp. 7–48; Dingding Chen, Xiaoyu Pu, and Alastair Iain Johnston, 'Debating China's Assertiveness', *International Security*, 38, no. 3 (2013), pp. 176–183.

China feel more threatened. This power shift has generated the dynamics of security dilemma between China and Japan.[28]

The following three sections will focus on the analyses of three cases of China's economics statecraft toward Japan. Each case will illustrate the ambivalent nature of Sino-Japanese relations.

Economic sanctions and rare earth export control

On 7 September 2010, after a Chinese fishing trawler collided with two Japanese Coast Guard patrol boats near the Senkaku/Diaoyu Islands, the Chinese captain of the trawler, Zhan Qixiong, was arrested by the Japanese government, sparking diplomatic tensions between Japan and China. According to a *New York Times* report, China reduced export quotas of rare earth metals to Japan.[29] It might be debatable if the timing of China's rare earth control was related to the territorial dispute between the two countries. Although officials from China's Ministry of Commerce denied such a relationship, the Japanese Ministry of Economy, Trade, and Industry (METI) announced that a number of trade companies had reported an embargo on the export of Chinese rare earth to Japan.[30] The Japanese government regarded China's action as a *de facto* trade embargo and decided to make contingency plans. There were tense negotiations between Chinese and Japanese officials on the rare earth issue. On 13 November, Japanese minister Ohata met with Zhang Ping, China's director of the Development and Reform Commission, on the sideline of the Asia-Pacific Economic Cooperation (APEC) Summit in Japan. Zhang noted that the rare earth issue would be probably resolved very soon. By December, shipments of rare earth to Japan returned to normal levels.[31]

---

[28]For the analysis of security dilemma in Sino-Japanese relations, see Thomas J. Christensen, 'China, the US–Japan alliance, and the security dilemma in East Asia', *International Security*, 23, no. 4 (1999), pp. 49–80.

[29]Keith Bradsher, 'China to Tighten Limits on Rare Earth Exports', *New York Times*, 28 December 2010, available at: http://www.nytimes.com/2010/12/29/business/global/29rare.html?_r=0.

[30]Sheila A. Smith, *Intimate Rivals: Japanese Domestic Politics and a Rising China* (New York: Columbia University Press, 2015), p. 192.

[31]*Ibid.*

In the fall of 2011, China seemed to use rare earth policies as eco-nomic statecraft in a different context. Beijing attempted to force Japanese companies reliant on rare earth to move their production center and tech-nology to China in exchange for a low-cost supply of rare earth. According to a Japanese publication, *Daily Yomiuri*, the then-Chinese vice premier Li Keqiang told a high-level delegation of Japanese officials visiting China in September 2011 that China wanted technological support from Japan in the rare earth industry.[32] The Japanese company Hitachi Met-als reportedly indicated in August 2011 that it was contemplating mov-ing production of some of its neodymium-based magnets to China.[33] This 'technology for resources' strategy fit closely with Beijing's goal of moving its rare earth industry to the more complex processing sec-tors.[34] In fact, many of these policy measures formed part of a larger set of industrial policies initiated by China to become the world's leader in technology.[35]

Regarding the strategic and diplomatic implications of China's action, we should evaluate China's rare earth control in a broader context. First of all, China has a dominant position in rare earth production, but its rare earth industry has to be reformed for various reasons. To improve economic effi-ciency and environmental standards, the Chinese government had imple-mented a more rigorous industrial policy on rare earth productions even before the 2010 diplomatic crisis. Consequently, China's export control of rare earth should be understood in such a broader context of China's indus-trial policy.[36] That said, if we assume China did implement a temporary embargo, this case indicates China's strong willingness to introduce a new

---

[32]Wayne M. Morrison and Rachel Tang, 'China's Rare Earth Industry and Export Regime: Economic and Trade Implications for the United States', *Congressional Research Service*, 30 April 2012, pp. 18–19.

[33]Yuko Inoue and Julie Gordon, 'Analysis: Japanese Rare Earth Consumers Set Up Shop in China', *Reuters*, 12 August 2011.

[34]Wayne M. Morrison and Rachel Tang, 'China's Rare Earth Industry and Export Regime', p. 19.

[35]*Ibid.*

[36]For the analysis of the problems and reform attempts of China's rare earth industry, see Wayne M. Morrison and Rachel Tang, 'China's Rare Earth Industry and Export Regime', pp. 10–12.

and more difficult challenge for Japanese policy makers to defend China's security interests.[37]

Regarding China's 'technology for resource' strategy toward Japan, one primary motive of China's rare earth policies is predominantly mercantilist.[38] As noted by China's *National Medium and Long-Term Program for Science and Technology Development* (2006–2020), China is interested in modernizing the structure of its economy by transforming the country from a world center of low-tech manufacturing to one that is a dominant center for innovation by 2020.[39] China sees developing technologies for manufacturing rare earth as being a key priority for the country's economic success. It seems that Beijing is using its rare earth policies to lure foreign investment to advance its rare earth sector with high-tech applications.

China's strategy to push for technological development through restrictive export policies has brought a tremendous concern to foreign companies. Although Beijing will continue to utilize its rare earth policies as a tool of economic statecraft, it will undertake precautions. China's capabilities in economic power are continually expanding along with its effectiveness in applying various economic statecraft options. However, its economic interdependence with Japan and other leading economic powers often checks its leverage in exercising economic power. Nevertheless, as China continues to modernize its economy by transforming the country to a dominant center for innovation, China might continue using coercive economic measures to advance its security interests.

Boycotting Japanese Goods (Dizhirihuo)

In 2012, a populist boycott of Japanese consumer goods coincided with the Chinese government's deployment of China's economic statecraft toward Japan. This reflects a larger pattern between the Chinese government and nationalist movements: the Chinese government sometimes represses anti-Japan protests and at other times, they tacitly approve or even encourage

---

[37] Sheila A. Smith, *Intimate Rivals: Japanese Domestic Politics and a Rising China*, p. 204.
[38] Wayne M. Morrison and Rachel Tang, 'China's Rare Earth Industry and Export Regime', p. 19.
[39] *Ibid.*

these protests. The key factor is whether those anti-Japan protests could strengthen China's bargaining leverage.[40] The 2012 consumer boycott represents an extension of the public's role in China's foreign policy.[41]

On 10 September 2012, Japanese prime minister Yoshihiko Noda announced that the Japanese government would nationalize the Senkaku/Diaoyu Islands by purchasing them from a private owner. Noda's announcement sparked violent protests across China. Japanese businesses were ransacked, Japanese-brand cars were smashed, and Japanese restaurants were set on fire. Thousands of Chinese demonstrated in front of the Japanese diplomatic embassy. As emotions swelled, many Chinese consumers declined to buy Japanese electronics and cars, and began canceling visits to Japan.

Boycotts of Japanese goods are not new in China. In the 1930s, a patriotic movement was led by Chinese boycotts in protest of Japan's invasion.[42] Sporadic calls for boycotts of Japanese goods reemerged in the 1985 protests.[43] In 2003, an online petition campaign opposing the award of contracts to Japanese firms to build China's high-speed rail lines.[44] A consumer boycott emerged in spring 2005 amidst the widespread demonstrations and online petition campaign protesting Japan's attempts to gain a permanent seat on the UN Security Council.[45]

In 2012, the Chinese government not only implicitly supported the consumer boycott, but also added its own economic weight. As the boycott grew stronger, the spokesman for China's Commerce Ministry offered implicit support because such boycotts were regarded as 'patriotic activities'.[46] Japanese companies had to handle the combined effects of the consumer

---

[40]For the analysis of this pattern, see Jessica Chen Weiss, *Powerful Patriots: Nationalist Protest in China's Foreign Relations* (New York: Oxford University Press, 2014).

[41]James Reilly, 'A Wave to Worry About? Public opinion, foreign policy and China's anti-Japan protests', *Journal of Contemporary China*, 23, no. 86 (2014), pp. 197–215.

[42]Dorothy J Orchard, 'China's Use of the Boycott as a Political Weapon', *The Annals of the American Academy of Political and Social Science* (1930), pp. 252–261.

[43]James Reilly, 'A Wave to Worry About? Public Opinion, Foreign Policy and China's Anti-Japan Protests', p. 212.

[44]*Ibid.*

[45]*Ibid.*

[46]*Ibid.*, p. 214.

boycott and official pressure. Japan suffered all kinds of economic losses. For instance, many Japanese companies in China closed their factories. All Nippon Airways announced that thousands of seats had been canceled for flights booked for the period between September and November. Many Chinese citizens had canceled trips to Japan. The production and sale of Japanese cars fell dramatically in China. By early October, Nissan, Toyota, and Honda had cut their China-bound production in half. Meanwhile, South Korean brands Hyundai and Kia experienced record sales in China in September. J.P. Morgan downgraded its projections for Japan's economy for the final quarter of 2012 from zero growth to 0.8% shrinkage.[47]

Some Chinese elites supported the idea of sanctioning Japan. For instance, a researcher from a Ministry of Commerce think tank who analyzed the prospect of sanctioning Japan from an economic perspective claimed: 'China should work out a comprehensive plan that should include imposition of sanctions and taking precautionary measures against any Japanese retaliation... [a]nd once China imposes sanctions on Japan, the government should ensure that all enterprises in the country, domestic and foreign, obey the rules'.[48]

China's economic statecraft is costly and sometimes counterproductive. If China's economic statecraft aims to promote China's national interests, it is hard to say that boycotting Japanese goods is really rational. Clearly, China's actions carries the risks of deterring foreign investment into China, undermining domestic manufacturing and tarnishing Beijing's global image.[49] In a highly interdependent context, China's boycott hurts both Japanese and Chinese economy. Many 'Japanese goods' are made by Japanese companies in China, and these Japanese companies have hired thousands of Chinese workers. Peking University professor Wang Zhengyi emphasized the importance of Sino–Japanese cooperation when he addressed the problem of previous anti-Japan protests. According to Wang,

[47] *Ibid.*

[48] Jin Baisong, 'Consider sanctions on Japan', *China Daily*, 17 September 2012, available at: http://www.chinadaily.com.cn/opinion/2012-09/17/content_15761435.htm.

[49] Keiko Yoshioka, 'China's economy could lose big-time if Japan firms suffer from isles row', *Asahi Shinbum*, 25 September 2012, available at: http://ajw.asahi.com/article/asia/china/AJ201209250103.

in the context of economic globalization, China must deal with its relationship with Japan appropriately if China wants to fulfil its national goal of sustainable economic growth.[50] Many 'Chinese internationalists' certainly share Wang's opinion. Chinese boycotting behavior has been counterproductive to China's economic interests because it erodes investor confidence, damages Chinese image. and hurts Chinese workers.

In terms of diplomatic implications, boycotting attempts did not achieve the desired result. Despite China's consumer boycotts and economic pressure, Japan refused to back down from its claims over the Senkaku/Diaoyu Islands. China's behaviors merely strengthened the Japanese sense of insecurity, and Tokyo has strengthened its cooperation with other Asian neighbors and has secured statements of support from the United States.

If boycotting attempts make no rational sense to both the economy and diplomacy, why did the Chinese government tacitly approve or support these attempts? Maybe it is useful to make a distinction between expressive and instrumental behaviors regarding the use of economic statecraft. Instrumental behavior is a means to an end; expressive behavior is an end in itself.[51] When applied to economic statecraft, some expressive measures 'were undertaken in order to pacify domestic public opinion and not because policymakers viewed them as instruments of statecraft'.[52] Whereas instrumental behavior is depicted as intended to shape the behaviors and policies of other countries, expressive behavior's primary function is to release internal tensions. Consequently, the Chinese government had to tacitly approve some behaviors of boycotting Japanese products, not because those nationalistic behaviors could really promote China's national interests, but because they are expressive behaviors that could potentially release the Chinese public's domestic anger towards the Japanese, in a high tide of diplomatic tensions.

---

[50]*Xinhua*, 'PKU Professor: Developing Sino-Japanese Relationship is the common goal of Chinese and Japanese people [Beida jiaoshou: Fuzhanzhongri youhao shi lianguorenmin gongtong yuanwang]', available at: http://news.xinhuanet.com/world/2005-05/05/content_2918072.htm.

[51]For the distinction of expressive and instrumental behaviors in statecraft, see David Baldwin, *Economic Statecraft*, p. 97.

[52]*Ibid.*

Contested Leadership and Asian regionalism

As the two largest economies in Asia, China and Japan have been struggling to achieve leadership in the East Asian region.[53] China and Japan have a very complicated relationship because of geopolitical, historical, and economic reasons. Economically, both China and Japan are important trading partners and both sides have strong incentives to cooperate with each other; politically, both sides have deep mistrust because of historical memory and territorial disputes.[54] China and Japan both cooperate and compete in the regional context.

Ever since its economic rise in the 1960s, Japan has been the most important economic power in Asia, providing much-needed trade and investment to a region largely composed of developing countries. Japanese companies built infrastructure to support emerging economies in Southeast Asia, and Japan's developmental state model became the model for many Asian countries. By the 1980s, Japan became a 'flying geese' model of Asian economies. Japan had also become a major player in regional integration. China's economic rise and active regional diplomacy have started to challenge Japan's leadership in regional affairs since the late 1990s.[55]

Before the mid-1990s, China was skeptical about the importance of participating in regional multilateral organizations and it preferred to deal with its neighbors and with the major powers on a bilateral basis. During the 1990s, while the fast growth of regionalism was achieved in the European Union and North American Free Trade Agreement (NAFTA), regionalism was stunted in East Asia. China's inactive policy toward regionalism was regarded as one of the major reasons for the failure of East Asian economic integration. In the mid-1990s a well-known expert commented, 'Today it is China and Japan who oppose rapid moves toward a formal

---

[53]Young Choi Ji, 'Power, Identity, and Asian Regionalism: Political Rivalry between China and Japan and a Contested Regional Identity in East Asia', *Conference Papers — International Studies Association (2008)*.

[54]Robert Sutter, *China's Rise in Asia: Promises and Perils* (New York: Rowman & Littlefield, 2005), pp. 125–153.

[55]Sheila A. Smith, *Intimate Rivals*, p. 21.

institutionalization of regional integration. China fears being trapped in institutions, not of its own making'.[56]

Since the late 1990s, China has changed its previous inactive policy toward regionalism and has actively participated in most regional multilateral institutions.[57] China is not only an active participant, but also an active leader in Asian regional cooperation. China has launched a regional dialogue between business leaders and government officials, the Boao Forum for Asia. The forum holds annual meetings in China's Hainan Province, where more than 1,000 political elites, business leaders, and experts from around the region meet to discuss economic cooperation in Asia.[58] China was one of the primary initiators of the Shanghai Cooperation Organization (SCO), whose members now include China, Russia, Kazakhstan, Kyrgyzstan, Tajikistan, and Uzbekistan. At the ASEAN–China Summit in November 2000, Chinese premier Zhu Rongji proposed to have an FTA with ASEAN. In late 2002, leaders of China and ASEAN signed the framework agreement to create a free trade area between China and ASEAN within 10 years.

During the Asian financial crisis in 1998, China provided financial assistance to its Asian neighbors, and also acted responsibly by not devaluating its currency (the Renminbi). These behaviors were widely praised by Asian countries. China also started to pursue a proactive regional diplomacy after the Asian financial crisis. China's regional diplomacy after the financial crisis was an important transformative moment. Chinese officials became more interested in the establishment of regional institutions.

---

[56]Peter J. Katzenstein, ed., *Network Power* (Ithaca, NY: Cornell University Press, 1997), p. 27.

[57]Although there are different interpretations of China's policy toward Asian regionalism, most Asian experts have largely agreed that China has become a more active participant. See for instance, Shambaugh, 'China Engages Asia: Reshaping the Regional Order', pp. 64–99; Shiping Tang and Yunling Zhang, 'China's Regional Strategy', in David Shambaugh, ed., *Power Shift: China and Asia's New Dynamics* (Berkeley, CA: University of California Press, 2005).

[58]China initiated the SCO primarily to deepen its regional cooperation with Russia and Central Asia. Although the SCO is different from other Asian regional institutions, it is still regarded as an important indicator of China's multilateral diplomacy in Asia. See Tang and Zhang, 'China's Regional Strategy', pp. 48–60.

Although China objected to Japan's Asian Monetary Fund (AMF) proposal,[59] China found itself increasingly drawn into closer cooperation with South Korea and ASEAN nations. Consequently, during the latter part of 1997, China projected the image of a responsible regional power through prudent responses, continued growth drives, and financial assistance for the region.[60] As China and some other Asian countries were dissatisfied with the response from the IMF, they started to maintain and establish regional multilateral arrangements to strengthen regional economic cooperation.

Although the reasons why China started to pursue a more active regional diplomacy since the 1990s are complex, competition with Japan is often regarded as an important driver for China's active regional diplomacy.

Regarding Asian regional cooperation, China not only competes but also cooperates with Japan. Most recently, China played a leadership role in establishing AIIB, which might rival the Japanese-led Asian Development Bank (ADB). It was reported that China offered Japan the post of the top-ranking vice president at the proposed AIIB. Although Japan did not accept the offer, both sides did try to cooperate. Jin Liqun, a senior Chinese official who is in charge of leading AIIB, had frequent exchanges with Takehiko Nakao, former Japanese official and current president of the ADB. Jin told Nakao that China wanted Japan to join the bank, and the Chinese side hoped Japan would provide at least manpower, if not money, for the new institution.[61] While Japan did not join AIIB as a founding member, the Chinese-led AIIB and the Japanese-led ABD are actively seeking cooperation. ADB President Takehiko Nakao said, "ADB will cooperate and co-finance with AIIB on infrastructure financing across Asia by using our long experience and expertise in the region".[62]

---

[59]For the analysis of Asian Monetary Fund, see Yong Wook Lee, 'Japan and the Asian Monetary Fund: An Identity–Intention Approach', *International Studies Quarterly*, 50, no. 2 (2006), pp. 339–366.

[60]Rosemary Foot, 'Chinese Power and the Idea of a Responsible State', *The China Journal*, 45 (2001), pp. 1–19.

[61]Nikkei Asian Review, 'China offered Japan No. 2 post at new bank', 15 April 2015, available at: http://asia.nikkei.com/Japan-Update/China-offered-Japan-No.-2-post-at-new-bank.

[62]Nikkei Asian review, 'Asia's largest development banks will act in concert', 1 May 2015, available at: http://asia.nikkei.com/Politics-Economy/International-Relations/Asia-s-largest-development-banks-will-act-in-concert.

Conclusion

As China's economy is expanding, it is inevitable that China will transform its economic power into diplomatic influence. China's expanding influence through economic statecraft has created much anxiety and uncertainty in Asia and the world. Through the case studies of China's economic statecraft toward Japan, this chapter identifies some patterns and limitations of China's behaviors.

As two leading economic powers in Asia, China and Japan have a complicated and delicate relationship. Sino–Japanese relationship is characterized by both competitive and cooperative elements. China must exercise great caution in its pursuit of economic statecraft toward Japan. For instance, in the 2012 diplomatic crisis, the Chinese government tacitly approved some protests, and some elites even endorsed the boycott of Japanese goods. However, in a highly interdependent context, the boycotting behaviors hurt China's economic interests directly or indirectly.

China's economic statecraft has achieved limited success and sometimes success can be counterproductive, especially when applied to large economies like Japan. In recent years, Japan has the tendency not to change its policy preferences toward Chinese economic pressure. Even when the Japanese backed down temporarily in the case of rare earth control, China's behaviors caused backlashes in the international community.

The limitations of China's economic statecraft reflect a dilemma of China's rise in a highly interdependent Asia. Compared with a military approach, economic statecraft does provide China with a relatively low-risk approach to defend its strategic and security interests. However, China must cooperate with other countries to create a peaceful international environment for its domestic development. If China pushes its economic statecraft too far, China's behaviors will damage its own image as well as its interests. Therefore, the pursuit of economic statecraft will continue to be a tricky art for Chinese policy makers.

Chapter 5

The Last Resort: China's Economic Coercion against North Korea

Xiaohe Cheng

There are numerous troubles on China's periphery. The ongoing war in Afghanistan causes deep concerns in Beijing that the growing chaos in that region might fuel unrest in China's western areas. Pakistan, China's long-term friend, struggles to cope with poverty and domestic disorder. In comparison with Afghanistan and Pakistan, North Korea causes much more concerns in Beijing for the following reasons: first, as the Korean Peninsula remains divided, the two Koreas are still at war and their competition constitutes a major source of tension in Northeast Asia; second, to the woe of Northeast Asia's security, North Korea (officially Democratic People's Republic of Korea, or DPRK) has detonated nuclear bombs four times and as a result, North Korea's nuclear weapons have become a bone of contention among major powers and further complicate the regional security situation; third, in addition to the dire security challenge, North Korea's dreadful economic situation and chronic poverty also pose a threat to China's and the region's prosperity.

As China becomes increasingly proactive in Pakistan's economic development and Afghanistan's peace-making process and as North Korea's nuclear and missile activities occupy a central position in Northeast Asia's security, the issue of reining in North Korea's provocations amid promoting peace and prosperity in Northeast Asia has become a significant challenge in China's foreign policies. China's initial soft approach of diplomatic persuasion plus material incentives pits it against the United States' tough measures against North Korea. China's soft approach proved to be less effective. As North Korea continued to defy opposition from the international community and pressed ahead with its missile and nuclear tests, China changed course and publically resorted to coercive measures such as supporting the United Nations Security Council's (UNSC) sanction resolutions and taking its own unilateral punitive actions. China's getting-tough approach has been moderate and incremental for a variety of reasons. Even though it is too early to make a reliable assessment of the new approach, as China is still North Korea's largest trading partner, its punitive economic actions will inevitably have a significant impact on North Korea, psychologically and materially within China and North Korea. This chapter explores the evolution of China's approaches to the denuclearization of the Korean Peninsula since the end of the Cold War.

Nuclear Issue Debuts

It is no secret that North Korea began to pursue nuclear weapons in the 1960s, but this nuclear quest grabbed the headlines as the Cold War began to fade into oblivion. North Korea's stepped-up nuclear drive resulted in a new geopolitical landscape in Northeast Asia: North Korea's relations with its traditional ally, China, ran into troubled waters when China exchanged diplomatic recognition with South Korea, North Korea's perennial rival. As the Soviet Union disintegrated or experienced dramatic regime changes, North Korea lost its major trading partners and sources of assistance; China's relations with South Korea, which had been locked in antagonism for decades, were normalized as China tried to break its diplomatic isolation after the June 4th Incident in 1989.

The dramatic changes tipped the balance of power on the Korean Peninsula to South Korea's advantage. North Korea was further isolated and its economic development stalled. In order to redress the loss of power balance, North Korea resorted to the ultimate weapon, the nuclear bomb, which triggered the first nuclear crisis on the Korean Peninsula in early 1990s.

The first nuclear crisis effectively scrapped the Joint Declaration of the Denuclearization of the Korean Peninsula and brought North Korea and the United States to the negotiating table. North Korea favored negotiations over the nuclear issue as a convenient mechanism to engage the United States and secure its diplomatic recognition. The negotiation resulted in the Agreed Framework in 1994: North Korea pledged to freeze its nuclear program development and abide by the Nuclear Non-Proliferation Treaty whereas the United States offered to build two light-water reactors for North Korea. The first Korean nuclear crisis thus faded away.

Failure of Diplomatic Persuasion

The United States and North Korea were the two key players that brought a temporary solution to the first North Korean nuclear crisis. Even though China is North Korea's immediate neighbor and long-term ally, China was a by-stander as the nuclear drama unfolded between the United States and North Korea. The reasons were mainly two-fold. First, China's relations with North Korea froze as China brushed aside North Korea's consistent opposition and granted a diplomatic recognition to South Korea, North Korea's perennial rival. Second, Sino–US relations had been in bad shape in the wake of the June 4th Incident. The two nations were deeply involved in a series of head-to-head diplomatic battles over human rights, trade, Taiwan, and Tibet.

Joining in the Nuclear Fray

China's hands-off approach came to an end when Sino–US relations improved in the wake of Li Denghui's visit. China joined in the Four Party Talks upon invitation from the United States and South Korea in 1996.[1] Even though the talks failed to address security concerns on the Korean Peninsula, China succeeded in walking out of the diplomatic isolation caused by the June 4th Incident,[2] and renewed its traditional interest in the Korean affairs. As a consequence of China's participation in the talks, Sino–DPRK relations began to rebound. In 1999, when Kim Yong-nam visited Beijing in

---

[1] Bill Clinton and Kim Young-sam jointly proposed four-party talks on 16 April 1996, in an effort to 'reduce tensions and build confidence on the Korean Peninsula with the aim of putting a formal end to the hostilities of the Korean War'.

[2] In the spring of 1989, massive student demonstrations took place in Beijing and in dozens of other Chinese cities. On 4 June, the Chinese government called in the military forces to end the demonstrations.

1999, Jiang Zemin quickly formulated the following 16-character guideline for Sino–DPRK relations: 'carrying forward the tradition, facing the future, developing the good-neighborly friendship and strengthening cooperation (*Jicheng Chuantong, Mianxiang Weilai, Mulin Youhao, Jiaqiang Hezuo*)'.[3] The guideline was a forward-looking political statement, which emphasized China's desire to further strengthen its relations with North Korea and paid little attention to economic matters.

Diplomatic Persuasion

At the turn of 21st century, the 1994 Agreed Framework fell apart and the Four Party Talks went nowhere. The second Korean crisis grabbed the headlines and gave birth to the Six Party Talks designed to fulfill what the Agreed Framework and the Four Party Talks could not do. China shook off initial hesitation to host and chair the Six Party Talks. At the same time, the leadership change in China enabled the new top leader to play a larger role in the Six Party Talks. When Hu Jintao assumed the position of the party general secretary, he fully inherited Jiang's legacy in the Korean affairs. In the Six Party Talks, China assumed multiple roles: (1) as a host to provide the conference venue and logistic assistance; (2) as an interlocutor to relay information among participating states; (3) as a consensus promoter to apply confidence-building measures and decision implementation that iron out differences among major participants and work toward a resolution; (4) as a participant to appoint its Special Representative on Korean Peninsula Affairs; and (5) to engage in intensive negotiations on its own.

With China's heavy involvement, the Six Party Talks produced a number of concrete results, including (1) the establishment of a multilateral-bilateral dialogue format; (2) formation of a basic organizational structure comprising five working groups; (3) formulation of 9.19 joint statements, which clearly stipulate the rights and obligation for the relevant parties, and its initial implementation; (4) creation of a 'commitment-for-commitment, action-for-action' guideline; and (5) formation of a community of government officials and academic researchers from various countries interested

---

[3] 'Qingzhu Zhonghua Renmin Gongheguo Chengli 52 Zhounian' (Celebrating the 52nd Anniversary of the Founding of People's Republic of China), *The People's Daily*, (28 September 2001).

in the Korean Peninsula affairs. Nonetheless, the Six Party Talks failed to persuade North Korea from going nuclear. In 2006, North Korea conducted its first nuclear tests. In 2009, after exploding its second test nuclear bomb, North Korean number 2 leader Kim Yong-nam announced that the Six Party Talks were finished forever in July 2009.[4]

Material Incentives

Even though the behind-the-door persuasion *plus* material incentive failed to convince North Korea to stay away from nuclear weapons, the Chinese government continued to stick to the approach of persuasion. In the wake of North Korea's second nuclear test, Wen Jiabao, the Chinese premier, paid a visit to the DPRK and once again set in motion China's policy of engagement with North Korea, a policy based on economic lure, diplomatic persuasion, and traditional friendship bond. Sino–DPRK relations quickly recovered, and in the next two years, it demonstrated remarkable progress in a number of ways.

On the political front, the frequent visits between top leaders became routine. Kim Jong-il made trips to China three times and two sitting members of the Standing Committee of the Politburo of the Communist Party of China (CPC) visited Pyongyang on important occasions.[5] For the first time, the CPC and the Workers' Party of Korea (WPK) set up the Strategic Dialogue for party-to-party relations to reach a new high. As another trend in their political interaction, the exchange of visits at the provincial level became increasingly visible. In October 2010, for the first time in Sino-DPRK's history, senior secretaries of all of North Korea's 11 metropolitan and provincial party committees visited China in one group.

In the diplomatic arena, China and the DPRK agreed to strengthen their communication, consultation, and cooperation over major international and regional issues;[6] as a result of China's persuasion, the DPRK reversed its

---

[4] Park Gayoung, 'N. Korea: Six Party Talks Are Dead', *Global Times* (17 July 2009).

[5] Zhou Yongkang and Li Keqiang visited North Korea in 2010 and 2011, respectively.

[6] Qian Tong, 'Hu Jintao Tong Jinzhengri Juxing Huitan (Hu Jintao Meets with Kim Jong-Il)', *Xinhuanet*, available at: http://news.xinhuanet.com/politics/2011-05/26/c_121463025.htm.

previous oath of not returning to the Six Party Talks forever and demonstrated a degree of flexibility for the resumption of the Talks. As a clear indication of diplomatic improvement on their bilateral relations, China came to behave like a protector of North Korea during two crises, the Cheonan and Yeonpyeong incidents in 2010. China refused to recognize the validity of a joint multinational investigation report of the Cheonan Incident by fending off possible new UN resolutions against the DPRK and watering down the presidential statement of the UNSC.

On the economic front, China's ties with DPRK have tangibly gained new momentum. In 2010, China and North Korea decided to jointly develop the Rason, Hwanggumpyong, and Wiwha economic zones. Chen Deming, China's commerce minister and Jang Song-thaek, director of North Korea's Central Administration Department, cochaired their joint steering committees. These committees are responsible for a number of big-ticket construction projects such as the 53.5-km-long road from Wonjeong-ri to Rason on a budget of 150 million Chinese yuan and the four-lane bridge across the Yalu River in Dandong that cost about 1.8 billion Chinese yuan. All the projects will be financed by the Chinese side to upgrade the infrastructure in North Korea's border areas. In 2011, The Hyesan Youth Copper Mine, the largest Sino–DPRK joint venture, came into operation. By 2010, Chinese businessmen have invested about US$290 million in the non-financial sector. The number of Chinese enterprises in North Korea was not less than 200.[7] The trade volume between the two nations in 2010 jumped almost 30% from the previous year. In 2011, the figure stood around US$5.64 billion, an annual increase of 62%.[8]

Hu Jintao managed to mend fences with Kim Jong-il and push the Sino–DPRK relationship to a new high. In August 2010, he made his personal mark on China's policy toward North Korea by announcing the 16-character guideline for Sino–DPRK relations: 'government guidance with enterprises playing a major role, market-orientation, and mutual benefit and win–win

---

[7] 'Chao 200 Jia Zhongguo Qiye Jinjun Chaoxian, Lu Guanqi Xiang Chaofang Xian Jintao' (More Than 200 Hundred Chinese Enterprises March to the DPRK, Lu Guanqiu Presents a Golden Peach to the DPRK), available at: Eastday.com, http://finance.qq.com/a/20120418/006856.htm.
[8] The numbers are available at www.customs-info.com, which is run by China Customs Information Center.

principle (*Zhengfu Yindao, Qiye Weizhu, Shichang Daoxiang, Huli Shuangying*)'.[9] This new guideline is aimed at putting Sino–DPRK economic relations on a normal state-to-state basis to free China from hefty economic assistance to North Korea and also to facilitate more sustainable bilateral business between the two nations.

During the Jiang Zemin–Hu Jintao era, China had already announced two sets of complementary guidelines for Sino–DPRK relations. One is designed to govern the two nations' political relations and the other for their economic interactions. The two sets of guidelines reflected China's deep desire to maintain good relations with North Korea and formed the cornerstone of China's policy on North Korea.

Coercive Diplomacy Kicks In

Throughout history, Sino–DPRK relations, previously cemented by blood in the Korean War, have not been free from problems. During the Cultural Revolution, Beijing and Pyongyang gave each other the cold shoulder. The two nations had no ambassadors in each other's capital for more than one and half a years. As China overcame North Korea's stubborn opposition, it gradually upgraded its trade relations with South Korea to diplomatic recognition. Instead of pressuring North Korea, China patiently persuaded Kim Il-sung to understand and support China's moves.[10] North Korea on the other hand made no effort to hide its strong displeasure with China's actions so its relations with China suffered a rapid decline.

The UNSC Sanctions

The rupture of Sino–DPRK relations caused by Beijing–Seoul rapprochement was finally repaired despite deep scars. The fence-mending between China and North Korea paved the way for China to chair the Six Party Talks

---

[9] 'Hu Jintao Zongshuji Tong Chaoxian Laodongdang Zongshuji Jin Zhengri Zai Changchun Junxing Huitan' (General Secretary Hu Jintao Meets General Secretary of KWP Kim Jong-il in Changchun), *Xinhua News*, 30 August 2010, available at: http://news.xinhuanet.com/politics/2010-08/30/c_12500145.htm.

[10] Qian Qichen, *Ten Stories of a Diplomat*, chapter V (Beijing: The World Affairs Press, 2003).

but the renewed friendship did not last very long. On 5 July 2006, North Korea fired testing missiles into the Japanese Sea. For the first time, China joined the United States, Britain, and France in endorsing a passage of UNSC resolution 1695 that denounced North Korea's missile tests. China also supported the UNSC to publish a strongly-worded presidential statement on 6 October 2006, calling North Korea to cancel its nuclear test plan. In the aftermath of North Korea's nuclear test, Liu Jianchao, a spokesman of the Chinese foreign ministry, announced:

> In disregard of the common opposition of the international community, the DPRK flagrantly conducted a nuclear test. The Chinese government strongly opposes this act. China strongly requires the DPRK to honor its commitment to denuclearization, stop all actions that may further worsen the situation and return to the Six-Party Talks.[11]

On 14 October 2006, with China's support, the UNSC passed resolution 1718, which demanded that the DPRK abandon all nuclear weapons and existing nuclear programs in a complete, verifiable, and irreversible manner. According to the resolution, a sanctions committee would be set up whereby all member states impose sanctions on luxury goods and certain types of heavy weapons and materials, equipment, goods and technology contributing to DPRK's nuclear-related, ballistic-missile-related, or other weapons-of-mass-destruction-related programs.

Clearly, the passage of resolution 1718 demonstrated a change in China's strategic thinking on its relations with North Korea. First, even though China had not abandoned the traditional persuasive approach, it realized that North Korea's nuclear activities should be punished. Second, the punishment should be moderate. China had reservations about the provisions for cargo checks on North Korean ships. For the first time, the Chinese government registered its open disapproval of North Korea's behavior by supporting UNSC sanctions against its traditional ally. Even though China was reluctant to take any unilateral punitive action against North Korea, it finally did so by resorting to the UNSC.

---

[11] Foreign Ministry Spokesman Liu Jianchao's Regular Press Conference on 10 October 2006, at this address, available at: http://www.fmprc.gov.cn/eng/xwfw/s2510/t275804.htm.

North Korea's detonation of its second nuclear bomb in 2009 further irked China. China claimed the following: 'The Democratic People's Republic of Korea, heedless of widespread international opposition, has again carried out a nuclear test, to which the Chinese government expresses its firm opposition'.[12] The UNSC resolution 1874,[13] endorsed by China, extended the arms embargo on North Korea. A ban was imposed on all weapons exports from the country and most imports, except for small arms, light weapons, and related materials. Financial services that could contribute to the nuclear or ballistic missile relations program were also prohibited. More importantly, the UN member states had to inform the Security Council of the steps they were taking to implement the sanctions within 45 days. Clearly, the Security Council stepped forward and further tightened its grip on North Korea. The scope of sanctions against North Korea increased and the implementation of the sanctions were further institutionalized.

Unfortunately, the tougher sanctions failed to intimidate North Korea into suspending its development of ballistic missile and nuclear weapon. The sudden leadership change in late 2012 revitalized North Korea's missile and nuclear drive. This time, China hastily took preventive measures. On 15 March 2013, when North Korea made public its satellite launch plan, Zhang Zhijun, China's deputy foreign minister, immediately summoned North Korea's ambassador to China, Ji Jae-ryong, to express China's concerns over DPRK's announcement of the satellite launch in mid-April. He asked North Korea to remain calm, exercise restraint and avoid bigger complexity caused by the escalation of situation.[14] Chinese official media, led by *Global Times*, became unprecedentedly vocal against North Korea's new provocations.

As China's call for calmness and self-restraint fell on deaf ears in Pyongyang, North Korea did what it wanted, and China was forced to endorse a UNSC presidential statement carrying the following trigger

---

[12]Justin McCurry and Tania Branigan, 'North Korea stages nuclear test in defiance of bans', *The Guardian*, 12 February 2013, available at: http://www.theguardian.com/world/2013/feb/12/north-korea-nuclear-test-earthquake.

[13]For full text of UNSC resolution 1874, see http://www.un.org/press/en/2009/sc9679.doc.htm.

[14]'Vice Foreign Minister Zhang Zhijun Meets with the DPRK Ambassador to China', available at: http://www.fmprc.gov.cn/eng/zxxx/t915503.htm.

clause: 'The Security Council expresses its determination to take action accordingly in the event of a further DPRK launch or nuclear test'.[15] In response to North Korea's third nuclear test on 12 February 2013, China also supported UNSC resolution 2094 to expand the scope of UN sanctions against North Korea by targeting the illicit activities of diplomatic personnel, transfers of bulk cash, and the country's banking relations.[16] According to the resolution, the Council was prepared to strengthen, modify, suspend or lift the measures as may be needed in light of the DPRK's compliance or to take further significant measures in the event of a further DPRK launch or nuclear test. Resolution 2094 was so tough that Susan E. Rice, US ambassador to the UN claimed, '[t]aken together, these sanctions will bite, and bite hard'.[17]

Since 2006, China has resorted to coercive diplomatic and economic measures under the auspices in an attempt to register its disapproval of and anger over Pyongyang's repeated nuclear and missile provocations.

Unilateral Punitive Action

China has been a principal source of aid to North Korea and remains its number one trading partner. Even though North Korea's nuclear program irritated China constantly, China carefully shielded its economic ties from North Korea's missile and nuclear issue. Although China denounced North Korea's detonation of its first nuclear bomb, Sino–DPRK trade still continued its growth momentum. In 2007, bilateral trade reached a record high of US$1.97 billion (16.1% increase from the previous year).[18] In the wake of North Korea's second nuclear test, bilateral trade was immune to the sanctions imposed by the UNSC. In 2011, bilateral trade volume jumped

[15]For full text of the Presidential Statement, see https://www.un.org/News/Press/docs/2012/sc10610.doc.htm.
[16]Full text of the UNSC Resolution 2094, see http://www.un.org/press/en/2013/sc10934.doc.htm.
[17]Colum Lynch and Joby Warrick, 'U.N. Security Council approves new sanctions against North Korea', The Washington Post (7 March 2013).
[18]'Liu Xiaoming Dashi Huijian Chaoxian Xinren Maoyixiang Li Longnan' (Ambassador Liu Xiaoming Meets DPRK's New Minister of Trade Ri Ryong Nam), (14 March 2008), available at: http://kp.china-embassy.org/chn/zcgx/jmhz/t418021.htm.

to US$5.629 billion, a dramatic increase from US$3.46 in 2010.[19] According to South Korea, North Korea's trade dependence on China surpassed 70%.[20]

The dynamic economic interactions between China and North Korea raised suspicion over China's true intention to punish North Korea for its nuclear provocations. The United States and South Korea have long pressured China to exercise economic leverage to restrain North Korea's behavior. China refused to put normal trade on the sanction list for two basic reasons. First, as North Korea's largest trading partner, had the UNSC imposed sanctions on China's normal trade with North Korea, China would have been the country that suffered most. Northeast China, whose economy lagged far behind many other parts of China, would have suffered the most negative impact. Second, any disruption of North Korea's normal external trade would have hurt the ordinary people most and may cause Humanitarian crisis in North Korea.

As the diplomatic persuasion *plus* material incentives failed to pull North Korea back to the Six Party Talks and prevent it from conducting new nuclear tests, China's traditional approach came under challenge. Chinese scholars and the mass media began to call for a change. Right before the third nuclear test, *Global Times* made an explicit warning: 'If North Korea conducts a new nuclear test or launches a 'satellite' again, China should not hesitate to reduce its assistance to North Korea'.[21] Sensing North Korea's upcoming nuclear test, *Global Times* made a last-ditch warning: 'If North Korea treats China harshly and unreasonably, we wish China would reciprocate in kind, and never coax and concede in order to appease it. If the Sino–DPRK

---

[19] 'Hanguo Tongjiting Cheng Chaoxian Duihua Maoyi Yicundu Shouci Chaoguo Qicheng' (South Korea's Statistics Office Claims North Korea's Trade Dependence on China is over 70% for the First Time), *Global Times* (28 December 2012), available at: http://world.huanqiu.com/exclusive/2012-12/3426410.html.

[20] *Ibid.*

[21] Editorial, 'Chaohe Weiji, Zhongguo Buxuyao Kan Renhe Yifang Lianse' (North Korea Nuclear Crisis, China Does Not Need to Pay Attention to Other Countries' Reactions), *Global Times* (25 January 2013), available at: http://opinion.huanqiu.com/editorial/2013-01/3581199.html.

relationship suffers any significant setback, let it be'.[22] More importantly, the official Chinese newspaper emphasized that if North Korea did not listen to advice and conducted the third nuclear test, it must pay a high price in the form of less assistance from China.[23] After North Korea went ahead with its third nuclear test, *Global Times* raised its voice:

> China should reduce its assistance to North Korea as a reaction to its third nuclear test. We oppose North Korea's nuclear test; such opposition should be expressed by action. No matter how unhappy Pyongyang might be, we must do so; Beijing should tell Pyongyang, if it launches any satellite again, or conducts any new nuclear test, we will further reduce assistance to it. China's attitude is unshakable.[24]

In an attempt to rein in North Korea's nuclear development, China substantiated its warning by implementing UNSC resolution 2094. China reinforced customs inspection of commodities to North Korea and intensified surveillance of North Korea's financial activities in China. The two-way trade between China and North Korea and the pace of China's investment in North Korea also slowed down. Given the volatile and dangerous situation on the peninsula and the uncertainties on Sino-DPRK relations, the slowdown was partially caused by the self-protection reactions from Chinese businessmen. On 17 April 2013, the Chinese Ministry of Transport sent out a circular, instructing all its affiliated units to strictly implement UNSC resolution 2094.[25] The ministry posted the circular online on 25 April. The Chinese media made the headline news to show that China was serious in

---

[22]Editorial, 'Zhongguo Zhenxi Zhongchao Youhao, Chaoxian Yexu Zhenxi' (China Treasures the Sino-DPRK Friendship, the DPRK Should Do the Same), *Global Times* (6 February 2013), available at: http://opinion.huanqiu.com/editorial/2013-02/3622838. html.

[23]*Ibid.*

[24]Editorial, 'Chaohe, Zhongguo Xu Buqienuo Buhuanxiang Bujizao' (North Korea Nuclear Issue, China Should Not Be Coward, Illusive and Irritable), *Global Times* (17 February 2013), available at: http://opinion.huanqiu.com/editorial/2013-02/3645628.html.

[25]'Guanyu Zhixing Lianheguo Anlihui Di 2094 Hao Jueyi De Tongzhi' (Circular on Implementing UNSC Resolution 2087), available at: http://www.moc.gov.cn/zizhan/siju/guojisi/duobianhezuo/guojiheyue/duobiantiaoyue/201304/t20130425_1402013.html.

carrying out the UNSC resolution. Earlier, on 21 February 2013, the Ministry of Transport had already posted a similar circular, calling its affiliated units to implement UNSC resolution 2087 which had been adopted on 22 January 2013, two months before UNSC resolution 2094,[26] but the circular went unnoticed.

No doubt about it, the 2014 satellite launch and nuclear test have further strained North Korea's relations with China. As China's public opinion became more polarized, recent North Korea behavior drove more and more Chinese to its opposition camp. Some of the leading Chinese scholars joined the public anti-North Korea chorus, calling the Chinese government to re-evaluate its policy toward North Korea and to give up on Pyongyang.[27] To make things worse, North Korea's domestic power struggles spilled over into foreign affairs, further complicating Sino–DPRK relations. In December 2013, Jang Song-thaek, former vice chairman of the National Defense Commission, was suddenly dismissed. Among all the crimes Jang allegedly committed, one stood out that annoyed China very much:

> He instructed his stooges to sell coal and other precious underground resources at random. Consequently, his confidants were saddled with huge debts, deceived by brokers. Jang made no scruple of committing such acts of treachery in May last year such as selling off the land of the Rason economic and trade zone to a foreign country for a period of five decades under the pretext of paying those debts.[28]

Although the accusation did not mention China's name, it is not difficult to identify the 'foreign country'. To raise China's ire, North Korea seemingly began to assess economic cooperation with China in the Rason economic and trade zone from an unfavorable angle.

---

[26] 'Guanyu Zhixing Lianheguo Anlihui Di 2087 Hao Jueyi De Tongzhi' (Circular on Implementing UNSC Resolution 2087), available at: http://www.moc.gov.cn/zizhan/siju/guojisi/duobianhezuo/guojiheyue/duobiantiaoyue/201302/t20130221_1369846.html.

[27] Deng Yuwen, 'China should abandon North Korea', *Finance Times* (27 February 2013), available at: http://www.ft.com/cms/s/0/9e2f68b2-7c5c-11e2-99f0-00144feabdc0.html#axzz2RzxJxkYW.

[28] 'Traitor Jang Song Thaek Executed', *KCNA* (13 December 2013), available at: http://www.kcna.co.jp/item/2013/201312/news13/20131213-05ee.html.

Exchange between top leaders came to a halt, as an indicator of the estranged Sino-DPRK relations. Xi Jinping reversed the age-old tradition of Chinese top leaders' visits to the two Koreas by making a state visit to South Korea first. Kim Jong-un who has ruled North Korea for more than four years, has not visited China yet. His request for a visit in early 2014 was met with a lukewarm response.

The development of the two joint economic cooperation zones has been suspended since 2013. As a result, the Hwanggumpyong and Wiwha Islands, designed to be the location of the second joint economic zone, remain severely underdeveloped. The construction of the New Dadong Bridge connecting Dandong and Sinuiju, a symbol of the renewed Sino–North Korean friendship, was completed in 2013 at a cost of 2.22 billion Chinese yuan, solely undertaken by China. However, the building of North Korea's corresponding railway system has not even started.

Trade between China and North Korea used to be a silver lining in their relations but even this has finally lost momentum. Even though the year of 2013 witnessed a record trade volume between China and North Korea accounting for 89.1% of North Korea's overall trade that year at about US$6.54 billion,[29] the annual growth rate was only slightly over 10%.[30] Although some scholars claimed that Sino–DPRK trade was 'business as usual' in comparison with previous years, the trade growth slowed down as a result of China's tightening economic grip on North Korea. In 2014, Sino–DPRK trade suffered a 2.4% decrease from the previous year. The drop was moderate but it marked the first decline since 2009.

In November 2014, this author visited the Rason and found that the economic interactions between Rason and Hun Chun, a Chinese border city, had cooled off significantly. The traffic on the highway between the two cities was lighter in comparison with what this author witnessed four years ago. It was reported that the oil pipeline connecting Dandong and Siniuju has already been eroded last year due to the long suspension of

---

[29] 'N. Korea's overall trade volume grows to a record high in 2013', *Yonhap News Agency* (22 May 2014), available at: http://english.yonhapnews.co.kr/northkorea/2014/05/21/16/0401000000AEN20140521003200320F.html.

[30] Scott Snyder, 'China–North Korea Trade in 2013: Business as Usual', *Forbes Asia* (27 March 2014), available at: http://www.forbes.com/sites/scottasnyder/2014/03/27/44/.

China's commercial oil supply to North Korea. Gasoline price in Rason skyrocketed. According to a local informant, one liter of gasoline cost about 20 yuan in Rason[31]; in China, it cost a little more than six yuan. In fact, the trade between China and North Korea continued to slide by 14.7% in 2015.[32]

China's commercial oil supply to North Korea has not yet resumed. Its fertilizer export, which could have helped North Korea to alleviate its food shortage, unfortunately decreased by 75.9% in early 2015.[33]

Obviously, as China adopted the coercive approach and tightened its grip on North Korea, their political relations deteriorated to the lowest point in years. Their economic ties, formerly immune to quarrels over the nuclear issue, began to bear the brunt of their nuclear disagreement. Even though their trade decline was not significant, the impact on North Korea's diplomacy was significant. The isolated North Korea must seek alternative trading partners to reduce its economic dependence on China. The ongoing tango between Pyongyang and Moscow is a recent example of North Korea's diplomatic effort to diversify its trade.

Although China is not a skillful practitioner of coercive diplomacy, it has already added coercive elements to its policy toward North Korea over nine years to rein in the latter's missile and nuclear provocations. China did so as other diplomatic means proved to be less effective.

But China's coercive diplomacy has been constrained by a number of considerations. First of all, by applying coercive measures on North Korea, China declares that it will not treat North Korea differently. If North Korea continues its missile and nuclear provocations, it must bear all the consequences. Second, China's trade with North Korea only accounts for a tiny fraction of its total external business, but it has a significant impact on the

---

[31] Information was collected through author's interview with local Korean people in November 2014.

[32] 'China's border city tightens customs check after N. Korea's nuke test', *Yonhap News* (2 February 2016), available at: http://english.yonhapnews.co.kr/search1/2603000000. html?cid=AEN20160202006100315.

[33] 'Tongji: 2015nian Diyijidu Chaozhong Maoyi Guimo Tongbi Jianshao 13%' (China's trade with N. Korea falls 13 pct on-year in Q1), *Yonhap News* (12 May 2015), available at: http://chinese.yonhapnews.co.kr/international/2015/05/12/0301000000ACK20150512001 700881.HTML.

North Korean economy and stability. China does not want any collective or unilateral punishment on North Korea to threaten the survival of the Pyongyang regime. Third, as other member states of the Six Party Talks have insignificant trading relations with North Korea, any further sanctions against North Korea, collectively or unilaterally, will hurt China the most. Last but not least, if history serves as a guide, the past economic coercive diplomacy barely produced the desired results. Usually, coercion alone is counterproductive.

China May Get Tougher on North Korea

North Korea's nuclear and missile weapon programs have become one of China's biggest diplomatic and security challenges along the former's periphery. Every time Pyongyang conducts its nuclear or missile tests, Beijing would automatically draw criticism from the outside world for its soft if not moderate responses toward North Korean provocations. Such an ironic phenomenon has made the Chinese leadership extremely uncomfortable. The fourth nuclear test and the satellite launch that followed has since elicited a tangible drift in China's policy toward North Korea, with Beijing showing unexpected readiness to punish Pyongyang much harder than many analysts anticipated.

Endorsing the Harshest Sanctions

Previously, China had been reluctant to adopt punitive measures toward North Korea even if the latter had violated UN resolutions and pressed ahead with its nuclear and missile tests for fear that harsher punishment may dim any hopes of Pyongyang's return to the negotiating table, lest such actions were to lead to unwanted consequences, including political instability. Beijing's endorsement of the UNSC Resolution 2270 clearly demonstrates China's willingness to impose harder measures to punish its defiant neighbor. This change of Chinese attitude was mainly caused by three basic considerations.

First, as the previous moderate sanctions against North Korea had failed to deter North Korea from developing its nuclear and missile programs, it was only to be expected that the UNSC would take further actions, such as closing the sanction loopholes and enlarging the scope of the sanctions.

Second, with South Korea determined to confront North Korea in a tit-for-tat fashion by shutting down the Kaesong industrial complex — the only remaining economic link between the two Koreas — China had to follow suit, lest any hesitation on its part were to risk alienating Seoul, with whom Beijing has been painstakingly cultivating friendship for the past several years. Third, North Korean provocations have become too frequent and too dangerous to be tolerated, and the United States and South Korea's patience with North Korean provocations have worn thin.

Resolution 2270 carries some hard-hitting elements that may hurt North Korea badly. It imposes sectoral sanctions targeting North Korea's trade in resources and bans transfers of aviation fuel to North Korea. Without doubt, such a new punitive measure can be expected to undermine Pyongyang's ability to continue its nuclear and missile programs, and also pose a threat to North Korea's economic and political stability. More importantly, the resolution could further impose new cargo inspection and maritime procedures to limit North Korea's ability to transfer UN-prohibited items. In fact, the Philippines recently took the lead in seizing a North Korea cargo ship right after the resolution was passed.

North Korea is at China's Mercy

Resolution 2270 represents the harshest sanctions the UNSC has ever imposed on North Korea. As results of the new sanctions unfold, some analysts have expressed their concerns that the sanctions may lack teeth since the resolution allows exceptions to the ban on mineral exports, leaving states to determine whether those exceptions are applied exclusively on goods that affect the livelihood of North Koreans, or whether they will have an impact on North Korea's nuclear or ballistic missile programs. Certainly, the exceptions will protect some Chinese companies from going bankrupt caused by sudden economic paralysis and avert high legal costs for any breach of contracts, but also offer China some maneuvering space to influence North Korean behavior. In other words, even as Beijing tries to reduce its own economic loss caused by the resolution, it has also put itself in a position to tighten or loosen its economic grip on Pyongyang, depending on the latter's external behavior. As such, the exceptions leave North Korea at China's mercy to some extent.

China May Resort to New Tougher Tools

In order to inflict pain on North Korea for its brinkmanship, China has no reasons to abuse the exceptions. So far, Beijing has been steadfastly implementing the UNSC resolutions. China's endorsement and implementation of the new resolution has angered North Korea, with the latter repeatedly making implicit criticisms of China for its 'unprincipled position' and 'collusion with the United States'.

Nevertheless, North Korea has continued to undertake a number of countermeasures in gross violation of the UNSC resolutions, including test-firing a submarine-launched ballistic missile. The signs point to the imminence of the fifth nuclear test, which can be expected to lead to another round of showdown between North Korea and the international community. Beijing and other global stakeholders may be forced to resort to heavier instruments in their diplomatic toolkit in an attempt to rein in Pyongyang. These may include banning North Korea from sending workers overseas and suspending tourism between China and North Korea. Adoption of either of these will be tantamount to rubbing salt into North Korea's wounds.

For China, imposing harsh sanctions against North Korea is the last resort in dealing with its nuclear and missile provocations and may cause unwanted consequences. But with China showing determination in persisting with these new North Korea-related sanction resolutions, it is more than likely that the new Chinese leadership is able to stomach all kinds of results, whether good or bad. Certainly, China does not want to punish North Korea just for the sake of it. Most importantly, the ultimate objective of the sanctions it has endorsed should help to drag North Korea back to the negotiating table and bring stability back to the Korean Peninsula.

Conclusion

The evolution of China's approaches in dealing with North Korea's nuclear program is clear and will continue to change in the future. The driving forces are multifaceted. First of all, China's policy toward North Korea's nuclear program is mainly driven by China's diplomatic posture. As long as China insists on maintaining a low profile on the world stage, it will be reluctant to get involved in the North Korean nuclear issue. But as China changes its course to pursue an active role in world affairs, its diplomatic posture undertakes a profound shift from 'maintaining a low profile' to 'actively doing something'. China's inherent desire to offer collective goods is growing strong. To pursue a nuclear-free Korean Peninsula is one of the best ways to exercise China's regional leadership as it offers a collective good to Northeast Asia.

Second, China's relations with the United States also play an important if not defining role in China's approach to North Korea's nuclear challenge. North Korea's nuclear program threatens both China and the United States, but they prefer different approaches to deal with it. As long as China and the United States are on good terms, they could easily forge common ground to deal with North Korea's nuclear issue. But when the two countries are locked in a rivalry, they can hardly speak in one voice and act in concert with each other. The relationship between China and the United States has reached a tipping point:[34] they either become adversaries or cooperative partners. How to deal with North Korea's nuclear weapons is a key litmus test of Sino–US relations. For China, North Korea has been China's strategic buffer zone and asset, and this could tie down a significant portion of US military and diplomatic resources on the Korean Peninsula. If China continues to pressure North Korea, it might lose North Korea to the US side, which seriously carries out the rebalance strategy to prevent China from becoming a dominant power in Asia-Pacific region. For the United States, Xi Jinping's promotion of the new type of major countries' relations should be backed by concrete cooperative actions. If China continues its soft approach toward North Korea's nuclear issue and refuses to take unilateral punitive action, the new type of major countries' relations would never been forged.

Third, China's relations with the two Koreas influence China's approach toward North Korea's nuclear issue. It is desirable for Beijing to maintain equally friendly relations with Pyongyang and Seoul, but as long as the Korean Peninsula remains divided and the two Koreas continues to play a zero-sum game, it is tremendously difficult for China to do so. This is proven by past history. Since the end of the Cold War, China and North Korea's

---

[34]David M. Lampton, 'A Tipping Point in U.S.–China Relations is Upon Us', a speech at the conference 'China's Reform: Opportunities and Challenges', *The Carter Center and the Shanghai Academy of Social Sciences*, 6–7 March 2015.

relations have shifted from a cold phase to a normal phase, and back to a cold phase. At the same time, China and South Korea's relations, which began as a partnership, have advanced to a comprehensive partnership and developed into a strategic partnership. As China leaned toward South Korea, China was more likely to be tough on North Korea. In contrast, as China leaned toward North Korea, it was less likely to resort to coercive measures to force North Korea to do something.

Since Hu Jintao's era, the Chinese government has tried to downplay its alliance with North Korea (codified by their 1961 Friendship, Cooperation, and Mutual Assistance Treaty). It has also tried to normalize their allied relations by putting their relations on the same footing as the one with South Korea. After coming to power, Xi Jinping replaced the old guideline of the 16-Chinese character with a new one: 'mutual respect, equal treatment, seeking common grounds while reserving differences and win–win cooperation (相互尊重 平等相待 求同存异 合作共赢)'.[35] The expression of 'seeking common grounds while reserving differences' has never been publicly applied to Sino–DPRK relations. Its inclusion in the guiding principle demonstrates China's intention to acknowledge their differences in public and normalize their relations. The expression 'reserving differences' is less positive than the expression 'settling differences (求同化异)' and it reflects China's realistic assessment: settling differences with North Korea is still not attainable in the near future.

Certainly, other factors also come into play and influence China's policy toward North Korea, but the three factors discussed jointly play an essential role in defining China's approach toward North Korea's nuclear issue. The driving forces will continue to influence the trajectory of China's approaches toward North Korea's nuclear issue, that of swinging between two basic poles: one pole stands for harsh sanction and another for soft persuasion.

In addition to all the possible changes, some elements in China's approach might remain unchanged. First, though economic coercive measures certainly can inflict pain on Pyongyang, it should be China's last resort. To effectively change North Korea's external behavior, coercion

---

[35] 'Li Jinjun Dashi Xiang Jin Yongnan Weiyuanzhang Dijiao Guoshu'(Ambassador Li Jinjun Presents His Credential to President Kim Yongnam), *The Chinese Embassy Bulletin*, available at: http://kp.china-embassy.org/chn/dshd/dshd/t1250501.htm.

should be combined with other policy tools. To achieve the denuclearization of the Korean Peninsula, China will continue to combine various diplomatic tools such as persuasion, material incentive and economic coercion. Second, even though China will continue to apply coercive measures such as sanctions on North Korea, the pressure cannot be too tough to jeopardize China's long-pursued three basic objectives of 'no nuclear, no war, no chaos' on the Korean Peninsula. Third, China's economic coercion against North Korea is designed to pull North Korea to the negotiating table rather than to choke Pyongyang's regime to death. Last but not least, even though China as an emerging world power has the innate desire to offer collective goods to Northeast Asia such as the denuclearization of the Korean Peninsula, the pursuit of a nuclear-free Korean Peninsula is a collective endeavor rather than China's sole responsibility. China will readjust its approach as other stakeholders respond to North Korea's nuclear issue in one way or another.

It is too early to make an accurate assessment of China's coercion against North Korea. Obviously China's economic coercive policy toward North Korea constitutes one of the most significant external pressures, given North Korea's heavy economic dependence on China. The pressure may deepen the rift within North Korea's ruling elites over policy preferences. It might also drive North Korea to cultivate relations with other actors even though North Korea's diplomatic maneuvering space is very limited. The critical issues are how long North Korea can sustain such pressure and if China is determined to keep the pressure on at any cost until North Korea gives up its nuclear weapons.

Chapter 6

China's Economic Statecraft in Sino-Southeast Asian Relations and the Security-Economic Nexus

Kheng Swe Lim

China's rapid economic rise has resulted in increased Chinese economic influence in its neighborhood, particularly in Southeast Asia. Both regions trade heavily with each other, and the manufacturing industries of both regions are heavily intertwined. China's economic influence in the region will only intensify, particularly given the development of initiatives such as the Belt and Road Initiative (BRI).

However, China's economic influence in the region may not merely be limited to the monetary gains or losses from trade and investment. China's influence opens the possibility that China would be able to use its economic clout for political ends; in other words, use 'economic statecraft' in order to achieve its political, diplomatic, or security goals. Although this would seem to be a natural development, the reality is more complex. China's initial decision to increase its level of economic intertwining with Southeast Asia was in itself a form of economic statecraft, as part of its charm offensive. However, it is often difficult to determine the extent to which China's deliberate attempts to improve its economic ties with Southeast Asia resulted in China's main political and strategic objective during this period, namely stable relations with Southeast Asia, as opposed to other factors such as the balance of power or constructivist norms. In light of this, it is no surprise that whether or not China's new wave of economic initiatives, encapsulated by the BRI, will have the desired effects with regard to China's relations with Southeast Asia.

This chapter is organized in the following manner. I first briefly define 'economic statecraft', looking at the scholarly literature that has been done on this topic; I also look at ideas behind economic interdependence in Sino–Southeast Asian relations. I will then attempt to describe the development of the Sino–Southeast Asian economic relationship from about 2000 to present, in light of China's pursuit of its political goals by using the 'Good Neighbor Policy'. Next, I will look at the introduction of the BRI and the South China Sea conflict. Finally, I will attempt to link these to theories about the security-economic nexus, while looking at how China's political, security, and geostrategic interests in Southeast Asia have been affected.

China's Economic Intertwining with Southeast Asia: The Influence of the Good Neighbor Policy

Throughout most of the 2000s, China's relations with Southeast Asia were sanguine. Both China and Association of Southeast Asian Nations (ASEAN) stressed the importance of trade and investment relations as the cornerstone of their relationship. Meanwhile, all parties in the South China Sea dispute had de-escalated it to the point where it was no longer seen as a flashpoint that could destabilize the regional order.[1]

The theories behind economic statecraft have been discussed in previous chapters; however, there are a few points to remember. Economic statecraft is ultimately defined as the use of economic means to achieve political purposes. Baldwin defines economic statecraft as consisting of three basic components: the type of policy instrument, namely economic; the domain of the influence attempt, which consists of other international actors; and the scope the attempt, which includes some dimension of the target state's

---

[1] Ralf Emmers, *The De-Escalation of the Spratly Dispute in Sino-Southeast Asian Relations*, RSIS Working Paper No. 129 (2007), available at: https://www.rsis.edu.sg/wp-content/uploads/rsis-pubs/WP129.pdf.

behavior.[2] In light of this definition, it can be argued that China has indeed engaged in economic statecraft towards Southeast Asia from 2000 to the present. Such statecraft mainly consists of increased economic engagement with Southeast Asia for political means.

During this period, China's economic outreach to Southeast Asia can be seen in light of its Good Neighbour Policy, which ultimately had political motivations. Robert Sutter writes that in 1997, China promulgated the 'New Security Concept' that argued against adopting a 'Cold War Mentality', instead emphasizing the 'Five Principles of Peaceful Coexistence, mutually beneficial economic contacts, and greater dialogue promoting trust and the peaceful settlement of disputes'. China emphasized the establishment of 'partnerships' or 'strategic partnerships' with neighboring countries. The main aims of China's new stance were as follows: to help stabilize China's external environment to allow for a greater focus on domestic economic growth and political stability; to calm regional fears of China's rising power and influence; and to boost China's power and influence both globally and in the Asia-Pacific region.[3] This also coincided with the development of China's "Going Out" policy, in which China would look for investment opportunities for its large and rapidly increasing foreign reserves.[4] The policy had the economic motives of resource-seeking, asset-seeking for managerial and technical expertise, and market-seeking by avoiding trade barriers or producing marketable products overseas; however, it also had the political consideration of strengthening China's position on the international stage.[5]

Going off these analyzes, China's motives behind its Good Neighbour Policy can be argued to have had diplomatic, geostrategic, and security motives. Diplomatically, China aimed to improve its relations with its Southeast Asian neighbors. Geostrategically, China wanted to stabilize its

---

[2] Richard Baldwin, *Economic Statecraft* (Princeton, NJ: Princeton University Press, 1985), p. 32.

[3] Sutter, Robert, 'China's Good Neighbor Policy and Its Implications for Taiwan', *Journal of Contemporary China*, 13, no. 41 (2004), pp. 719–720.

[4] Raphael Shen and Victoria Mantzopoulos, 'China's "going out" policy: inception, evolution, implication', *Journal of Business and Behavioral Sciences*, 25, no. 2 (2014), pp. 121–122.

[5] *Ibid.*, p. 124.

relations with its immediate southern neighbors; this ultimately had a security motive, as it would serve to reduce threats and uncertainty in China's Southeast Asian backyard, allowing it to focus on domestic reform.

How did China try to go about achieving these motives? China needed to assuage worries among its Southeast Asian neighbors that it had caused in the 1990s by incidents such as the Taiwan Straits Crisis of 1997 and its actions in the South China Sea.[6] From an economic point of view, China needed to assuage concerns that Southeast Asian countries had over China's accession to the World Trade Organization (WTO), which sparked fears that Foreign Direct Investment (FDI) would flow away from Southeast Asia and toward China.[7] Therefore, during the 2000 ASEAN–China Summit, Chinese premier Zhu Rongji proposed the establishment of the CAFTA (China–ASEAN Free Trade Area).[8] The agreement was negotiated over a period of years and finally came into full effect in 2010. However, many of the effects of the treaty had actually come into effect before it was officially signed, due to the agreement of 'early harvest packages' between China and Southeast Asia. These early harvest packages were primarily aimed at easing the burden on the poorer Southeast Asian countries, particularly those in mainland Southeast Asia. By this, both sides agreed to liberalize early tariffs on mainly agricultural goods such as livestock, vegetables, fruits, and nuts.[9] This program was specifically designed to alleviate ASEAN's concerns about the negative repercussions of the CAFTA.[10]

How effective, ultimately, was the CAFTA as a political tool? This is difficult to measure. The implementation of this agreement can be taken as an independent variable while the prevailing warm relations between China and Southeast Asia during this period, which fulfilled all of China's

---

[6] Ian Storey, *Southeast Asia and the Rise of China* (London and New York: Routledge, 2011), p. 65.

[7] Joseph Cheng, 'The ASEAN–China Free Trade Area: genesis and implications', *Australian Journal of International Affairs*, no. 58(2), (2004), p. 258.

[8] *Ibid.*

[9] 'Is early harvest good for RP?' *Embassy of the People's Republic of China in the Republic of Philippines* (24 November 2004), available at: http://ph.chineseembassy.org/eng/sgdt/t171568.htm.

[10] Seungjoo Lee, 'The economy-security nexus in East Asian FTAs', in Vinod K. Aggarwal and Kristi Govella, eds., *Linking Trade and Security: Evolving Institutions and Strategies in Asia, Europe, and the United States* (New York: Springer-Verlag, 2013), p. 142.

diplomatic, geostrategic, and security motives, can be taken as a dependent variable. The difficulty lies in disentangling this from other possible confounding variables. For example, during this period, the South China Sea conflict was placed on the back burner to the point that it could no longer be considered a flashpoint.[11] In addition, the United States was involved in disputes in the Middle East, thereby reducing its great power presence in East Asia and thus the possibility of great power conflict. There was also the fact that China's military and economy were weaker than they are today, therefore reducing the possibility of assertive behavior on the part of China to get what it wanted. The intent behind China's promulgation of the CAFTA was clear, namely to stabilize its political relations with Southeast Asia, and this can be linked back to the broader Good Neighbor Policy that China was encouraging with regards to its relations with Southeast Asia during the period. Its effectiveness, though, is difficult to disentangle from the broader geopolitical landscape of the time.

The CAFTA has been the most significant economic tool that China used toward Southeast Asia for political means; however, it was not the only one. In keeping with China's Going Out policy, Chinese companies, both state-owned and private, have invested significant amounts of money in many of the less economically developed Southeast Asian countries, particularly in the Greater Mekong Subregion (GMS) countries of Myanmar, Laos, Thailand, Cambodia, and Vietnam. Chinese companies have significant investments in Cambodia, having put a total of US$9.7 billion in the country from 1997 to 2012, as well as US$2.7 billion in loans and grants.[12]

Meanwhile, in neighboring Laos, Chinese companies have a very heavy footprint. Most Chinese investments in Laos are the result of top-down agreements between the Chinese and Lao central governments, by which Chinese state-owned companies invest in industries in Laos ranging from hydropower to agriculture to retail. In 2013, China became the largest foreign investor in Laos, with over US$5 billion in investments, in areas

---

[11] Ian Storey, "The United States and ASEAN-China relations; all quiet on the ASEAN Front", (Strategic Studies Institute, United States War College, 2007), p. 4, available at: http://www.dtic.mil/cgi-bin/GetTRDoc?AD=ADA473640.

[12] Pheakday Heng, 'Chinese investment and aid in Cambodia a controversial affair', *East Asia Forum* (16 July 2013), available at: http://www.eastasiaforum.org/2013/07/16/ chinese-investment-and-aid-in-cambodia-a-controversial-affair/.

ranging from energy, raw materials, transport, and real estate.[13] Before Myanmar's sudden opening to the West, China was the largest investor in that country, making up a third of the US$44 billion in foreign investment in the country from 1988 to 2013.[14] Within the GMS region, China has been involved in the construction of a series of highways and railways in the North–South Corridor, contributing about a third of the US$97 billion required to build Route 3 in Laos, thus completing the road linkages between Singapore and Beijing through mainland Southeast Asia.[15]

Many of these investments, while they have a strong economic focus, can also be argued to have a political motive of stabilizing China's relations with these countries. In general, these investments largely fit into China's broad policy directive of stabilizing relations with its periphery, thus serving goals that are ultimately non-economic. It is also true that most mainland Southeast Asian countries are, on the whole, accommodating of China's political and strategic interests. For example, Cambodia deported Uighurs detainees back to China in 2009.[16] Thailand did so likewise in 2015.[17] In 2012, Cambodia, widely seen as being under China's influence, took a strong stance on the South China Sea at an ASEAN foreign ministers' meeting, resulting in the grouping not issuing a joint communiqué for the first time in its history.[18] In 2013, Laos, Myanmar, and Thailand cooperated

---

[13] Suwatchai Songwanitch, 'China's strong investments in Laos bringing a transformation', *The Nation* (8 June 2015), available at: http://www.nationmultimedia.com/opinion/Chinas-strong-investments-in-Laos-bringing-a-trans-30261822.html.

[14] Song Sophie, 'Myanmar FDI: China accounts for one third of foreign investment in Myanmar with $14 billion', *International Business Times* (29 October 2013), available at: http://www.ibtimes.com/myanmar-fdi-china-accounts-one-third-foreign-investment-myanmar-14-billion-1446282.

[15] Tin Seng Lim, 'China's active role in the Greater Mekong Sub-region: challenge to construct a "win-win" relationship', *East Asian Policy*, 1, no. 1 (January/March, 2009), p. 41.

[16] 'US concern after Cambodia deports 20 Chinese Uighurs', *BBC News* (20 December 2009), available at: http://news.bbc.co.uk/2/hi/8422022.stm.

[17] Catherine Putz, 'Thailand deports 100 Uyghurs to China', *The Diplomat* (11 July 2015), available at: http://thediplomat.com/2015/07/thailand-deports-100-uyghurs-to-china/.

[18] Jane Perlez, 'Asian leaders at regional meeting fail to resolve disputes over South China Sea', *New York Times* (12 July 2012), available at: http://www.nytimes.com/2012/07/13/world/asia/asian-leaders-fail-to-resolve-disputes-on-south-china-sea-during-asean-summit.html?_r=0.

with Chinese law-enforcement authorities in order to hunt down and arrest Naw Kham, a druglord accused of killing 13 Chinese sailors on the Mekong; such a move was in keeping with China's interest in safeguarding its citizens' movements on its periphery.[19]

Once again, though, the challenge of assessing the effectiveness of China's interactions in achieving its political goals lies in the difficulty of establishing causality between China's investments and the target countries' policies. There is little evidence that China actively used its investments in these countries in order to actively pressure them to change their behavior on these individual incidents. It is easier to argue that China's general stance of encouraging good relations with these countries has resulted in warmer opinions toward China, making them more likely to defer to China's interests on issues that China treats seriously. Even so, it is difficult to disentangle this factor from other possibilities. For instance, the mainland Southeast Asian countries could be 'bandwagoning' with a rising China. Scholars like Martin Stuart-Fox may argue that they could have fallen into a 'tributary-system' pattern of relations.[20] There is also the possibility of the pure economic motive; especially given that many Southeast Asian countries are rapidly developing, thus making them good investment destinations regardless of politics. Nevertheless, we must not forget that the definition of economic statecraft is more a result of motivations, and there is enough evidence to suggest that a large China's motivations do, broadly speaking, have a political and strategic edge in addition to their economic motive.

A New Era of Chinese Foreign Policy Proactiveness: 2012 to Present

Since about 2012, though, there have been some changes in China's approach to economic statecraft in Southeast Asia. The South China Sea

---

[19]Jane Perlez and Bree Feng, 'Beijing flaunts cross-border clout in search for drug lord', *New York Times* (4 April 2013), available at: http://www.nytimes.com/2013/04/05/world/asia/chinas-manhunt-shows-sway-in-southeast-asia.html.

[20]Martin Stuart-Fox, 'A Short History of China and Southeast Asia: Tribute, Trade and Influence', Crow's Nest, NSW (Australia: Allen and Unwin, 2003).

has influenced China's relations with several Southeast Asian claimant countries. A pattern can be detected where China's economic relations with certain countries worsens along with the South China Sea disputes in some areas. In tandem with this, China has more actively advanced its own economic initiatives, with the development of the BRI and the AIIB; unlike the CAFTA in the early 2000s, these initiatives are mainly targeted at infrastructure investments and large-scale projects with target countries; and as of the time of writing have had little interaction with ASEAN's institutional setup.

The effect of China's new economic initiatives, namely the Asian Infrastructure Investment Bank (AIIB) and the Maritime Silk Road (MSR), on Southeast Asia, is worthy of further discussion, though neither initiative is purely Southeast Asia-focused. The former, with members from all around the world, focuses on developing a new multinational lending institution focused on filling the infrastructure deficit in the Asia-Pacific region. The latter, backed up by a US$40 billion Silk Road Fund, aims to break Asia's 'infrastructure bottleneck', and consists of an overland 'Silk Road Economic Belt' and a 'Maritime Silk Road'.[21] The Asian Development Bank estimates that, on the whole, Asia is suffering from an US$8 trillion infrastructure deficit.[22] Many Southeast Asian countries are in particularly bad shape when it comes to their infrastructure development. Indonesia's infrastructure, for example, has lagged behind its economic growth; its infrastructure stock grew by only 3% annually from 2001 to 2011, against GDP growth of 5.3%.[23] Vietnam only inaugurated its first deepwater port in 2009, despite its long coastline and interests in the South China Sea.[24]

---

[21] Jeremy Page, 'China to contribute $40 billion to Silk Road Fund', *Wall Street Journal* (8 November 2014), available at: http://www.wsj.com/articles/china-to-contribute-40-billion-to-silk-road-fund-1415454995.

[22] 'Who will pay for Asia's US$8 trillion infrastructure gap?', *Asian Development Bank* (30 September 2013), available at: http://www.adb.org/news/infographics/who-will-pay-asias-8-trillion-infrastructure-gap.

[23] *Development Policy Review 2014: Indonesia: Avoiding the Trap* (Jakarta: The World Bank, 2014), available at: http://www.worldbank.org/content/dam/Worldbank/document/EAP/Indonesia/Indonesia-development-policy-review-2014-english.pdf.

[24] 'Vietnam's first deep sea port inaugurated', *ASEAN Affairs* (31 May 2009), available at: http://www.aseanaffairs.com/vietnam_daily_news_updates/infrastructure/vietnam_s_first_deep_sea_port_inaugurated.

Therefore, there is a natural overlap between China's desire to invest in infrastructure overseas, and that of many Southeast Asian countries to improve their domestic infrastructure and thus spur on economic growth.

Economically, by getting involved in infrastructure projects overseas, China is hoping to soak up some of the economic overcapacity that has resulted due to the slowdown in China's economic growth, particularly in the steel, coal, and cement sectors, which are facing up to 30% overcapacity.[25] Furthermore, China also hopes that total trade volumes along the BRI would come up to US$2.5 trillion a decade after its establishment.[26] However, this leaves the question of whether, aside from economic motivations, there is also a political or strategic angle to these initiatives. The main difficulty with analyzing the relationship between the MSR and economic statecraft, though, is the fact that the MSR has not been fully developed on an operational level. As of the time of writing, the central government has set out a broad general directive, but there seems to be no central masterplan that lays out exactly what projects China will invest in and in which countries. There are as many as 12 government agencies involved in the MSR, and 20 provinces have made their own proposals for the BRI. From the point of view of Southeast Asian countries, this has resulted in a lack of clarity, which has given rise to much speculation that, for example, the Philippines has been left out of the MSR due to the South China Sea disputes (which China has denied).[27]

Any analyses of the MSR's motives with regards to Southeast Asia will therefore, by necessity, remain somewhat speculative. According to an official document released by China's State Council, the MSR is mainly aimed at increasing 'win–win cooperation' between China and its

[25]Brenda Goh and Koh Gui Qing, 'China's "One Belt, One Road" looks to take construction binge offshore', *Reuters* (6 September 2015), available at: http://uk.reuters.com/article/2015/09/06/uk-china-economy-silkroad-idUKKCN0R60X820150906.

[26]Wee Sui-Lee 'China's Xi: trade between China and Silk Road nations to exceed $2.5 trillion', *Reuters* (29 March 2015), available at: http://www.reuters.com/article/2015/03/29/us-china-economy-oneroad-idUSKBN0MP0J320150329.

[27]Irene Chan, 'China's Maritime Silk Road: the politics of routes', *RSIS Commentaries* (12 March 2015), available at: https://www.rsis.edu.sg/rsis-publication/rsis/co15051-chinas-maritime-silk-road-the-politics-of-routes/#.VjwxcrSqqkp.

neighbors.[28] Fu Mengzi and Lou Chunhao echo these statements, and add that the MSR would serve to strengthen China's economic lifeline, which includes securing China's sea lines of communication and overcoming the 'Malacca Trap'.[29] They point out that the countries along the MSR, particularly in the Middle East, North Africa, and Australia, are strategically important to China, as they are natural resource producers.[30] In light of this, it would make sense for China to secure its sea lanes of communication that run through Maritime Southeast Asia. Zhou Bo has written that, in the Indian Ocean, China is only interested in access and securing its sea-lanes of communication; however, he does not touch on China's interests in Southeast Asia.[31] Shannon Tiezzi, meanwhile, believes that China's MSR could be potentially used as a tool of economic coercion in the South China Sea dispute, particularly given China's blurring of the lines between civilian and military aspects. She writes that China's strategy of using civilian or paramilitary vessels to advance its claims in disputed maritime regions would blur the lines between a military-focused 'String of Pearls' strategy and an economics-focused MSR.[32] From what these analysts have written, we can develop a tentative list of China's political, geostrategic, and security interests in developing the MSR. Politically, it is fair to say that China is hoping to use the MSR in order to set a new tone with regard to its relations with Southeast Asia, especially in light of the problems in the South China Sea, thus helping in the maintenance of cordial relations with them. Geostrategically and security-wise, China is hoping to use the MSR

---

[28] 'Jingguowuyuan shouquan san buwei lianhe fabu tuidong gongjian "yidai yilu" de yuanjing yu xingdong', *Gov.cn* (28 March 2015), available at: http://www.gov.cn/xinwen/2015-03/28/content_2839723.htm.

[29] Mengzi Fu and Chunhua Kou, 'Guanyu 21 shiji "haishang sichou zhilu" jianshe de nuogan sikao', *Xiandai guoji guanxi* (Contemporary International Relations), p. 3, (2015), available at: http://www.cicir.ac.cn/UploadFile/files/20150609095445961.pdf.

[30] *Ibid.*, p. 3.

[31] Zhou Bo, 'The String of Pearls and the Maritime Silk Road', *China–US Focus* (11 February 2014), available at: http://www.chinausfocus.com/foreign-policy/the-string-of-pearls-and-the-maritime-silk-road/.

[32] Shannon Tiezzi, 'The Maritime Silk Road vs. the String of Pearls', *The Diplomat* (13 February 2014), available at: http://thediplomat.com/2014/02/the-maritime-silk-road-vs-the-string-of-pearls/.

to secure its sea lines of communication, and possibly provide itself with additional advantages in the South China Sea dispute.

How effective have these new economic initiatives been at advancing China's aims? As of the time of writing, it is too early to tell; once again, these analyses remain somewhat speculative. From a geostrategic point of view, China has focused on Indonesia and Malaysia, countries that sit on important sea lines of communication running through the Malacca Strait. The MSR was announced in a speech that Xi Jinping made to the Indonesian parliament in 2013, in which he made specific reference to ASEAN using the China–ASEAN Maritime Cooperation Fund in order to jointly build the MSR.[33] The MSR would involve China supporting the development of stronger marine connectivity through the construction of ports infrastructure, as well as enhancing cooperation in the marine industry by supporting the construction of industrial parks and economics and trade cooperation zones, as well as develop port economic zones and free trade zones along the MSR.[34] These seem to mesh naturally with Indonesia's plan to turn itself into a 'Global Maritime Axis', focusing on increasing inter-island connectivity in Indonesia and shifting Indonesia's security focus from an army-based territorial defense posture to building a strong navy.[35] This has resulted in Indonesia's president Joko Widodo announcing a Maritime Partnership with China.[36]

Malaysia, meanwhile, has also been on the receiving end of Chinese attention in the same way that Indonesia has. What is interesting is that, though Malaysia is also one of the claimant countries to the South China Sea and has expressed its worries over China's activities there, their bilateral

---

[33] Jiao Wu and Yunbi Zhang, 'Xi in call for building of new "maritime silk road"', *China Daily* (10 April 2013), available at: http://usa.chinadaily.com.cn/china/2013-10/04/content_17008940.htm.

[34] Cigui Liu, 'Reflections on maritime partnership: building the 21st century Maritime Silk Road', *China Institute of International Studies* (15 September 2014), available at: http://www.ciis.org.cn/english/2014-09/15/content_7231376.htm.

[35] Vibhanshu Shekhar and Joseph Chinyong Liow, 'Indonesia as a maritime power: Jokowi's vision, strategies, and obstacles ahead', *Brookings Institute* (November 2014), available at: http://www.brookings.edu/research/articles/2014/11/indonesia-maritime-liow-shekhar.

[36] Shannon Tiezzi, 'Indonesia, China seal "maritime partnership"', *The Diplomat* (27 March 2015), available at: http://thediplomat.com/2015/03/indonesia-china-seal-maritime-partnership/.

relationship seems to be smoother than China's relations with the Philippines and Vietnam. Both the China–Malaysia Industrial Parks in Qinzhou and Pahang are examples of actual Sino–Malaysian investment cooperation. Malaysia has allowed the China Construction Bank to list RMB 1 billion worth of MSR bonds, which will come due in 2017.[37] Guangdong Province and the state of Malacca, which lends its name to the Malacca Straits, are working on an industrial park and port project, which covers two manmade and one natural island and which aims to include a deep-sea port, a shipyard, and a duty-free trade zone.[38]

China's official language on the MSR has been largely conciliatory. The announcement of the MSR initiative in Jakarta highlighted the importance of win–win cooperation and the need to expand practical cooperation, as well as the importance of peacefully resolving territorial disputes in the South China Sea.[39] At the 17th ASEAN Summit in Naypyidaw, premier Li Keqiang spoke about the MSR as one of the pillars of the '2 + 7 cooperation' framework between China and ASEAN.[40] As of the time of writing, there have also been one or two cultural exhibitions of the MSR held in Southeast Asia. The Quanzhou Maritime Museum and Brunei Museums Department have held a MSR exhibition in Brunei.[41] The Thai national gallery of art has also showcased a series of paintings on the theme of the MSR.[42] However,

---

[37]C.K. Tan, 'China throws troubled state fund a lifeline, pledges more', *Nikkei Asian Review* (25 November 2015), available at: http://asia.nikkei.com/Politics-Economy/Economy/China-throws-troubled-state-fund-a-lifeline-pledges-more?page=2.

[38]Xiaoshu, Quan and Jun, Shang, 'Spotlight: Chinese premier visits Malacca to send message of peace amid U.S. meddling in South China Sea', *Xinhua News Agency* (22 November 2015), available at: http://news.xinhuanet.com/english/2015-11/23/c_134842767.htm.

[39]'Speech by Chinese President Xi Jinping to Indonesian Parliament', *ASEAN–China Centre* (2 October 2013), available at: http://www.asean-china-center.org/english/2013-10/03/c_133062675.htm.

[40]Keqiang Li, 'Take China–ASEAN relations to a new height', *The State Council, People's Republic of China* (13 November 2014), available at: http://english.gov.cn/premier/speeches/ 2014/11/15/content_281475010415762.htm.

[41]'China's Quanzhou "Maritime Silk Road" exhibition opens in Brunei', *China.org.cn* (27 March 2015), available at: http://www.china.org.cn/world/Off_the_Wire/2015-03/24/content_35133736.htm.

[42]Lisheng, Zhan, 'Feng Shaoxie's "Maritime Silk Road" oil paintings on show in Thailand', *China Daily* (7 July 2015), available at: http://www.chinadaily.com.cn/regional/2015-07/07/content_21203105.htm.

aside from the general tone of official pronouncements and these exhibitions, there does not seem to be a cohesive soft-power strategy behind China's approach toward Southeast Asia with regard to the MSR.

However, from a strategic point of view, the MSR proposal will likely not affect the formal regional security or economic structures. The economic architecture of the Asia Pacific is characterized by a 'noodle bowl' of networks that bind the region together into 'factory Asia', a just-in-time supply chain of manufacturing components.[43] This was made possible by the tangle of preferential trade agreements (PTAs) that criss-cross the Asia-Pacific region, bringing tariffs between countries to levels below that required by the WTO.[44] Meanwhile, the formal security architecture of the Asia-Pacific is defined by two factors. First, there are the many non-binding multilateral security forums that involve countries across the Asia-Pacific, usually ASEAN-centered. These include initiatives such as the ASEAN Defence Ministers' Meeting (ADMM)-Plus, the ASEAN Regional Forum and the East Asia Summit. Second, there are the formal or informal bilateral alliances between the United States and several countries in the region; the United States has formal alliances with Thailand and the Philippines, has good security interactions with Singapore and Malaysia, and is increasing its level of security cooperation with Vietnam. What is interesting is that the MSR will affect neither of these. It is not a series of new military alliances or a new multilateral forum, and will therefore not affect the formal security structures of the region. Neither is it a series of new trade arrangements, as it is not aimed at cutting tariffs. The infrastructure-focused nature of the MSR therefore aims at going over and above the more traditional structures of regional integration, focusing more on facilitating economic development in the target countries as opposed to creating new structures.

What should be asked, therefore, is whether or not the aims of the central idea behind developing the MSR have overtones of economic statecraft. The answer is that they do, inasmuch as China hopes to use its economic tools of infrastructure building, port development, and the development of special

---

[43]Richard Baldwin, 'Managing the noodle bowl: the fragility of East Asian regionalism', *The Singapore Economic Review*, 53, no. 1 (2008), p. 470.
[44]*Ibid.*, pp. 468–469.

economic zones to secure its strategic interests in Maritime Southeast Asia, as well as reduce the negative attitudes toward China that resulted from the South China Sea disputes. The effectiveness of this statecraft, however, is yet to be determined, given the current inchoate nature of the MSR in Southeast Asia. As of now, according to Li Mingjiang, the countries of Southeast Asia can be roughly divided into supportive, largely supportive and less supportive groups (Vietnam and the Philippines), and there are concerns among the second and third groups that China is trying to create a Sino-centric regional order.[45]

China's diplomatic, geostrategic, and security motives are more difficult to disentangle during this current period, as analysts do not have the benefit of hindsight as they did for the period between 2000 and 2012. However, judging by China's current stance, it is possible to make some tentative guesses as to China's objectives. It is fair to say that China remains interested in maintaining cordial, peaceful diplomatic relations with its Southeast Asian neighbors; no one wants armed conflict to break out. In tandem with this, though, China's recent actions in the South China Sea suggest that it is interested in pressing its sovereignty claims more vigorously; this may have geostrategic and security motives, as China has an interest in securing its sea lines of communication. Furthermore, the entry of the United States into the dispute has resulted in an element of great power conflict, and it would be fair to say that China is seeking to develop in stature as a great power in the Asia-Pacific vis-à-vis the United States.

The South China Sea disputes began heating up in about 2010, when in light of maritime confrontations between China and Vietnam, Hillary Clinton gave a speech at the ASEAN Regional Forum in Hanoi that touched on the South China Sea, thus introducing an element of great power politics into the conflict. It is not for this chapter to go into the details of the sovereignty dispute. However, it can be noted that during sensitive periods in the South China Sea dispute, there is usually an uptick in problems in economic cooperation between China and the Philippines and Vietnam. In

---

[45]Esther Ng, 'Slow and steady ambition', *The Star Online* (18 October 2015), available at: http://m.thestar.com.my/story.aspx?hl=Slow+and+steady+ambition&sec=news&id= %7B7515CDEB-4AF0-4AEA-8EBA-0D44B2D0E49D%7D.

the wake of the Scarborough Shoal standoff of 2012, there were reports that China quarantined imports of Philippine's bananas into the country and began slowing imports of other fruit from the Philippines; Chinese tour groups also stopped sending tourists to the Philippines, allegedly over safety concerns. In response, the Philippine business community placed pressure on the government to come to an agreement with China, which resulted in the Philippine navy pulling out of the shoal.[46] During the Haiyan Shiyou incident in 2013, when China placed an oilrig in waters disputed between China and Vietnam, there were reports that large consignments of lychee exports to China were left to rot on the China–Vietnam border.[47] Furthermore, in the aftermath of riots in Vietnam in 2014, Chinese lenders effectively froze credit lines to a number of Vietnamese infrastructure projects.[48]

Bonnie Glaser has described these incidents of China blocking agricultural imports as 'a new and worrying trend', particularly in light of similar actions over rare-earth exports to Japan in 2010 over the Diaoyu/Senkaku Islands dispute.[49] However, the significance of these incidents, while causing real economic damage to some sectors, is too easily blown out of proportion. First, the actual mechanisms by which these import restrictions were implemented are not clear. It is not obvious whether the initiative was passed down from the central government, was developed on the local level as a nationalist reaction to the general political atmosphere, or was the initiative of individual firms and individuals on the border reflective of more local concerns. Second, these import bans are only restricted to a small sector

---

[46]Bonnie Glaser, 'China's coercive economic diplomacy: a new and worrying trend', *CSIS* (6 August 2012), available at: http://csis.org/publication/chinas-coercive-economic-diplomacy-new-and-worrying-trend.

[47]'After China woes, Vietnam's lychee farmers head to new markets', *AFP* (15 July 2015), available at: http://www.thanhniennews.com/business/after-china-woes-vietnams-lychee-farmers-head-to-new-markets-47985.html.

[48]Gavin Bowring, 'Vietnam yields cautionary tale over Chinese investment', *Financial Times* (27 November 2014), available at: http://blogs.ft.com/beyond-brics/2014/11/27/vietnam-yields-cautionary-tale-over-chinese-investment/.

[49]Bonnie Glaser, 'China's coercive economic diplomacy: a new and worrying trend', *CSIS* (6 August 2012), available at: http://csis.org/publication/chinas-coercive-economic-diplomacy-new-and-worrying-trend.

of Philippine and Vietnamese exports to China. According to Philippine's statistics, in 2011, the Philippines exported US$6.237 billion to China; in 2012, this figure was US$6.169 billion; in 2013, this was US$7.025 billion; while in 2014, this figure was US$8.467 billion.[50] Philippine exports to China have been on a steady rise despite the South China Sea tensions. The same can be said for Vietnam; according to figures from Vietnam's General Statistics Office, Vietnam exported US$7 billion to mainland China in 2010, US$11 billion in 2011, US$12 billion in 2012, US$13 billion in 2013, and US$15 billion in 2014.[51] The figures for Vietnam would increase by a significant amount if the figures for Hong Kong SAR were included, given that it is likely that a significant portion of exports to Hong Kong end up in mainland China. Suffice to say that the 'new and worrying trend', while possibly significant on the level of certain individual industries or exporters, does not seem to affect the general nature of trade flows between China and these two countries.

The general impression of China's use of economic statecraft in the most recent years has therefore been a mixed one, and no discernable pattern can be ascertained as of now. There have been instances in which China's economic exchanges with certain Southeast Asian countries took a turn for the worse just when the South China Sea disputes were becoming more sensitive, but the causation between the former and the latter remains unclear. China's overall trade volumes with the Philippines and Vietnam have remained strong, though there has been difficulty in advancing further trade and investment mechanisms. Meanwhile, China's launching of the MSR seems to be motivated by a combination of economic and strategic motives, and can therefore be counted as a form of economic statecraft. However, as of the time of writing, aside from China's diplomatic outreach to Indonesia and the MSR being mentioned in China's speeches at ASEAN forums, there has been little progress in the plan's implementation given its early stages, making the results of the MSR's economic statecraft difficult to establish.

---

[50]All statistics on the Philippines come from the Philippine Statistics Authority website.

[51]All statistics for Vietnam come from the General Statistics Office of Vietnam website.

Country-Level Perspectives on China's Economic Policy Assertiveness: Public Opinion, Hedging, and Strategic Realignments

The section above detailed China's economic statecraft towards Southeast Asian in a broader sense. This broader picture, while important, obscures some interesting country-level empirics. Southeast Asian countries want to reap the benefits of China's economic expansion, while also balancing these off against a variety of factors including nationalism and national security. This influences their overall alignments in the international system. The country-level pictures reflect the general trend that China's economic statecraft is just one of the many factors that shapes the foreign policy considerations of Southeast Asian countries.

Many Southeast Asian governments adopt a hedging strategy, choosing to strengthen some aspects of their relations with China while maintaining cordial relations with other powers such as the United States, Japan, and India. However, the exact nature of this hedging varies from country to country. The presence of the United States was far less evident from 2000 to 2010. During this period, the United States was accused of benignly neglecting Southeast Asia.[52] The country had closed its last military base, Subic Bay, in Southeast Asia. The Bush administration's 'War on Terror' caused Washington to focus on Afghanistan and the Middle East, and much US rhetoric toward Southeast Asia was aimed at supporting countries such as the Philippines against terrorism.

It would be a gross exaggeration, of course, to say that Southeast Asia cut all links with the United States during this period and entered into a Sino-centric regional order, driven by China's promotion of the CAFTA. Throughout this period, Thailand and the Philippines remained major non-NATO US allies, and the United States continued to conduct military

---

[52] 'For much of the past two decades, many Southeast Asians have expressed frustration that US policy treated their region with benign neglect or indifference, and that the United States' attention was episodic rather than consistent'. See John J. Brandon, 'A strategic pivot in U.S.–Southeast Asia relations in 2012', *The Asia Foundation* (4 January 2012), available at: http://asiafoundation.org/in-asia/2012/01/04/a-strategic-pivot-in-u-s-southeast-asia-relations-in-2012/.

exercises such as Cooperation Afloat Readiness and Training (CARAT) and COBRA-Gold with its Southeast Asian partners. Furthermore, the United States continued its International Military Education and Training (IMET) training program with Southeast Asian militaries and governments. Many of Southeast Asia's ties with the United States had already been institutionalized, resulting in the US presence existing in parallel to China's expanding economic power. It can be debated whether Southeast Asian countries made a conscious decision to maintain their ties with the United States to hedge against Chinese economic policy-making, or whether they were just maintaining the preexisting links due to inertia while seeking to take advantage of China's economic openness. The fact of the matter remains that the United States maintained its presence in Southeast Asia even through the years of 'benign neglect'. From about 2010, it is easier to analyze the extent to which China's economic proactiveness has shaped the strategic alignments and hedging behavior of different Southeast Asian countries. No Southeast Asian country, regardless of their diplomatic or territorial disagreements with China, has frozen its links with China. At the same time, no Southeast Asian country, regardless of how close its relations with China, has voluntarily downgraded ties with other powers, be it the United States, Japan, India, or other ASEAN members. Almost all Southeast Asian countries hedge to some extent, maintaining their economic relations with China while building diplomatic or military ties with other powers.

Hedging can be defined as a strategy by states to handle uncertainties in the future behavior of their partners by using a set of policy tools that include both competitive and cooperative measures, in order to both foster cooperation as well as guard against potential threats to their security.[53] The extent to which countries 'lean China' — having their security and economic foreign policies aligned with that of China — differs depending on their domestic and strategic considerations, which vary given the large variety of countries and interests within ASEAN. In addition, the factors affecting their hedging strategies and alignments are constantly shifting, making any representation a mere snapshot of the situation at a point in time. It is difficult to sort the hedging strategies of the different Southeast Asian countries into

---

[53]Long Hiep Le, 'Vietnam's hedging strategy against China since normalization', *Contemporary Southeast Asia*, 35, no. 3 (2013), p. 227.

a neat typology, as doing so would obscure the fine variations in the mix of factors acting on each country's foreign policy. Keeping these limitations in mind, instead of trying to group all 10 ASEAN countries into categories, I look more closely at how a few countries have reacted to China's increased economic assertiveness, in order to achieve a reasonable cross-section of Southeast Asian views. The cases of the Philippines and Vietnam, both claimant states to the South China Sea, have been discussed earlier. To briefly recap, China's economic strategies aimed at these countries should not be taken out of proportion, and their strategic alignments and hedging behavior are as much a result of broader geopolitical shifts, domestic policy considerations, and their interests in the South China Sea as they are a product of China's economic policies. In addition to these countries, we can also look at the strategic alignments of some other Southeast Asian countries.

The first is Indonesia, with which China, as mentioned in the previous section, is currently hoping to boost its diplomatic and economic ties. Indonesia requires large amounts of capital in order to jump-start its infrastructure, and China is willing to supply this. Indonesia's willingness to involve China in its infrastructure development can be seen by its decision to allow China to build a high-speed railway from Jakarta to Bandung, the first in the country.[54] However, the economic benefits that Indonesia can gain from China will not change Indonesia's long-entrenched policy of non-alignment. Indonesia values its foreign policy independence. Evidence of this can be seen in Indonesia's dealings with the other great power, the United States. Both countries announced a strategic partnership in October 2015, which signaled Indonesia's intent to strengthen its strategic relations with the United States.

However, Indonesia has not always voiced support for US foreign policy initiatives in Asia. For example, after the United States staged its freedom of navigation operation (FONOP) in the South China Sea, Indonesia's president called on all parties, including Washington, to 'exercise restraint'. Luhut Pandjaitan, a close advisor, equated US 'power projection' in the

---

[54]Wahyudi Soeriatmadja, 'Indonesia, China sign $7.6 billion high-speed rail deal', *The Straits Times* (17 October 2015), available at: http://www.straitstimes.com/asia/se-asia/indonesia-china-sign-76-billion-high-speed-rail-deal.

South China Sea to its interventions in Iraq and Afghanistan.[55] In addition, Michael Buehler argues that Indonesian politics is dominated by a streak of 'resource nationalism'.[56] This was most recently evident in Indonesia's complete ban on raw mineral ore exports in 2014, which halted nickel and bauxite exports to China.[57] Ultimately, Indonesia is hedging, strengthening its strategic relations with the United States while taking advantage of China's economic policies. However, Indonesia's deep-seated nationalism and its free and active foreign policy will remain, regardless of the development in its economic relations with China or its strategic relations with the United States.

Thailand's strategic reactions involve the interaction between domestic politics, great power politics, and economic interests. Thailand is also interested in benefiting from its relations with China, particularly in infrastructure connectivity. The Kunming–Singapore railroad passes through Thailand, and there is also chatter about the feasibility of constructing a canal through the Isthmus of Kra, which would bypass the Straits of Malacca (though this idea remains in the realm of speculation). China's economic advances in Thailand are but one major component of a broader warming of relations; the Chinese and Thai militaries have also strengthened their relations by holding joint military exercises.[58] Despite the draw of China's economy, Thailand's decision to strengthen its relations with China is also influenced by its cooling relations with the United States. In the wake of its military coup, Thailand's relations with the United States have cooled.

---

[55] Prashanth Parameswran, 'The new U.S.–Indonesia strategic partnership after Jokowi's visit: problems and prospects', *Brookings Institute* (8 December 2015), available at: http://www.brookings.edu/research/opinions/2015/12/08-new-us-indonesia-strategic-partnership-parameswaran.

[56] Michael Buehler, '"Resource Nationalism." clouds Indonesia's economic prospects', *The Diplomat* (7 September 2012), available at: http://thediplomat.com/2012/09/resource-nationalism-clouds-indonesias-economic-prospects/.

[57] Andy Home, 'RPT-COLUMN-Bauxite and the limits of resource nationalism: Andy Home', *Reuters* (29 March 2015), available at: http://www.reuters.com/article/indonesia-bauxite-ahome-idUSL6N0WT1TS20150330.

[58] Patpitcha Tanakasempipat and Jutarat Skulpichetrat, 'China, Thailand joint air force exercise highlights warming ties', *Reuters* (24 November 2015), available at: http://www.reuters.com/article/us-china-thailand-military-idUSKBN0TD0B120151124.

At the same time, Thailand will not sever its links with the United States, and remains a major non-NATO ally. The country plays host to the annual COBRA-Gold exercise; the exercise went ahead, albeit 'scaled down', in 2015, highlighting the continuing strategic links between Thailand and the United States.[59] Therefore, while Thailand's economic relationship with China is one factor influencing its decision to strengthen its ties with Beijing, its cooling relations with Washington over issues of Thai domestic politics are also explanatory factors for the particular nature of its strategic alignment.

Laos also benefits from China's overseas economic activities. China is now the third-largest investor in Laos, having invested a total of over US\$5 billion in the country as of 2014.[60] China also has a strong interest in Laos's natural resources and central location in mainland Southeast Asia. In 2012, over half of China's foreign direct investment stock in Laos was in mining and natural resources, particularly in the copper industry.[61] China's high-speed railroad from Kunming to Thailand passes through Laos. It would be wrong, though, to say that these investments give China political dominance over Laos. The Lao government has historically strong ties with Vietnam, dating back to the Cold War, when the Lao–Vietnamese Treaty of Friendship and Cooperation resulted in heavy Vietnamese influence in Laos.[62] Stuart-Fox notes that China and Vietnam are not in competition in Laos, as China's interests are primarily economic while Vietnam's are strategic.[63] Nevertheless, the net result is that Laos has a space between the great powers, using its relations with China to develop its economy

---

[59] Prashanth Parameswaran, 'US–Thailand Relations and Cobra Gold 2015: what's really going on?' *The Diplomat* (5 February 2015), available at: http://thediplomat.com/2015/02/us-thailand-relations-and-cobra-gold-2015-whats-really-going-on/.

[60] Li Yan, 'China becomes largest investor in Laos', *Chinanews.com* (30 January 2014), available at: http://www.ecns.cn/business/2014/01-30/99461.shtml.

[61] Phanhpakit Ophanhdala and Terukazu Suruga, *Chinese Outward FDI in Agriculture and Rural Development: Evidence from Northern Laos*, GSICS Working Paper Series No. 25 (2013), available at: http://www.research.kobe-u.ac.jp/gsics-publication/gwps/2013-25.pdf.

[62] Martin Stuart-Fox, 'Laos: the Vietnamese connection', *Southeast Asian Affairs* (1980), p. 191.

[63] Stuart-Fox, Martin, 'Laos: the Chinese Connection', *Southeast Asian Affairs* (2009), p. 151.

while benefiting from its political ties with Vietnam. Whether this was a conscious decision by Laos, or an unintended, but natural, consequence of the region's power structures is up for debate. It is interesting, though, that even in the absence of the United States, which has a relatively weak presence in Laos, Vientiane can still strike such a balance between China and a second country in its foreign relations.

The interplay of economic relations and other political and strategic considerations is complex enough on the macro-level. These three case studies demonstrate that this complexity is reflected on the state level. Economic considerations, particularly with regard to China, do help shape the alignments and strategies of individual Southeast Asian countries. However, these also contend and interact with geopolitical and domestic considerations. The interaction of these factors determines the ultimate strategic alignments of Southeast Asian countries. China's economic influence over them is not one definite 'independent variable' shaping their alignment or hedging behavior. Rather, it is one of a larger set of factors acting on these countries' foreign policies.

Meanwhile, in light of China's economic policy assertiveness, Southeast Asian public opinion has remained largely positive towards China, with a few exceptions. The Pew Research Center's Global Indicators Database collects data on how different countries around the world view China, including five Southeast Asian countries. For these five countries, the data is patchy, as information for some of the years is missing. The country with the most comprehensive data is Indonesia, ranging from 2012 to 2015. Favorable Indonesian opinions of China fluctuated between a high of 73% in 2005 and 58% in 2008 and 2010; the most recent figure was 63% in 2011. In 2015, 78% of Malaysians had a favorable view of China. For Thailand, the only available figure was in 2014, where 72% of the population held a favorable view. Even Philippine public opinion, despite the South China Sea disputes, is not as unfavorable as would be expected. The 2015 figure of 54%, while lower than the 2002 figure of 62%, is still significantly higher than the corresponding 2015 figure for Vietnam, a very low 19%.[64]

The main difficulty about this data is correlating it with China's economic interactions with these countries. The Pew Report's question, which

---

[64]All data taken from the Pew Research Center's Global Indicators Database.

was 'Please tell me if you have a very favorable, somewhat favorable, some-what unfavorable or very unfavorable opinion of China', does not let the respondent explain their opinion on China's economic policies toward their country.[65] Given this, we can tentatively, and broadly, analyze the figures for each country in relation to its economic relations with China. All five countries are major economic partners with China, both exporting and/or importing large volumes to and from China. Assuming that the economic relations between China and these countries remains more or less constant, what varies would therefore be the political relationship between them; hence Vietnam, which has historically been wary of China, and the Philippines, which is caught up in the South China Sea disputes, have a less favorable public opinion of China than the other three countries, which do not have such disputes. To actually delve into the causal links between China's economic policies and public opinion in Southeast Asia would require a detailed study on its own, which is beyond the scope of this book chapter. It would suffice to say that, if economic considerations do shape Southeast Asian public opinion toward China, they would act in tandem with other political and historic considerations.

Linking China's Economic Statecraft to the Security-Economic Nexus: China's Geostrategic, Political, and Security Interests

China's use of economic statecraft in Southeast Asia has some overlap with debates on the security-economic nexus in the region. China's foreign policy towards its neighbors in the early 2000s had the political aim of stabilizing its relations with them in order to create a peaceful external environment. This furthermore had the security and geostrategic aims of ensuring a stable periphery, which would enable China to concentrate on its economic growth. It is true that for much of the first decade of the 2000s, relations between China and Southeast Asia were, on the whole, very good. However, was China's economic strategy of using access to China's large and growing economy to secure peace the main driver of this era of relative harmony?

---

[65] 'Opinion of China, Global indicators database', *Pew Research Center* (2016), available at: http://www.pewglobal.org/database/indicator/24/.

The causal relations behind this are difficult to tease out, and there are a variety of possible mechanisms. It could be that domestic coalitions within both China and Southeast Asia lobby their governments to adopt less provocative policies towards each other; that China is being socialized into cooperative norms of behavior by its economic interactions with ASEAN; that China does not need to fight for what it wants when it can do so through trade; or that the countries of Southeast Asia would not want to provoke China due to their increased levels of economic interdependence. Regardless of which mechanism is correct, if it was true that increased economic interdependence did bring about peace, China's economic policies towards Southeast Asia can be said to have fulfilled its geostrategic, political, and security interests. However, there is the alternative possibility that the warm relations during the early 2000s were not the result of China's economic outreach, but rather due to other geopolitical factors. A number of alternative explanations can be posited. For example, the relative lack of tensions may have been due to the United States focusing more attention on the Middle East, thus decreasing levels of great power rivalry; the desire by Southeast Asian countries to focus on their economic development, as opposed to their territorial claims in the South China Sea; the fact that China did not have a strong navy as compared to the present period; or the relative lack of nationalist feeling towards the South China Sea in all of the claimant countries.

With regard to China's relations with the GMS countries, a similar question can be asked. China's main geostrategic objective with regard to these countries, in addition to ensuring a stable periphery, was to ensure China's access to their natural resources and trade routes. However, were China's good relations with Cambodia, Laos, and Myanmar, thus helping China gain access to their resources and markets, due to its economic outreach towards these countries, to the decisions of these countries to 'bandwagon' with a rising great power, or to domestic pressures within them? In the case of Myanmar, for example, despite China's significant investments in the country, it has moved away from China's orbit, marked by the cancellation of the Myitsone Dam project in 2011.[66] It is difficult to say whether or

---

[66]Thomas Fuller, 'Myanmar backs down, suspending dam project', *New York Times* (30 September 2011), available at: http://www.nytimes.com/2011/10/01/world/asia/myanmar-suspends-construction-of-controversial-dam.html?_r=0.

not Myanmar's warm relations with China were a result of China's economic outreach toward it, of Myanmar's lack of access to diplomatic and economic support from the West, or to the fact that nationalist tendencies within Myanmar were suppressed during this period. Nevertheless, it is true that China has been able to derive much strategic value from its investments in Myanmar, such as the oil and gas pipeline that runs from the Indian Ocean on the Burmese coast into Yunnan province, thus helping China in its quest to diversify its sources of energy resources.[67]

These debates, meanwhile, will have significance for the MSR's broader geostrategic, political, and security objectives as well. Politically, the MSR is aimed at reducing negative perceptions of China due to the South China Sea. Geostrategically, China hopes to cement warm relations with particular Southeast Asian countries that are strategically important, especially the Maritime Southeast Asian countries of Indonesia and Malaysia that lie on the Straits of Malacca. Security-wise, the main assumption appears to be that increased economic integration will reduce tensions with these countries. If China's development of the MSR constitutes a form of economic statecraft towards Southeast Asia, its effects on the region's security will be due to indirect mechanisms such as these, as opposed to any direct impacts on the formal security and economic architecture.

With regard to China's political aims towards Southeast Asia though, the MSR's effectiveness would depend on the nature of the South China Sea disputes. If the disputes intensify in nature, this would undermine the positive political effects that the MSR would have on China's relations with Southeast Asia. The geostrategic effects of the MSR will also be difficult to determine. Its economic outreach and attempts to develop joint projects with Southeast Asian governments is contingent upon many domestic and international factors that are often out of China's control. For example, China's economic relations with Indonesia and Malaysia seem to be going relatively smoothly, especially in light of the joint Sino-Malaysian industrial parks. Furthermore, China has recently announced plans to build a high-speed railway on the island of Java in Indonesia. The problem, though, is that

---

[67]Eric Meyer, 'With oil and gas pipelines, China takes a shortcut through Myanmar', *Forbes* (9 February 2015), available at: http://www.forbes.com/sites/ericrmeyer/2015/02/09/oil-and-gas-china-takes-a-shortcut/.

these Chinese-backed projects are dependent on the goodwill of national and local governments, which could be withdrawn due to the vagaries of domestic politics, as the case of China's loss of influence in Myanmar has made clear.

Meanwhile, the MSR's security impacts will likely not come about by altering the formal security structures of Southeast Asia, but would result from more indirect impact on regional security, bypassing the formal security architecture and operating via other mechanisms.[68] One possible means would be by changing the preferences of domestic actors in the target countries in order to get them to adopt policies more in favor of China. Another would be by binding the countries of Southeast Asia into a Sino-centric economic relationship, such that they will be unwilling to harm China's security interests in the South China Sea or along its land border with Southeast Asia for fear of hurting their own domestic economy. Meanwhile, the complex nature of the regional architecture, partially constructed by China in the 2000s, has restricted China's use of trade sanctions as a punishment for countries that are not cooperative over the South China Sea. The level of trade interdependence between China and its neighbors is such that by sanctioning trade with its partners, China would only hurt itself economically. The 'just-in-time' nature of the manufacturing networks as suggested by Baldwin would preclude the sudden severing of trade ties as a weapon against these countries.

After all is said and done, the nature of China's economic statecraft in Southeast Asia is complex, and cannot be separated from the security-economic nexus in the region. In the early 2000s, China's economic policy toward Southeast Asia definitely had a strong political, geostrategic, and security angle to it. Whether or not China's aims (a peaceful, stable region) were a result of China's means (increased economic outreach) or a result of broader shifts in the international system is unclear. After 2012, China's economic statecraft towards Southeast Asia has mainly taken on the form of the MSR, which aims to counter some of the more negative sentiments

---

[68] A more detailed description of the theoretical background can be found in Miles Kahler, 'Regional economic institutions and East Asian security', in Avery Goldstein and Edward Mansfield, eds., *The Nexus of Economics, Security, and International Relations in East Asia* (Palo Alto, CA: Stanford University Press, 2012), pp. 66–95.

arising from the South China Sea, as well as to cement China's geostrategic position in the region. Given the early stages of this initiative, the results are unclear, though it is likely that the complexity of the regional situation will cause some difficulties in China achieving its goals. In general, given the difficulty of determining the causal mechanisms between China's actions and the development of the international situation, it is difficult to say whether or not China's new economic statecraft will be successful in furthering its interests.

Chapter 7

China's Rise and Geo-Economic Push into the Heart of Eurasia

Roman Muzalevsky

Despite a slowdown of China's economy over the last years, many view the rise of the 'Middle Kingdom' as an unstoppable development challenging the US global position and international order. High-economic growth since 1970s has turned China — from an isolated actor confined to East Asia and constrained by the Cold War — into one of the largest economies benefiting from globalization. China has lifted hundreds of millions out of poverty by becoming the largest trading partner of more than 120 countries and producing US\$1.5 trillion more in GDP than the output of the rest of the BRICS (Brazil, Russia, India, China, and South Africa) economies combined.[1] In 2014, China overtook the United States as the largest economy based on purchasing power parity (PPP) calculations. By 2040, its economy is projected to be three times the size of the US economy and producing 40% of the global output.[2]

Beijing's expanding capabilities and global role have caused concerns worldwide, including Central Asia that borders China's Uyghur

---

[1]Minghao Zhao, 'March Westwards and a New Look on China's Grand Strategy,' paper presented at Workshop IV of the Peking University–University of Chicago Summer Institute on International Relations Theory and Method, Beijing, 18–22 August 2014, p. 2.
[2]Aaron Friedberg, *A Contest for Supremacy: China, America, and the Struggle for Mastery in Asia* (New York, NY: W.W. Norton & Company, 2011), p. 33.

Autonomous Region of Xinjiang, representing a periphery for Beijing, a backyard for Moscow, and a fore-post for Washington. Long viewed as a backwater, the Central Asian region is now being turned by China into its 'Silk Road Economic Belt' ('Belt') component linking dynamic centers in the East and the West and advancing the region's internal and external economic integration. Beijing relies on the Belt to reduce its dependence on maritime routes; claim a geopolitical stake in the region; enhance regional stability; exploit trade, investment, and energy resources development opportunities; and ensure a more even development of its coastal and continental zones. China's overall regional strategy hinges on its geo-economic expansion, which has made it the dominant regional economic actor accelerating the region's geo-economic and geopolitical realignment.

Beijing's reliance on bilateral and multilateral frameworks of cooperation in Central Asia fits the logic of a Chinese proverb that it 'must walk with both legs'.[3] The region is emerging as a second 'leg' — in addition to Beijing's 'leg' in East Asia — and a springboard for China to develop its restive and poor areas of Xinjiang, Tibet, and Inner Mongolia and to expand its westward development push. China is now the largest trading partner of Russia, Kazakhstan, and Turkmenistan, the second-largest partner for Uzbekistan and Kyrgyzstan, and the third-largest partner for Tajikistan.[4] More than 75% of external trade of China's Xinjiang is with Central Asia. As China's economic growth model changes from one predominantly based on savings and exports to one largely based on domestic consumption and export of high-tech products,[5] China will need to rely on nearby economic zones to sustain its economic expansion. This task is imperative given the slowdown of China's economic growth rate, looming debt, and difficulties with management of popular political and economic expectations inside China.

---

[3]Zhou Huasheng, 'China's Central Asia Policy', in Charles Hawkings and Robert Love, eds, *The New Great Game: Chinese Views in Central Asia* (Fort Leavenworth, KS: Foreign Military Studies Office, 2006), p. 21.

[4]Vladimir Blinkov, 'Izmenenie ekonomicheskoi modeli razvitiya Kitaya I ego vliyanie na kitayskuiu vneshneekonomicheskuiu politiku', *Russian Institute of Strategic Studies* (30 June 2014).

[5]*Ibid.*

China's growing geo-economic advances are perceived as constraining the Russia-led Eurasian Union, India's 'Connect Central Asia' policy, and US New Silk Road Strategy (NSRS). Points of convergence exist within regional policies and initiatives of these states, and select components thereof contribute to regional development. But the designs of these powers could also produce exclusive policies, outcomes, and conditions for instability due to external rivalries for regional influence. On the one hand, Russia and China, two authoritarian powers with imperial histories, are seeking to retain and project dominance in the region. Moscow and Beijing are advancing alternative and opposing geopolitical visions for Central Asia, while working in concert and individually to keep Washington and Delhi out. On the other hand, the United States and India, the democratic superpower from across the high seas and the global power-in-the-making based in South Asia, are struggling to anchor their regional presence, while trying to break Moscow's security monopoly and shape China's geo-economic expansion.

Converging and diverging capabilities and goals of these powers and attempted multi-vector policies of the regional republics prompt reconfiguration of Central Asia's geopolitics by producing multidirectional 'push-pull' forces and shifting economic flows that simultaneously 'glue' the regional states and their partners together and pull them apart in a continuously shifting mode of geopolitical and geo-economic interaction. A result is a functional division of labor among external powers: Russia retains a predominant security role; China gains the pre-eminent economic role; the European Union (EU) positions itself as an economic, democratic, and development partner; the United States leads a military role in Afghanistan while advancing South–North integration; and India pursues its assumed role of interconnector for Central and South Asia. These dynamics position China as the major force potentially capable of projecting hegemony in Central Asia should other players sleep through another round of the new 'Great Game'.

That said, China faces significant social, environmental, and economic challenges as well as agendas of other powers that could derail or constrain its global rise. But if China were to succeed in projecting a potentially hegemonic influence in the region, it would likely draw on the legacy of its tributary system of relations with 'peripheral' territories, Confucian values propagated via already proliferating Confucian Institutes, and ideas and practices favoring open markets and state control. And the more China imbeds itself economically and culturally in the region, the more likely it will project a military presence to protect its interests. The nature of China's own transformation is important in this regard. Its projected rise to the high-income status may spur democratization of its political system, generating beneficial effects on Central Asian regimes. Alternatively, China may demonstrate a sustained capacity to be simultaneously wealthy and authoritarian, impeding democratization of the regional countries. If China's potential hegemony brought development and prosperity to the region (and it could), historians would term it a benevolent one. If it brought subjugation and exploitation (and it may), it would prove to be yet another episode of imperial expansion. Central Asian states are expected to continue building diverse ties with external powers to prevent one power from dominating the region.

China's Needs, Interests, Goals, and Capabilities

In his *Foreign Affairs* article, an advisor to Chinese leadership Zheng Bijian articulated the concept of China's 'peaceful rise' (later changed to 'peaceful development'). According to the concept, China should achieve the status of a great power without wars that have marked the rise to power of other states and by promoting 'incremental reforms' and 'democratization of international relations'.[6] This overarching framework has guided China's increasingly active foreign policy in Central Asia, which has rested on a deferential treatment of Russia as a traditional regional security guarantor and China's strategic partner on global issues. Yet, China's activities in Central Asia are designed to advance China's internal development and promote its westward expansion as an aspiring global power,[7] raising concerns for Moscow.

China has already been outperforming Russia economically, and has also started assuming a more confident security role in the region as it

---

[6]Henry Kissinger, *On China* (New York, NY: The Penguin Press, 2011), p. 499.

[7]A. Mal'tsev, 'Osobennosti Politiki KNR v Tsentral'noi Azii v Otsenkakh Rossiiskikh I Zapadnykh Utchenykh', *Sravnitel'naia Politika*, 4, no. 10 (2012), p. 21.

seeks to address the threats of 'three evils' (terrorism, extremism, and separatism), prepare for a post-2016 Afghanistan, exploit Central Asia's vast energy resources and transit potential as its implements its Belt initiative, and position itself favorably vis-a-vis other powers in the heart of Eurasia. China is especially concerned that a premature exit of the United States and coalition forces from Afghanistan without a durable solution to the conflict would increase the threat of regional and domestic terrorism and separatism. Beijing views the possibility of Uyghur and other militants infiltrating Xinjiang with alarm and has stepped up its counter-terrorism and military collaboration both within and, importantly, increasingly outside the framework of the SCO (Shanghai Cooperation Organization) co-led by Beijing and Moscow.

To achieve the above objectives, Beijing relies on the Belt, a geo-economic initiative seeking to develop and link trade, energy, and transit networks across Eurasia with those in China. In 2013, China's president Xi Jinping signed US$50 billion in deals with Central Asian counterparts as he unveiled the strategy. Months later, Xi announced China's Maritime Silk Road strategy to complement the country's geo-economic push throughout Eurasia. Beijing aims to link the Belt and Maritime Silk Roads via a planned China–Pakistan Economic Corridor and the Bangladesh–China–India–Myanmar Economic Corridor. It also seeks to build a commercial network through the Arctic as a third Silk Road initiative.[8] China has called for improving currency convertibility and entered currency swap arrangements with Russia, Kazakhstan, and Uzbekistan in Central Eurasia and South Korea and Japan in East Asia as part of its Silk Road initiatives.[9] China's currency, the RMB, was ranked as the fifth most traded in the world in 2014, positioning Beijing well in the contest for the title of global reserve currency in the next few decades.[10] China is also leveraging its world's largest foreign currency reserves to pursue "Going Out' (a.k.a. "Going Global")

---

[8] Stephen Blank, 'China's Silk Roads and their challenges', *Central Asia-Caucasus Analyst* (7 January 2015).

[9] Flynt Leverett, Hillary Mann Leverett, and Wu Bingbing, "China looks West: What is at stake in Beijing's "New Silk Road" project', *The World Financial Review* (25 January 2015).

[10] Geoff Dyer, *The Contest of the Century: The New Era of Competition with China — and How America Can Win* (New York, NY: Alfred A. Knopf, 2014), p. 229.

investment strategy. It plans to invest US$1–2 trillion overseas by 2020, with Central Asia as its destination for resources, infrastructure, and energy investments.[11]

China provides Central Asian countries with access to East Asia through 11 trade ports, the second Trans-Eurasian railway, and the Uzbekistan–Kyrgyzstan–Xinjiang highway. It helped finance the North–South Corridor linking China, Tajikistan, Kyrgyzstan, and Kazakhstan, and is building a rail line via Kyrgyzstan, Tajikistan, and Afghanistan, which will form the Trans-Asian Railway (TAR) network. China further helped construct the North–South road and the port at Gwadar in Pakistan, facilitating linkages with Afghanistan, the Arabian Sea, Central Asia, and Southeast Asia. In 2013, China agreed to build a railroad from China to Kyrgyzstan and Uzbekistan, planning to extend links to China, Turkey, and Iran. 'It is not important for China as to who will be building this railway line. The most important thing is that it is built', Chinese ambassador to Kyrgyzstan Wang Kaiwen remarked on the US$2 billion project.[12] Beijing has also been actively building roads and highways in the region, while supporting the Western Europe–Western China International Transit Corridor to improve main roads linking China and Europe. Notably, Russia announced that it would not build its portion of the line until 2020.[13]

China also invests heavily in the region's energy markets to reduce its dependence on the Indian Ocean and the Strait of Malacca (which the US and Indian navies patrol) for energy imports and to undercut the perceived US policy of 'strategic exclusion' of China. In 2011, 77% of its oil imports passed through the Strait of Malacca.[14] By 2025, its dependence on oil imports is projected to reach 68.8%.[15] Ensuring safe access to Central Asia's

---

[11] David Shambaugh, *China Goes Global: The Partial Power* (Oxford: Oxford University Press, 2013), pp. 174, 178–181.

[12] Quoted in Roman Muzalevsky, 'China–Kyrgyzstan–Uzbekistan Railway scheme: Fears, hopes and prospects', *Eurasia Daily Monitor*, 9, no. 102 (30 May 2012).

[13] Roman Muzalevsky, *Central Asia's Shrinking Connectivity Gap: Implications for US Strategy* (Carlisle, PA: Strategic Studies Institute and US Army War College Press, November 2014), p. 33.

[14] *Ibid.*, Shambaugh, *China Goes Global*, p. 163.

[15] *Ibid.*, Dyer, *The Contest*, p. 29.

energy resources is a major aspect of China's Belt initiative,[16] which also seeks to facilitate exports to Europe and the Middle East. The share of the region's gas climbed to 65% of China's gas imports, constituting 17.6% of China's gas consumption in 2012. China also imports almost all of its uranium from the region.[17] Building infrastructure in the region further allows China to expand the use of its Xinjiang–Shanghai gas pipeline linking China's west and east.[18] Potential participation of Japan and South Korea in this and other projects could foster a dynamic connection between Central and East Asia, with China turning into the node of Eurasia's expanding infrastructure[19] — a geo-economic role it has been seeking in East Asia and the Pacific over the last three decades.

China's economic reach in Central Asia is especially pronounced in Kazakhstan, where its China National Petroleum Corporation (CNPC) acquired energy firms Petrokazakhstan for US$4.18 billion and half of MangistauMunaiGas for US$2.6 billion. CNPC also bought an 8.33% share of Kashagan oil field, the largest discovered field in the last three decades, solidifying its presence in the country's energy market. China provided US$10 billion in loans to Kazakhstan in 2009 during the global financial crisis and, along with Kazakhstan, launched the Beineu–Bozoi pipeline in 2014 to deliver up to 14 million tons of Kazakh oil to China annually. As a Kazakh official explained, 'The Chinese have told us quietly but clearly that their energy demands are massive and urgent, and that they are willing to pay a steep price to address them.'[20]

---

[16] Liyan Hu and Ter-Shing Cheng, 'China's Energy Security and Geo-Economic Interests in Central Asia', *Central European Journal of International and Security Studies*, 2, no. 2 (2008), p. 52.

[17] Aleksandra Jarosiewicz and Krzysztof Strachota, *China vs. Central Asia: The Achievements of the Past Two Decades*, no. 45 (Warsaw: Center for Eastern Studies, October 2013), pp. 47, 51.

[18] Pan Guang, 'China and Central Asia: Charting a new course for regional cooperation', *China Brief*, 7, no. 3 (7 February 2007).

[19] Peter Pham, 'Beijing's great game: Understanding Chinese strategy in Central Eurasia', *American Foreign Policy Interests*, 28 (2006), p. 58.

[20] Parag Khanna, *The Second World: Empires and Influence in the New Global Order* (New York, NY: Random House, 2008), p. 87.

China lent about US$4 billion to Turkmenistan for developing the South Yolotan fields, and provided US$6.7 billion for the construction of the Turkmenistan–China gas pipeline with a capacity of 40 billion cubic meter per year that runs via Kazakhstan and Uzbekistan. Beijing and Ashgabat now plan to build a new pipeline to supply gas to China via Uzbekistan and Kyrgyzstan. China invests heavily in the transport market in Uzbekistan, and has become the country's second-largest trade partner. In Kyrgyzstan, China is actively involved in the trade facilitation and oil-processing business.[21] In Afghanistan, China is focused on developing transit and trade infrastructure and has become the country's largest investor. It won rights to develop the world's second-largest undeveloped copper reserves located in Afghanistan at Aynak — a project worth US$4.4 billion.[22]

China's growing geo-economic presence and rising threats to this presence have prompted debates in China on the issue of military expansion to protect China's interests.[23] In 2014, China agreed to provide US$6.5 million in military assistance to Kyrgyzstan and more than a hundred million dollars to Tajikistan for police uniforms and training.[24] In 2015, China delivered anti-missile defense systems HQ-9 to Uzbekistan and Turkmenistan, which became the first-ever recipients of Chinese anti-missile defense systems.[25] Previously, it provided training, military uniforms, and communications equipment to Kabul, Dushanbe, and Bishkek. It also increased the number of military exercises and its military aid to the countries' security sectors.[26] China-led SCO held a total of 13 separate military exercises in each member state, with the number of personnel ranging from 800 to 10,000.[27] China's growing military profile signals concerns with the situation in Afghanistan and the start of a shift in the politico-military balances in Central Asia traditionally shaped by Moscow as the region's main weapons supplier.

[21] *Ibid.*, Muzalevsky, *Central Asia's Shrinking Connectivity Gap*, pp. 34–35.
[22] Andrew Scobell, Ely Ratner, and Michael Beckley, *China's Strategy toward South and Central Asia: And Empty Fortress* (Santa Monica, CA: RAND, 2014), p. 57.
[23] *Ibid.*, Shambaugh, *China Goes Global,* pp. 201–202.
[24] Sarah Lain, 'China's Strategic Presence in Central Asia', *IHS Jane's* (August 2014).
[25] Yuri Chernogaev, 'Oruzhie "made in China"', *Ankhor.uz* (3 February 2015).
[26] Niklas Swanstrom, 'China and Central Asia: A new great game or traditional vassal relations?' *Journal of Contemporary China*, 14, no. 45 (November 2005), p. 582.
[27] *Ibid.*, Scobell *et al.*, *China's Strategy*, p. 41.

The SCO serves as China's vehicle for promoting its geo-economic and geopolitical role in Central Asia. Its members collaborate against the 'three evils' and seek to promote regional stability in conflict-ridden parts of Afghanistan, Pakistan, and Xinjiang. China has used the Shanghai Cooperation Organisation (SCO) platform to challenge the US regional military presence. In 2005, the SCO called for eviction of US military bases from Central Asia. The SCO is also a new concept and model of security cooperation that China is experimenting with,[28] while deflecting negative perceptions about its growing military capabilities in the region. The membership of Russia in the organization supports this conclusion, just as it also helps the regional countries and Moscow to shape China's evolution as an economic giant and a nascent military force in the wider region.

China increasingly views stability in broader Central Asia and Xinjiang as key to its emergence as a global power. These poorly developed areas serve as barriers to China's expanded development and domestic security. Only by consolidating itself internally by ensuring a more even economic development between coastal and continental zones can China mitigate concerns about social implosion and marshal far more internal resources for the pursuit of geostrategic objectives of continental proportions. This is an imperative familiar to China's sages and strategists preoccupied with questions of unity and prosperity throughout China's long history as the world's only continuous civilization to date. So far, and unlike its geo-economic advances, China's military influence in Central Asia has been limited, even if steadily growing. China has publicly acknowledged Russia's predominant security and military role. At this stage, it is still China's geo-economics that is primarily defining Beijing's rise in Central Asia and throughout the world.

China's Geo-Economics versus Russia's Geopolitics

China and Russia are dissatisfied with the global status quo and seek to adjust the US-led international order. They cooperate in the UN Security Council, oppose interventionism in rhetoric, and support state sovereignty,

---

[28]David M. Finkelstein, *China and Central Asia: Enduring Interests and Contemporary Concerns* (Washington, DC: CNA), pp. 9–10.

while working against US alleged attempts to project global hegemony. They are also concerned about prospects of 'color revolutions'. Both have boosted their economic ties significantly in the last decade, planning to increase bilateral trade to US$200 billion by 2020. But the two powers have major differences, which will surface more clearly as China expands its role in Russia's 'zone of privileged interests'. Their base of power and foreign policy approaches in Central Asia differ in substance and emphasis. Both rely on geo-economics and geopolitics, but Beijing's approach to national development and foreign affairs has predominantly favored the former as a tool of statecraft. In a way, this division of labor is mutually reinforcing as it undercuts the perceived US global pre-eminence using both economic and geopolitical means. But this division has also influenced the development and strategic potential of China and Russia in Central Asia and elsewhere differently.

China's significant reliance on geo-economics has achieved far more significance in the 21st century than Russia's persistent grip on geopolitics. President Obama had a point when he described President Putin as being stuck in the 19th century. The communist China in 1970s made a bet on 'opening up', expecting that it would allow it to modernize and compete globally and enabling it to amass power to deflect encroachments that had previously humiliated China. Beijing has been expanding its economic development and influence globally ever since, becoming the largest economy in 2014 based on PPP calculations and also the biggest trading nation. China seeks to redress past injustices and reclaim its lost leadership position.[29] It has adhered to policy advice of Deng Xiaoping and subsequent leaders to 'bide its time, hide its brightness, not seek leadership, but do some things', avoiding costly geopolitical entanglements and focusing on exports-led economic growth. As it has enmeshed itself in global trade, China's economic drive at home has been predicated on economic expansion abroad. Starting with the collapse of the Soviet Union and especially since 2000s, this expansion has increasingly affected Central Asia. China has been marching west in search of new markets, resources, investment opportunities, and ways of reclaiming its position as the central power.

---

[29] *Ibid.*, Kissinger, *On China*, p. 546.

China's push westward has unnerved Russia, which is now preoccupied with warding off the US military influence and Chinese economic expansion in greater Central Asia. But Russia lacks tools to do so, suffering as it is from shrinking economic power base. Its post-Soviet influence eroded significantly due to its imperial foreign policy and authoritarian rule. In the 1990s, Russia experimented with liberalization but failed to consolidate democratic gains and project power effectively at home and abroad. In late 1900s and early 2000s, Russia accumulated substantially more wealth and power under Putin's leadership. But the sources and fundamentals of that power have rested on petro-revenues and a skewed economic model favoring energy exports. Instead of fixing economics and politics at home, Russia resorted to using 'hard power' abroad to settle scores in the 2008 Russian–Georgian war and has relied on geopolitics in Ukraine. Western sanctions on Russia in response to its seizure of Crimea, Moscow's involvement in the conflict in Ukraine, and a roughly 60% decline in oil prices since June 2014 have weakened its economy, causing a substantial outflow of capital, depreciation of ruble, and spike in inflation, undercutting its accumulated wealth and power base.

Russia's preoccupation with geopolitics has undermined its regional geo-economic initiatives. It spearheaded the creation of the Eurasian Union in 2015, which comprises Russia, Belarus, Kazakhstan, Armenia, and Kyrgyzstan. But it has failed to secure participation of other post-Soviet states. Ukrainian leadership's decision in 2014 to pursue a free trade association deal with the EU rather than join the Union prompted Moscow to rely on geopolitics to advance its interests in Ukraine. Russia dismembered Ukraine by seizing Crimea and has supported pro-Russian rebels in the east of Ukraine — actions partly motivated by the perceived expansion of the West and NATO to Russia's borders, militarily and economically. Given its weak economic base, Russia was unable to use 'soft power' and resorted to the use of 'hard power' to impose its will on its neighbors. Despite symbolic statements of support by a select few, the post-Soviet states have not approved Russia's actions in Ukraine weakening the appeal of Russia's initiatives, including the Eurasian Union. And while Yerevan and Bishkek decided to join the Eurasian Union, they still have strong apprehensions about Russia's regional intentions and ambitions. Russia's airstrikes in Syria conducted by air and navy forces have meanwhile signaled to unruly rulers of Central Asian states that Moscow still has geopolitical tools in its arsenal.

Like any regional project of a major power, the EU initiative has a geopolitical subtext: It helps Russia expand its influence and guard against Western and China's advances in the post-Soviet space. In regards to China, the EU mission to facilitate free movement of labor, capital, and technologies conflicts with China's plans to expand trade westward, allowing Moscow to constrain Beijing's geo-economic advances and explain its caution in approaching China's proposal on cooperation between the European Union and the Belt initiative.[30] Whether out of despair or hope, China and Russia issued a statement in 2014 stating this about the Belt initiative: 'Russia believes that China's initiative to form a Silk Road Economic Belt is very important and highly values the willingness of the Chinese side to keep Russian interests in mind during its development and implementation'.[31] Unless Beijing implements its proposed free trade zone with the Union, which Central Asian states could resist,[32] its Belt could falter.

For now, China's reliance on geo-economics has ensured a winning position vis-à-vis Russia in Central Asia. It has become the top trading and investment partner for the region, with its trade in 2011 amounting to US$39 billion compared to Russia's at US$16.5 billion and its FDI hitting US$2.9 billion in 2010 compared to Russia's US$3.17 billion. In 2012, China's trade with the region reached US$46 billion, 100 times of its amount in 1992. Beijing's energy trade and investments have particularly challenged Russia's positions. Russia now seeks to purchase gas and oil distributions networks to be able to control energy resource deliveries. In 2015, Russia's Gazprom announced a reduction of gas purchases from Turkmenistan and Uzbekistan, planning to buy 4 billion cubic meters of gas from the former and up to 1 billion cubic meters from the latter, as opposed to previously planned 10 billion cubic meters and 4 billion cubic meters respectively.

---

[30]Alina Terekhova, 'Moskva distantsyruetsya ot kitayskogo proekta novogo Shelkovogo puti', *Nezavisimaya Gazeta* (20 January 2015).

[31]Wang Shuchun and Wan Qingson, 'The Silk Road Economic Belt and the EEU: Rivals or Partners?' *Central Asia and the Caucasus Journal of Social and Political Studies* (3 January 2014), p. 7.

[32]*Ibid.*, Scobell *et al.*, *China's Strategy*, p. 44.

Beginning in 2009, Russia has been reducing purchases of regional gas, just as China has been buying up gas and investing in related infrastructure. The same year, China, Turkmenistan, Uzbekistan, and Kazakhstan opened the first-ever regional gas pipeline with Beijing's involvement since 1991, breaking Russia's monopoly on energy resources deliveries. China and Kazakhstan now plan to open a second oil pipeline.

Just as Russia has been leveraging geo-economics to advance its interests in the post-Soviet space, China has also relied on geopolitical instruments to pursue its agenda. And while Beijing lags behind Russia's military influence in Central Asia, it has recently stepped up its geopolitical involvement due to the unstable security situation in Afghanistan and its growing economic stake in the region. China's sale of its own new generation medium-to-long range HQ-9 air defense systems and its percussion unmanned aerial vehicles *Yilong*-1 to Uzbekistan and Turkmenistan in return for reduced gas prices[33] demonstrates its growing military influence, especially considering the sophistication of the systems and their interoperability issues with the predominantly Russian weapons systems. It has trained Afghan forces[34] and also stepped up military collaboration with its regional partners within and outside the framework of the SCO, which nevertheless lacks the spirit of multilateralism, with China and Russia preferring bilateral deals with other members to bypass each other's opposing responses. The upshot is, for the first time in the last two centuries, Moscow is constrained to leverage its position in Central Asia to expand its geopolitical influence vis-à-vis China.[35]

Unlike Russia, China has not secured military bases in the region largely due to Russia's overwhelming regional military role; the lack of a substantial economic stake by China; and nascent formation of China's geopolitical interests driving decisions on the deployment and use of military force. Moreover, the Chinese military has not yet developed effective logistics and combat capabilities for military deployment and overseas basing. China's regional geopolitical and military roles will thus remain limited

---

[33] *Ibid.*, Chernogaev, 'Oruzhie "made in China"'.

[34] William Dalrymple, 'Afghanistan: As China forges new alliances, a New Great Game has begun', *The Guardian* (18 March 2014).

[35] *Ibid.*, Jarosiewicz and Strachota, *China vs. Central Asia*, p. 22.

in the intermediate term. This is in contrast to its geoeconomic role and expansion in the region that are very likely to grow in the coming years, raising questions about the sustainability of the Sino-Russian partnership in Central Asia.

China's West–East 'Pull' versus India's South–North 'Push'

China's growing presence in Central Asia also worries India as one of few states capable of challenging China's preeminence in the decades ahead.[36] Unlike Russia, India is a latecomer to the region's 21st Century 'Great Game'. Unlike China, it is starting its ascendance from a lower base and at a lower rate due to its relatively unsuccessful policies. It is also a cumbersome actor constrained by democratic yet highly bureaucratic politics at home and unstable security dynamics in its neighborhood. It does not share a border with Central Asia. Nor has it managed to substantially improve its trade links with the region since the collapse of the Soviet Union.[37] Delhi views presence and influence in Central Asia as key to its great power status, but it cannot attain them without resolving regional security challenges that limit its ambitions. India will thus remain largely confined to South Asia and the Indian Ocean in the intermediate term, despite Central Asian countries' growing interest in diversifying their external ties and securing access to the Indian subcontinent and the Indian Ocean.

This is not to discount India's plans to gain deeper foothold in Central Asia. In 2012, it launched the 'Connect Central Asia' policy to link South and Central Asia via energy, trade, and transit corridors, while positioning Afghanistan as a hub of Central and South Asian economic integration. As part of the policy, India planned to set 14 flight links with the Central Asian states, develop local IT, energy, banking, and pharmaceutical industries, and to build energy infrastructure and e-networks linking the two regions.[38] In Kazakhstan, Indian firms are involved in coal, oil, and

---

[36] *Ibid.*, p. 65.

[37] Ambrish Dhaka, 'Factoring Central Asia into China's Afghanistan policy', *Journal of Eurasian Studies*, 5 (2014), p. 101.

[38] *Ibid.*, Muzalevsky, *Central Asia's Shrinking Connectivity Gap*, p. 37.

uranium industries. As of 2014, India imported more than 3,500 tons of uranium from Kazakhstan since 2009. In Tajikistan, Indian companies are involved in a hydropower project to help boost the 1000 Electricity Transmission and Trade Project for Central Asia and South Asia (CASA-1000 initiative) to bring electricity from Central to South Asia. In Kyrgyzstan and Tajikistan, India plans to open an Indian-Central Asian University and a military hospital, respectively. In Uzbekistan, Indian companies are present in the pharmaceuticals, IT, construction, energy, and mining sectors.

As the sixth largest energy consumer, India is also a major party to the Turkmenistan–Afghanistan–Pakistan–India (TAPI) project, seeking an active role in the development of the region's energy reserves to reduce its dependence on energy imports from the Middle East. Delhi has expressed interest in a proposed gas pipeline from southern Kazakhstan to India and the IPI gas pipeline. But instability in Pakistan and Afghanistan and the standoff between Iran and the West have impeded India's attempts to import energy resources from Central Asia and Iran.[39] India's economy, projected to overtake that of China's around 2050, requires access to the region's vast energy resources. But India has yet to catch up with China. China has already secured rights to develop the Galkynysh gas field in Turkmenistan, launched a pipeline in 2009 to supply Turkmen gas to China, and in 2013 secured an 8.4% stake in Kashagan oil field worth US$5 billion that Kazakhstan planned to give to India.

To gain unimpeded access to Central Asia's markets, India has to ensure the development and integration of Afghanistan into the broader region as part of its 'connect' policy. Related initiatives are underway. Delhi planned to invest US$100 million to develop the Iranian port at Chabahar and connect it to Afghanistan and on to India via railways and roads. It has spent at least US$136 million to connect the port with the 'Ring Road' in Afghanistan, where it has invested US$2 billion in local infrastructure over the last decade and sought to develop the Hajigak iron deposits. The port would enable Delhi to access Central Asian markets without relying on Pakistan and position it favorably vis-à-vis China, which can help build a rival Pakistani port at Gwadar linking China and the Persian Gulf. The Chabahar port is but one link in the India's North–South Transit Corridor connecting

---

[39] *Ibid.*, p. 38.

Indian-built Zaranj–Delaram highway in Afghanistan and providing an outlet for Indian exports to Central Asia. In case of entente between Iran and
the West, the corridor would facilitate India's trade with the region along a
North–South route.[40]

India's positioning as an autonomous actor and unwillingness to be a perceived US 'pawn'[41] has limited its presence in Central Asia. In 2014, India's
trade with the region stood at approximately US$1.24 billion compared to
China's US$50 billion. The same year, Indian exports and imports to Central
Asia constituted less than 2% and 1.5% of its overall exports and imports on
average. India gained an SCO observer status to enhance its influence and
applied for full membership in 2014, but it perceives that China is blocking
its membership to prevent it from any active engagement in Central–South
Asia. India's relative failure in projecting comparable influence in Central
and South East Asia, as well as concerns about China's policy of containment, have prompted Delhi to start reconsidering its obsession with the
non-alignment positioning in international affairs and enhancing strategic
cooperation with the United States. In 2015, Delhi and Washington concluded an additional deal on nuclear energy and are increasingly perceived
as working together to keep China's rise in check. That said, India is likely
to retain the role of an autonomous actor in world affairs seeking deeper
ties with all powers.

India's status as the last major Asian economy to join the Asian economic renaissance also explains its limited regional presence. In the 1990s
and 2000s, India started advancing economic reforms to unleash private
forces to accelerate economic development, but it undertook such measures
a couple of decades later than China. It did so in an external environment
that saw the collapse of the Soviet Union, ever-expanding US-led global
economic integration, running the risk of increasing marginalization if it
failed to reform. By the end of the 20th century, India had become one

---

[40]For in-depth discussion, see Roman Muzalevsky, *From Frozen Ties to Strategic Engagement: US–Iranian Relationship in 2030* (Carlisle, PA: Strategic Studies Institute and US
Army War College Press, 2015).

[41]For growth comparisons, see Sandy Gordon, 'Sino-Indian Relations and the Rise of
China', in Roy Huisken, ed., *Rising China: Power and Reassurance* (Canberra: The
Australian National University Press, 2009), p. 59.

of the fastest-growing economies with much more enhanced capabilities to start projecting a more active foreign policy and influence in Central Asia.[42]

India views Central Asia as a geopolitical prize in the contest for global primacy, perceiving China's maritime and continental expansion as a double threat to its plans to emerge as a global power, despite a significantly improving relationship with China cultivated over the last three decades. And just as China views the US 'Pivot to the Pacific' and military presence in Central Asia as containing China's rise along its perimeter, so does Delhi consider China's engagement with India's neighbors as a stratagem to contain India. Beijing has been effectively building military ties with countries surrounding India — all in the context of the 1962 Sino–Indian Border War and continued unresolved political tension between the two countries. As part of its countermove and overall foreign policy agenda in Central Asia, Delhi has been seeking enhanced military ties and presence in the broader region. It has cooperated with regional forces against Taliban in the 1990s and after 9/11; developed a strong relationship with Uzbekistan as its major arms supplier; opened a mountain biomedical research center in Kyrgyzstan; sought rights to the use of the Ayni airbase in Tajikistan; assisted with training of the Kazakh Caspian fleet; and has participated in counterterrorism exercises with Kyrgyz special forces in Kyrgyzstan.[43] But India's poor relationship with Pakistan (China's ally) and the volatile security situation in Afghanistan have prevented it from assuming an even more active military and security role in greater Central Asia, forcing it to apply more effort compared to China.

India's South–North 'push' will thus continue to be less pronounced than China's West–East geo-economic 'pull'. However, Delhi has committed itself to enhancing the development and stability of Afghanistan and reconnection of Central and South Asia. The resolution of the security and economic challenges centered on Afghanistan and Pakistan would lead to a more active and influential regional role played by India in the future. China's interest in developing links between the Middle East and

---

[42] *Ibid.*, Friedberg, *A Contest*, p. 26.

[43] Yu Jianhua, 'Competition for Caspian energy development and its relationship with China', in Charles Hawkings and Robert Love, eds., *The New Great Game: Chinese Views in Central Asia* (Fort Leavenworth, Kansas: Foreign Military Studies Office, 2006), p. 149.

Central–South Asia and growing economic cooperation with India would also facilitate India's regional policy if Delhi plays the Pakistan card right and better exploits its long-term advantages over China: Indian democratic system, its use of English, and perceived unimposing approach to foreign policy-making vis-à-vis Central Asia, among others.

China's Expansion versus US Containment?

China's rising influence worldwide puts a question mark on the US status as a superpower and protector of the global order. Ironically, the US attempts to promote globalization and global order have facilitated China's rise ever since the signing of the Shanghai Communique in 1972. Beijing has tapped into globalization ever since to achieve for itself the status of the largest economy based on PPP calculations in 2014. As the second-largest counter-defense spending nation after the United States, China spent US$106 billion on defense in 2012. China's economic and military expansion is accompanied with the sense of pride and opportunity to redress the perceived humiliation China suffered under Japanese and Western powers in the past two centuries. And while it largely continues to 'bide its time and capabilities' and pursue 'peaceful development', China has recently displayed a notably assertive stance, as frictions have intensified with Japan, Vietnam, and the Philippines over contested islands in the South and East China Seas. Such posturing has evoked fears of China's economic drive complemented by growing military prowess, which Beijing is expected to display more assertively when the period of its 'strategic opportunity' (a.k.a. favorable external and internal conditions) ends by 2020.[44]

China's ascendance is reconfiguring international relations, especially in East Asia and increasingly Central Asia, prompting Washington to 'rebalance' to Asia as part of its 'Pivot to Asia-Pacific' launched in 2012. From a policy of containment since 1949 and engagement since 1969, the United States has pursued a China policy displaying elements of both containment and engagement since 1989. Some describe the current US strategy toward

---

[44] *Ibid.*, Kissinger, *On China*, pp. 497–498. Also see Friedberg, *A Contest*, p. 147.

China as 'congagement'.[45] China has countered by initiating in 2013 its own 'pivot' in the form of overland and Maritime Silk Road initiatives in East and Central Asia[46] and by enhancing pressures toward multipolarity. China has been seeking to adjust or create alternative economic and security institutions, challenging the post WWII structures created by the United States.

China seeks to create the new security architecture without US participation in broader Asia. As Xi stated at a conference in 2014, "[i]t is for the people of Asia to run the affairs of Asia, solve the problems of Asia, and uphold the security of Asia'.[47] China has yet to succeed in the economic area. Along with BRICS nations, it launched the New Development Bank (NDB) with the capital of US$100 billion in order to level the playing field where the World Bank (WB), with capital of US$223 billion and the International Monetary Fund (IMF) have traditionally reigned supreme. It also spearheaded the Asian Infrastructure Investment Bank (AIIB) involving 21 Asian nations with a capital of US$160 billion, challenging the Asian Development Bank led by the United States and Japan.[48] Britain's application in 2015 to join AIIB displeased Washington, prompting a US official to say that the United States is 'wary about a trend toward constant accommodation of China'.[49] Through its China Development Bank, China also issued US$10 billion more in loans than the WB between 2008 and 2010.[50] Its support for the Chiang Mai Initiative has challenged the position of the IMF by seeking to create a regional lender of last resort.[51]

[45] *Ibid.*, Friedberg, *A Contest*, pp. 58–59.

[46] *Ibid.*, Leverett *et al.*, 'China looks West'.

[47] Elizabeth C. Economy, 'China's imperial president Xi Jinping tightens his grip', *Foreign Affairs* (2 November 2014).

[48] 'Why China is creating a new "World Bank" for Asia', *The Economist* (11 November 2014).

[49] Nicholas Watt, Paul Lewis, and Tania Branigan, 'US anger at Britain joining Chinese-led investment bank AIIB', *The Guardian* (12 March 2015).

[50] *Ibid.*, Zhao, 'March Westwards', p. 2

[51] C. Fred Bergsten, Charles Freeman, Nicholas R. Lardy, and Derek J. Mitchell, *China's Rise: Challenges and Opportunities* (Washington, DC: Peterson Institute for International Economics and Center for Strategic and International Studies, 2008), p. 224.

Economic imperatives have often prevailed over geopolitics in Asia in the last three decades.[52] But this is about to change in the next three decades, as China translates its economic capabilities into military ones and prompts more focus on geopolitics with neighboring states increasingly uneasy about China's rise. Already, Japan is debating its self-defense clause, which may open the way for a more active security role by Tokyo. India, a member of the Nuclear Club but not of the Non-Proliferation Treaty (NPT), is starting to assume the role of Washington's strategic partner to ensure the peaceful rise of China and promote a stable global order. Delhi and Washington signed a Civil Nuclear Cooperation Agreement in 2006, and India may soon start importing nuclear reactors and fuel from the United States. The deal is critical because it enables Washington to help Delhi develop ballistic and anti-ballistic missile technology.[53] Vietnam, no longer facing a full arms embargo by Washington, looks forward to receiving US arms supplies while relying on Russia as a major arms supplier and building stronger defense ties with India.[54]

But it is the evolution of the US–China relationship that is viewed as the major factor for global stability. One can describe the relationship as a 'competitive coexistence', with both countries suffering from the deficit of 'strategic trust'.[55] Should the United States contain or engage China? Unlike during the Cold War when it misapplied the concept of containment developed by George Kennan to keep the Soviet Union in check, the United States today is in an intertwined economic relationship with China that enjoys strong and growing economic ties with US allies in Asia and Europe. China is thus more likely to deflect than succumb to any US containment.[56] Washington would be unable to alter the balance of power and contain

---

[52]Zhiqun Zhu, 'Zhu on Kueh, "Pax Sinica: Geopolitics and Economics of China's Accidence"', review of Y. Y. Kueh, *Pax Sinica: Geopolitics and Economics of China's Accidence*, *H-Diplo, H-Net Reviews* (September 2013).

[53]*Ibid.*, Gordon, 'Sino-Indian Relations', p. 60.

[54]Carl Thayer, 'The Philippines, Malaysia, and Vietnam Race to South China Sea defense modernization', *The Diplomat* (23 January 2015).

[55]*Ibid.*, Shambaugh, *China Goes Global*, p. 74.

[56]*Ibid.*, p. 77. Also see Wang Jisi, 'China's changing role in Asia', in Kokubun Ryosei and Wang Jisi, eds., *The Rise of China and a Changing East Asian Order* (Tokyo: Japan Center for International Exchange, 2004), p. 17.

Beijing without undermining its own economic base. By the same token, China's attempt to exclude the United States from Asia would face resistance from Washington and Asian states.[57] This does not mean that China will not attempt containment or that the United States will not seek hegemony.

With the United States 'Pivot to the Pacific' and China's expansion and consolidation of its strategic position in Asia, Beijing finds it timely to march westward into Central Asia in search of resources to fuel its internal development, expand its global economic footprint, and deflect US pressure in the east. Unfortunately for Washington, the US regional economic influence is insignificant and its military role is under question, as US military forces plan to withdraw from Afghanistan in the near future. China, in turn, sees Central Asia as an outlet for its untapped development and geo-economic expansion, years after it has attained a leading geo-economic position in Southeast Asia. China is actively pursuing its Belt initiative, which overshadows the US NSRS in reach and commitment, and may sooner or later deploy military infrastructure in Central Asia to safeguard its bourgeoning economic interests in the broader region.

While China's Belt across Central Asia feeds into US strategy of enhancing global connectivity, it also supports the 'comprehensive national power' of the country that may emerge as the mightiest economic and military actor by 2050 and 2100, respectively. Why does all this matter? Central Asia is of strategic importance to US allies in Europe and Asia and for the United States to sustain its leading position and global order amid the rise of new centers of power. To preserve the sinews of the international system, the United States has sought to adjust the system by involving China and other parties. But unlike in East Asia, it has failed to live up to related expectations in Central Asia. As a sea-based power that defeated Japan in WWII, the United States is far more comfortable in Asia-Pacific where it has built a network of allies and economic partnerships. In Central Asia, however, the US institutional influence and country partnerships are weak. Even the collapse of the USSR and the 9/11 attacks may prove to be fleeting drivers of its presence in Central Asia, where Russia's predominant security role and China's growing economic influence have impeded US attempts to 'grow roots'.

---

[57] *Ibid.,* Kissinger, *On China*, p. 526.

Unlike China, which spearheaded the creation of the SCO, reinvigorated the Kazakhstan-initiated Conference on Interaction and Confidence-Building Measures in Asia, and launched the Belt initiative, the United States has largely failed to create, sustain, or involve itself in new or reshaped regional institutions. It negotiated Trade and Investment Framework Agreements and has sought to advance TAPI, Baku–Tbilisi–Ceyhan (BTC), and NATO's Partnership for Peace (PIP) programs. It has also advanced the Northern Distribution Network (NDN), proposed the creation of a counternarcotic initiative, and launched the NSRS. Aside from the BTC and NDN, other initiatives have not materialized while some failed to effectively advance US interests. The BTC and NDN have fostered the integration of the Caspian and Central–South Asia with the global economy, but the US role in sustaining the NDN and unleashing the NSRS potential is unclear.

On balance, China's geo-economic expansion is proving more active and influential than US projection of regional economic influence. The expected US military withdrawal from Afghanistan may well create a geopolitical opening for China as well, with pertinent implications for US and Chinese presence in the heart of Eurasia.

If China Succeeds or Fails: The Future of Security and Economic Order in Central Asia

The 'push-pull' forces exerted by external powers reconfigure Central Asia's geopolitics at a much more rapid and profound pace and extent than it had been after the collapse of the Soviet Union. The forces are simultaneously 'gluing' and tearing the region apart, potentially creating conditions for instability. Russia drags the region northwards; India pulls it southwards; the EU, westwards; the United States, westwards and southwards; and China, eastwards. At this stage, no power is able to wield an overwhelming influence across all domains. But both China's current rise and India's ascendance in the long term are bound to transform the regional landscape beyond recognition if current dynamics continue. In this case, the failure of Central Asian states to organize collectively to promote intraregional integration would prove an omission that had traditionally cost them dearly during imperial expansions by Russia since the 19th century and China under various dynasties. Only a strong pole of intraregional organization can withstand these pressures and mitigate the conditions that could otherwise lead to externally-driven conflicts and internal wars in the broader region.

Of these pressures, China's rise is more multifaceted and powerful, promising to tilt the balance of power further in favor of Beijing, as China expands its regional geo-economic footprint in the next decades. Already, the region's shifting economic flows indicate that China's 'pull' on Central Asia is a stronger force, realigning the region along an eastern vector. China's expansion could be a major advantage to the economic development of the regional countries or a threat to their sovereignty. Central Asian states are expected to continue taking advantage of the division of labor among external players to ensure that the region's geopolitical reconfiguration is not a one-sided process driven by a single all-powerful actor. They are also expected to leverage China's rise to advance their economic development as well as internal and external integration.

Of course, China's dreaded hegemony may never pass. China faces immense domestic and external challenges that could derail or delay its rise to the ranks of the most powerful. The wealth China has amassed has made the internal social dislocations and inequality more pronounced, exposing its economic model and making it vulnerable to external influences. Its economy is in the process of readjustment from traditionally double-digit growth rates in the previous decades to single digits today and years ahead. Some thus view China as a 'partial' global power pursuing an 'Empty Fortress' stratagem in Central–South Asia by positioning itself as a strong and rising power despite facing major challenges constraining its global rise.[58]

Unless it implements profound reforms successfully and lessens its vulnerability to 'exogenous developments', China may not make it as a hegemon or a 'comprehensively' great power. To translate its 'economic weight into power and influence' will require it to embrace the same or similar concepts and modes of operation pursued by the United States and similar major powers.[59] Latest plans unveiled by the leadership indicate that China is moving in this direction. Beijing seeks to modernize its financial system, enhance labor mobility, reduce corruption, and advance sustainability and

---

[58] *Ibid.*, Scobell *et al.*, *China's Strategy*, pp. xii–xiii.

[59] *Ibid.*, Dyer, *The Contest*, pp. 276–277.

governance mechanisms.[60] As China gets closer to obtaining a 'comprehensive national power' status, it is likely to change its current strategy to tap into external environment to generate internal development.[61] It is at this point that the choice of its strategy toward neighbors and the world will be of paramount importance. Until then, China will continue its geo-economic push while seeking enhanced geopolitical influence, potentially redrawingx the cultural, economic, political, and security fabric of Central Asia in the long term.

---

[60] *Ibid.*, Zhao, 'March Westwards', p. 3.

[61] Michael Swaine and Ashley Tellis, *Interpreting China's Grand Strategy: Past, Present, and Future* (Santa Monica, CA: RAND, 2000), pp. 152–153.

Part Three
China's Economic Statecraft in Key Bilateral Relations

Chapter 8

China's Economic Statecraft in Sino-American Relations

William J. Norris

The Sino-American bilateral relationship is the single most important economic and diplomatic relationship for the United States and for China. 'The United States is China's second-largest trading partner, after the European Union (EU), and China is the fourth-largest trading partner for the United States (after the EU, Canada, and Mexico)'.[1] This mutual interdependence extends beyond trade alone. Chinese ownership of US national debt and the growing pools of outward direct investment (ODI) capital from China suggest that both states share abiding common economic interests as well.[2] In many of these aspects of Sino-American relations, it may seem like the United States is disproportionately dependent upon its Chinese partner. However, the United States is no less indispensable to China. The Sino-American bilateral relationship is the single most important economic and diplomatic relationship for China. From the diplomatic and security perspective, the United States continues to be the world's sole superpower. This unique position in international affairs means that successfully managing

---

[1] From the US Department of State, Bureau of East Asian and Pacific Affairs, 'US Relations with China', *Fact Sheet* (5 June 2012), available at: http://www.state.gov/r/pa/ei/bgn/18902.htm.

[2] Chinese ODI into the United States doubled from 2012 to 2013 to US$14 billion.

the relations with the United States is crucial for China to rise to great power status. But the centrality of relations with the United States for China extends beyond the realm of grand strategy alone. China's export-driven growth model has been highly dependent on the world's largest consumer economy. Of China's net exports, about a quarter goes to the United States — more than any other nation.[3] In addition to China's 'flow' dependence on the United States, China also has a 'stock' dependence on the United States. The large portion of China's foreign exchange reserves that are held in dollar-denominated assets means that China has a significant portion of its national wealth now inextricably linked with American monetary and fiscal policy. At the end of 2013, China held US$1.27 trillion of its US$3.82 trillion foreign exchange reserves in US debt. China's total 2013 GDP was about US$9.4 trillion. By 2015, China's GDP had grown to US$14 trillion while China still held about US$1.2 trillion of its US$3.33 trillion of foreign exchange reserves in US debt.[4]

Given the massive levels of economic contact between both countries and the sometimes contentious strategic relationship, one might expect to find that this dyad would be rife with instances of economic statecraft. However, in preparing this paper, I was struck by the comparative lack of recent cases of Chinese economic statecraft directed against the United States. This seemed puzzling. Why would there be so little Chinese economic statecraft vis-à-vis the United States when China seems to have little difficulty exercising economic statecraft across a wide range of partners and issue areas?

My answer to this puzzle is two-fold. First, the terms used to think about economic statecraft within the political science subfield of international relations tends to be too narrow. Generally, our field tends to focus on coercive leverage when discussing economic power. Examples of coercive

---

[3]For a visually appealing depiction of China's net exports see: the MIT Observatory of Economic Complexity, available at: http://atlas.media.mit.edu/explore/tree_map/hs/export/chn/show/all/2011/ (last accessed 4 May 2014).

[4]These shifting compositions reflect a larger set of economic transformations underway in China. For more on the strategic ramifications of such shifts, see William J. Norris, 'Geostrategic implications of China's twin economic challenges', *Geoeconomics Report* (New York, NY: Council on Foreign Relations, 2016) available at: http://www.cfr.org/thinktank/cgs/reports.html.

leverage include sanctions, blockades, travel bans, withholding payments (as the United States did with tolls collected for the Panama Canal as part of its effort to oust Noriega), freezing bank accounts, and many of the types of negative economic statecraft that are highlighted in Baldwin's work. In fact, much of the work on the use of economic power in international relations has been confined to coercive leverage.[5] Moscow's recalling of technical experts, cutting of trade ties and aid and abrogating a loan agreement to Yugoslavia in 1948 and the US pressure on the pound sterling in response to the 1952 Suez Crisis are both historical examples of coercive leverage. A more recent example of coercive leverage was China's 2006 decision to cut off oil flows into North Korea. In that instance, North Korea was dependent on Chinese supplies of oil for approximately 90% of its oil. China cut supplies to force North Korea back to the negotiating table following its nuclear test on 9 October 2006. Under the right circumstances, coercive leverage is an important and a potentially powerful path through which economic interaction affects security. However, I show elsewhere that coercive leverage is only the tip of the iceberg when considering the full range of the impact of economics on security.[6] If our understanding of Chinese economic statecraft were limited strictly to instances of coercive leverage, then the puzzle posed by Sino-American relations is hardly surprising at all.

China's relationship with the United States does not have the necessary asymmetric dependence elements that would enable China to effectively exercise coercive leverage. In the realm of trade, China relies on American consumer demand to fuel its export-oriented growth model. China's 2012

---

[5]For a good work on what I call the externality of coercive leverage, see Daniel W. Drezner, *The Sanctions Paradox: Economic Statecraft and International Relations* (Cambridge: Cambridge University Press, 1999). Drezner looks at the application of economic power in the context of coercion. His work focuses mainly on what I call *Coercive Leverage* security externalities and is very much in keeping with the field in its thinking about economic statecraft in these relatively limited terms. His work, like much of the field, was limited to the sanctions paradigm. Views of economic statecraft that are too myopic fail to engage the full range of the various types of economic interaction that generate security externalities.

[6]For example, see William J. Norris, *Chinese Economic Statecraft: Commercial Actors, Grand Strategy and State Control* (Ithaca, NY: Cornell University Press, 2016); see also, William J. Norris, 'A Theoretical Framework for Understanding the Relationship Between Economics and National Security'. Unpublished working paper.

GDP growth rate of 8% was driven in no small part by its net exports (about 220 basis points of this 8% growth can be attributed to net exports).[7] The United States is the major destination of this trade accounting for about a quarter of all of China's net exports. At the same time, about 70% of the US$17 trillion GDP is attributed to personal consumption so the US economy is more reliant on domestic consumer confidence than on external trade relations. Trade comprises only 23% of US GDP (mostly imports which actually decrease the bottom-line GDP figure). But for China, trade accounts for almost double that amount.[8] Compared to the United States, China is much more reliant on external trade.[9] In the monetary arena, China's foreign exchange reserves represent a significant store of China's national wealth. There are few assets capable of absorbing this level of investment other than US Treasuries. The result is that these foreign exchange reserves are highly concentrated in US dollars. China's position is substantial enough so as not to be liquid for practical purposes.[10] First, financial coercion rarely works against great powers, and China's attempts at financial coercion against the United States would likely be futile. As the two largest economies, they are tied together to such an extent that hurting the United States also hurts China. Second, US Treasury Notes would still be very attractive to many other potential creditors even if China decides to stop supporting the Treasury auctions. Third, the United States is in a position to impose high-retaliatory costs on China. China needs the United States at least as much as the United States needs China.

---

[7]OECD, *Economic Outlook for Southeast Asia, China and India 2014: Beyond the Middle-Income Trap* (OECD Publishing, 2013), p. 47, available at: 10.1787/saeo-2014-en (last accessed 4 May 2014).

[8]Trade makes up 42.8% of China's 2013 GDP.

[9]In response to the 2008 Financial Crisis, China engaged in a massive investment stimulus to offset the softening international demand for China's exports. Although this cushioned the impact on China, it ought to be noted that these measures have since come under fire for their own potentially destabilizing and distorting characteristics. For better or worse, China's economy remains a primarily export-oriented growth model as of this writing. Measures have been implemented to move away from that model of economic development toward more of a domestic consumption-driven growth model.

[10]Daniel Drezner, 'Bad debts: Assessing China's financial influence in great power politics', *International Security*, 34, no. 2 (2009), pp. 7–45.

However, if we broaden our aperture and understand that economic statecraft can take on several forms beyond simple coercive leverage, then the issue of Chinese economic statecraft vis-à-vis the United States becomes more interesting. This brings me to the second part of my answer to the puzzle. A full accounting of Chinese economic statecraft in its relations with the United States requires an understanding of economic statecraft that includes at least two other types of phenomena: what I will call *bolstering* and *strategic transfer*. But before we can delve into these logics, we ought to take a step back and specify what I mean by 'economic statecraft'.

Defining Economic Statecraft

Before delving into a full analysis of economic statecraft in Sino-American relations, we should establish what I mean by the term 'economic statecraft'. When discussing the international use of economic power, commercial actors ought to feature prominently. Commercial actors are those entities that actually carry out international economic transactions (such as buying and selling commodities, making investments, selling products, building factories, purchasing assets, employing workers, and so forth). They are often but not always multinational corporations (MNCs). States, strictly speaking, do not actually conduct the vast majority of today's international economic interaction; firms do. In some instances, states themselves may directly engage in economic transactions (foreign aid, procurement, and so forth) but for the most part, states write the rules of the game and define the conditions under which multinational firms operate.

Being a referee or designing the playing field is not the same thing as being a player in the match, even though both have an influence over the outcome of the game. Sharpening our understanding of how states use economics to pursue their strategic objectives requires a more explicit focus on the role of commercial actors — the entities that actually conduct the vast majority of international economic interaction. The concept of externalities captures the notion that a given transaction may also produce effects that are not fully internalized among the parties that are directly involved in the transaction. I use the term *security externalities* to denote those security effects that are not fully internalized among the parties directly conducting any given economic interaction. Security externalities are the security implications arising as a by-product of economic interaction.[11] Strictly speaking, whether or not states or firms are conscious of these security externalities does not matter. Whether these security effects are intended or not also does not affect the security consequences of the economic interaction.[12] In short, neither intentionality nor awareness matters.

An example may help to illustrate. Air pollution is often an environmental externality resulting from a factory employing its workers to produce steel. A common consequence of high levels of air pollution is asthma. Strictly speaking, whether or not local citizens are aware of the presence (or the cause) of air pollution does not affect the incidence of asthma in the general population. Nor does it matter that the factory owners are aware that their economic activity of employing workers to produce steel is producing an environmental externality. The likelihood of developing asthma would be the same whether or not owners or citizens are conscious of the environmental externality. In the same way, whether the factory owners intended to inflict asthma is unrelated to the fact that asthma resulted.

An externality was produced because there were effects generated that were exogenous to the transacting parties. This exogeneity is what makes these effects externalities, irrespective of the intentions or awareness of the transacting parties. Just as environmental externalities may result from economic activity, security externalities may be thought of as the security

---

[11] Of course, not all security externalities are a consequence of economic activity. There may be security externalities that stem from environmental activities, social changes, demographic trends, or any other number of factors. This work, however, will be limited to those security externalities resulting from economic activity. When the term 'security externalities' is used, it is used to denote the security consequences arising as a by-product of economic interaction.

[12] Intentionality is merely likely to influence the degree to which *manipulation of the externality* occurs — such manipulation is defined below as economic statecraft and is conceptually distinct from the notion of security externalities (see my definition of 'Economic Statecraft' below). What really matters from the point of view of the strategic outcomes are the security externalities themselves — whether or not they were deliberately generated or simply the unintended by-product of normal commercial behavior does not really affect the security consequences *per se*. Whether or not intended, the casual logic of security externalities holds; that is, commercial actors can and do generate security consequences as a result of economic interaction. When states seek to deliberately manipulate that economic interaction, they are engaging in economic statecraft.

consequences stemming from economic activity. Some examples of types of security externalities arising from economic interaction include transfer of sensitive technology, loss of strategic industries, dependence on concentrated supply or demand (in areas of trade, investment, and monetary relations), the forging of common interests resulting from currency unions, joint ventures, macroeconomic coordination, or even simple trade complementarity. My understanding of economic statecraft builds on this concept of security externality.

I define *economic statecraft* as the state manipulation of economic interaction to capitalize on or to reduce the associated security externalities. In this way, economic statecraft is conceptually distinct from the security externalities that result from the activities of commercial actors. States are, in varying degrees, aware of these security externalities. Some externalities may be beneficial while others may be detrimental.[13] Since the externalities are generated by commercial actors that are subject to incentive structures at least partly determined by states, states can seek to influence the behavior of commercial actors to promote their strategic objectives. When states seek to manage security externalities, they are engaging in what is known as economic statecraft. This is where intentionality plays a role. Security externalities may simply result from the autonomous activities of commercial actors pursuing profits (without any direction by the state). However, economic statecraft is the intentional attempt of the state to deliberately incentivize commercial actors to act in a manner that generates security externalities that are conducive to the state's strategic interests.[14] Economic

---

[13] For a seminal work on security externalities arising from trade, see Joanne Gowa and Edward D. Mansfield, 'Power Politics and International Trade', *American Political Science Review*, 87, no. 2 (1993), pp. 408–420. It should be noted that Gowa and Mansfield use the term to describe one particular type of security externality — that of the efficiency benefits stemming from Ricardian gains. Although such bolstering is undoubtedly an important security externality, I suggest that it is only one particular type of security externality.

[14] Note that economic statecraft is analytically distinct from the security externalities themselves. Security externalities may be (inadvertently) generated by commercial actors engaging in various types of economic interaction simply for their narrow commercial rationales. With economic statecraft, there is an element of intentionality present. When engaging in economic statecraft, the state seeks to direct and manipulate the economic activity so as to generate the associated security externalities.

statecraft often occurs as part of a state's grand strategy.[15] Such manipulation of commercial actors and the economic interaction they conduct occurs through a range of state policies including sanctions, taxation, embargoes, trade agreements, asset freezing, engagement policies, currency manipulation, subsidies, tariffs, trade agreements, and so forth. Economic statecraft encompasses the scope of state actions taken to manipulate economic interaction and the security externalities associated with that economic interaction. In this manner, states may use commercial actors to achieve foreign policy objectives by creating incentives for commercial actors to behave in a way that carries with it security externalities that advance a state's strategic interests.

How China Uses Economic Statecraft in Its Relations with the United States

Based on this paper's analysis, China's use of economic statecraft in its US relations consists mainly of attempts to encourage and capitalize on two different types of security externalities: *bolstering* and *strategic transfer*. In this section, I define these causal logics before moving on to a review of several recent cases that reflect these types of security externalities.

Bolstering is the category of security externalities that result when economic interaction with the United States makes China's economy stronger. China's export-oriented growth model relies heavily on what is effectively outsourced, global aggregate demand. The US consumer-driven economy is a key pillar of that global demand. Much of the 'economic statecraft' that China engages in with regard to the United States is simply designed to advance China's own economic well-being. An exhaustive survey of the various ways that international economic interaction might improve the economic health of a state could occupy volumes. A few simple examples will suffice to illustrate how *bolstering* works. The most prominent

---

[15]Broadly speaking, states have four objectives when they employ economic statecraft to achieve their strategic objectives: (1) limit the good done to rivals/enemies; (2) maximize the bad done to rivals/enemies (including transformation); (3) limit the bad done to themselves/allies; and (4) maximize the good done to themselves/allies. I am indebted to Barry Posen for this characterization.

way economic interaction produces a more powerful economy is through the concepts depicted by Ricardo as 'gains from trade' which are Pareto improvements resulting from complementary specialization. Competition stemming from international economic interaction is also an important source of macroeconomic strength as weaker firms are removed from the economy and supporting resources are more productively redeployed elsewhere. Chinese government policies can incentivize Chinese MNCs to acquire strategic assets (expertise, technology, and proprietary information) in order to make up for the shortcomings of Chinese industry.[16] The list could go on. As China has integrated into the international system, it has sought to move steadily up the value chain. This is a natural state of affairs in the economic evolution of developing economies. China has taken this a step further and actively encourages investment in R&D that is specifically designed to indigenize innovation. To the extent that the Chinese state has explicitly designed policies and strategies to facilitate China's own economic growth, one could say that China has engaged in economic statecraft that has been designed to encourage *bolstering* types of security externalities.

There are several types of this kind of Chinese economic statecraft that are often cited in the US context. Allegations of China's currency manipulation (a particularly attractive talking point during electoral cycles and in the US Congress) are classic examples. The logic of this accusation suggests that the Chinese state, by artificially holding down the value of the RMB's exchange rate, effectively engages in an across-the-board subsidy for Chinese exporters. Another frequently cited criticism of Beijing lies in the state's proclivity for industrial planning. Chinese efforts to identify and support national champions and to target strategic emerging industries for national promotion raised concerns over Chinese economic statecraft that is designed to facilitate *bolstering* dynamics. Another type of Chinese economic statecraft that reflects the *bolstering* logic is market-access restriction

---

[16]Deng Ping, 'Why do Chinese firms tend to acquire strategic assets in international expansion', *Journal of World Business*, 44 (2009), pp. 74–84. The Chinese government apparently offers favorable financing and tax regimens to companies which follow these mergers and acquisitions (M & A) policies, and may punish those that resist the government (Deng, p. 76).

that is designed to tilt the playing field in favor of domestic Chinese firms. Google's experience in China was one very public airing of how foreign firms often feel that they are asked to compete on unfair terms against favored domestic competitors in China. To the extent that the Chinese government engages in tactics that are designed to discriminate against foreign firms in favor of bolstering domestic rivals, China engages in this type of economic statecraft.

Strategic transfer is the category of security externalities that results from economic interaction which enhances a target state's war-making capabilities through the acquisition of strategic goods, expertise, resources or dual-use, and/or dedicated military technologies. The enhanced military capabilities result from the transfer (of goods, technologies, strategic resources, etc.) that takes place in the course of economic interaction. The causal pathway is one in which economic interaction — in this case mostly trade and investment in militarily significant sectors — engenders a transmission of ideas, expertise, cutting-edge technologies and methodologies, or even raw materials and components that have military applications. Such transfers enhance China's military capabilities, thus producing security externalities that fall into the category *strategic transfer*.

A strategy that seeks to employ this security externality would encourage economic interaction that is likely to entail the transfer of sensitive technologies, processes, designs, or other strategic goods and resources. The likelihood of success of this type of strategy is dependent on several factors: how critical the particular technology or resource is for improving China's military capabilities; how easily China can absorb and make use of the technology or resource; and how effectively can certain economic interaction facilitate technology acquisition. Encryption technology exports, Loral satellite launches, and 12-inch semiconductor wafer production technologies are all examples of the transfer of sensitive technologies. Strategic goods or resources are fairly broadly defined across time and space but at various times and in various regions, have included saltpeter, fissile material, cod, bauxite, horses, oil, coal, iron ore, rubber, water, wheat, and gold. Although a universal definition is difficult to come by, strategic goods generally involve some combination of: (1) the ease with which the good or service can be substituted; (2) the ease with which the service or good can be converted into military capabilities; and (3) the relative scarcity of the good or service.

States may pursue a variety of strategies to exploit *strategic transfer* externalities. These economic policies can range from subsidies of less strategically significant goods (with the goal of displacing the more strategically valuable substitute goods) to tariffs designed to dissuade consumption of strategic goods, to outright restrictions and bans on trade of sensitive items. The issue of what does or does not constitute 'strategic' is of fundamental importance for this category of externalities. If a good or service is very critical to improving a target state's military capabilities (like fissile material), states will likely seek to engage in economic statecraft to prevent the acquisition of such goods and services by rival states. In addition, states will consider the degree to which a certain good or service enhances the target's military capabilities and the degree to which a certain type of economic interaction is likely to encourage the transfer of strategically valuable knowledge, material, or expertise when determining the sort of economic statecraft policies to pursue. In addition to preventing others from acquiring strategic goods, states will often seek to ensure, improve, or expand their own ability to access strategic goods through strategic stockpiling or measures to gain self-sufficiency in a particular area.

In China's economic statecraft that targets the United States, the logic of capitalizing on *strategic transfer* security externalities features prominently. Because so much of modern warfare relies on integrated information technology that frequently can have both military and non-military commercial applications, the problem of dual-use technologies is one example in which *strategic transfer* security externalities looms large. When Chinese companies obtain access to dual-use technology, they can augment China's war-fighting capabilities. Additionally, this kind of *strategic transfer* can also have the effect of degrading US military capabilities. In addition to normal commercial activity in the dual-use realm, China has been accused of conducting industrial espionage against US targets. Another aspect of Chinese economic statecraft that reflects the *strategic transfer* logic concerns China's foreign direct investment (FDI) in the United States. At various times, elements of the US government have raised concerns about Chinese attempts to acquire technology, intellectual property, technical processes, and sensitive expertise. To the extent that these investing activities are motivated, encouraged, or supported by the Chinese government with the explicit intention of facilitating *strategic transfer* types of security externalities, this activity also could be classified as Chinese economic statecraft.

Having defined economic statecraft and specified the two prominent security externalities that seem to underpin Chinese economic statecraft in relation to the United States, in the next section, I explore a few specific recent cases that might qualify as Chinese economic statecraft. Admittedly, just because an investment takes place in potentially sensitive sectors (such as technology, energy, infrastructure, or aerospace) does not necessarily imply that this qualifies as a clear-cut case of Chinese economic statecraft. At best, most of these observations listed below can only be classified as 'potential cases of Chinese economic statecraft' given the dual-use nature of their industries. In addition, state intentionality is notoriously difficult to gauge in the Chinese context. The extent to which the state has deliberately incentivized commercial actors to behave in a way that carries with it security externalities that advance China's strategic interests remains an open but critical question.

Cases that May Be Considered Chinese Economic Statecraft in the US Context

Huawei has been a favorite target of critics of Chinese economic statecraft in the United States. Its activities were the subject of a lengthy report by the US Congressional Permanent Select Committee on Intelligence.[17] In September 2007, Huawei, in conjunction with Bain Capital Partners, announced plans to buy the US firm 3Com Corporation for US$2.2 billion. The company 3Com was a provider of data networking equipment. Following a review of the deal by the Committee on Foreign Investment in the United States (CFIUS), the proposed merger was withdrawn in February 2008. Huawei and its partner failed to adequately address US national security

---

[17]Along with ZTE, Huawei was examined for its ties to the Chinese security apparatus. See US House of Representatives 112th Congress, *Investigative Report on the US National Security Issues Posed by Chinese Telecommunications Companies Huawei and ZTE* (8 October 2012), available at: https://intelligence.house. gov/sites/intelligence.house. gov/files/documents/Huawei-ZTE%20Investigative%20Report%20(FINAL).pdf.

concerns raised by CFIUS members. In a separate incident, CFIUS also asked Huawei to rescind its May 2010 offer to buy intellectual property assets from 3Leaf Systems.

In February 2010, Emcore Corporation, a provider of compound semiconductor-based components, subsystems, and systems for the fiber optics and solar power markets, announced it had agreed to sell a 60% interest of its fiber optics business (excluding its satellite communications and specialty photonics fiber optics businesses) to China's Tangshan Caofeidian Investment Corporation (TCIC) for US$27.8 million. Four months later, Emcore announced that it was scrapping the deal due to concerns raised by CFIUS. In 2004, Lenovo Group Limited signed an agreement with IBM Corporation to purchase IBM's personal computer division for US$1.75 billion. Some US officials raised national security concerns over the possibility of espionage activities that could occur at IBM research facilities in the United States if the deal went through. A review of the agreement by CFIUS took place in which IBM and Lenovo were able to address certain national security concerns. The result was the completion of the acquisition in April 2005.

Sensitive sectors are not limited to the computer/information technology space. In 2005, Chinese state-owned enterprise (SOE) China National Offshore Oil Corporation (CNOOC) made a bid to buy US energy company Union Oil Company of California (UNOCAL) for US$18.5 billion, but widespread opposition in Congress led CNOOC to withdraw its bid. Critics of this deal argued that the proposed takeover represented a clear threat to the energy and national security of the United States. Specifically, there was concern that the deal would place vital oil assets in the Gulf of Mexico and Alaska in the hands of a Chinese state-controlled company. Other opponents were concerned that the acquisition could transfer advanced technologies to China. Finally, reflecting concerns about Chinese state support, some expressed reservations that CNOOC's bid to take over UNOCAL would be heavily subsidized by the Chinese government. CNOOC officials referred to US political opposition to the sale as 'regrettable and unjustified'.

A good deal of Chinese FDI in the United States in recent years focused on the energy space. In 2012, Sinopec bought a US$2.5 billion stake in Devon Energy (shale assets in Ohio and Michigan) and in 2013, Sinopec bought a billion-dollar interest in Chesapeake Energy's Mississippi

Lime holdings (unconventional liquids play in Oklahoma). This followed CNOOC's US$2.2 billion deal with Chesapeake Energy in 2010. Also in 2013, CNOOC was cleared by CFIUS for its US$15 billion purchase of Canadian-based Nexen which has one of the largest holdings of deep-water leases in the Gulf of Mexico. Not wanting to be left out in the cold, Sinochem Group bought a 40% stake valued at US$1.7 billion in the Wolfcamp Shale assets in West Texas from Pioneer Natural Resources Company in 2013.

Chinese companies have also expressed an interest in the US aviation industry. Advancing China's own aviation industry is a strategic focal point for Chinese economic planners. Superior Aviation Beijing Company's US$1.79 billion bid to purchase the corporate jet propeller plane operations of Hawker Beechcraft out of bankruptcy in 2013 fell apart due to security concerns. Another aviation deal fell apart due to financing issues: a five-member consortium of Chinese buyers failed to generate the funds to support a US$4.2 billion purchase of American International Group (AIG)'s 80% share of International Lease Financing Corporation.

While the acquisition of certain sectors might prompt *strategic transfer* security concerns, CFIUS has also blocked attempted Chinese investments in the United States on the basis of simple real estate proximity. In July 2009, China's Northwest Nonferrous International Investment Company offered US$26 million for a 51% stake in the Firstgold Corporation. But some of the mines controlled by Firstgold were located near US military installations. Concerns raised by CFIUS caused the Chinese firm to withdraw its bid five months later. Moreover, in an unusual move, the US president barred a Chinese-owned company from building wind farms near a US Navy base in Oregon in September 2012. This was the first time in 22 years that a US president blocked a transaction because it was deemed to be a national security risk.

In a classic political reaction to perceived Chinese economic statecraft, US steel companies mobilized congressional support against the attempt of Anshan Iron and Steel Group Corporation (Ansteel) to partner with Steel Development Company, a US firm in Mississippi. The two were planning to build and operate four mills to produce reinforcing bar and other bar products used in infrastructure applications, and one mill that would be capable of producing electrical and silicon grades of steel used in energy applications. Fifty members of Congress signed a letter to secretary of the

Treasury Tim Geithner, expressing concerns over the effect the investment would have 'on American jobs and our national security'.

Of course, not all major Chinese investment deals in the United States raise issues of economic statecraft. Increasingly, Chinese FDI in the United States is coming from private rather than state-owned companies. Moreover, the last couple of years have seen an increase in Chinese investment in consumer-oriented sectors. Both of these features help assuage national security concerns that might stem from Chinese investing activities in dual-use or security-sensitive sectors. For instance, one would be hard-pressed to find legitimate national security concerns stemming from Dalian Wanda's US$2.6 billion purchase of AMC Cinemas or from Shuanghui International Holdings' US$7.1 billion acquisition of Smithfield Foods (even though that does not mean there were none raised).

In addition to these investment cases, a number of Sino–American trade disputes have noteworthy implications for bilateral relations. Given the historical importance of the US trade relationship for China's overall growth trajectory, potential trade disruptions threaten to undermine Beijing's access to a vibrant, dynamic source of aggregate demand. On 15 September 2010, the Office of the United States Trade Representative (USTR) announced that it was bringing two World Trade Organization (WTO) cases against China: the first, for China's improper application of anti-dumping duties and countervailing duties against US flat-rolled electrical steel exports; the second, for China's discrimination against US suppliers of electronic payment services. The USTR also announced that it would bring a case to the WTO against Chinese subsidies for Chinese wind-power equipment manufacturers who were using China-made components instead of foreign-made components. This case seems to provide additional evidence of Chinese economic statecraft designed to bolster domestic Chinese performance in a strategic renewable energy industry. Other trade dispute cases have included subsidies for China's semiconductor manufacturers, penalties on tire imports from China, and poultry-trade barriers.

China has also engaged in economic statecraft to help its own firms to successfully compete internationally. For example, China created a domestic surplus of critical raw materials by restricting the export of certain critical raw materials (e.g., rare earth elements, bauxite, coke, fluorspar, magnesium, manganese, silicon carbide, silicon metal, yellow phosphorus, and zinc). This domestic glut could lower material costs for Chinese producers, giving them an international competitive advantage. The Chinese state has also engaged in economic statecraft to strengthen Chinese brands. As part of China's *bolstering* effort, the government provided subsidies, tax cuts, and incentives to encourage technological upgrades and foster a vigorous indigenous innovation program. The state directed banks to provide financing and designed advantageous government procurement policies to support these programs. Finally, the extension of export credits and other sources of low-cost funding helps Chinese firms compete and invest overseas.

Analysis

Based on this evidence, there seems to be at least four objectives of Chinese economic statecraft in the American context. First and foremost, China seeks to abide by the Hippocratic oath: 'First do no harm' to its critical economic and strategic relationship with the United States. Simply by maintaining stability and sustaining prosperous economic engagement across a wide range of trade, investment, and monetary relations with the United States, China serves its primary objective of continued economic growth necessary to fuel its rise to great power status. As long as its relationship with the United States remains strong and prosperous, China will stand to benefit immensely.

Second, assuming that primary objective can be maintained, China also seems to provide some evidence of pursuing secondary economic statecraft policies designed to encourage and harness *bolstering* types of security externalities at the margin. These have included manipulating monetary and fiscal policy tools to provide unique advantages to Chinese companies and interests. These efforts may exhibit higher or lower levels of transparency, but generally seek to tilt the Chinese playing field in favor of Chinese firms.

Third, there seems to be evidence of Chinese economic statecraft designed to facilitate *strategic transfer* types of security externalities. *Strategic transfer* seems to be a fairly consistent theme across many of these cases. Dual-use technologies create attractive potential commercial targets. Such duality also makes it difficult for host nations to know where appropriate boundaries ought to be set for Chinese investment and acquisition activities. Chinese economic statecraft does not seem to be the exclusive mechanism for pursuing this objective. The goals of this strategy to acquire high-technology assets and knowledge also seem to be supported by Chinese cyber and industrial espionage.

Finally, the recent patterns of Chinese deals to acquire interests and partnerships in the US energy sector seem to reflect a fourth Chinese objective: securing reliable access to strategic resources such as energy. The boom in unconventional shale oil and gas recovery in the United States has attracted the interest of Chinese oil majors. These partnerships are likely to contribute important technical skills transfer and expertise that one day may help China to unlock its own shale deposits.

How Successful has China Been in Its US-Oriented Economic Statecraft?

In my opinion, Chinese economic statecraft directed at the United States is actually quite limited given what it could be. Considering the size of the two economies, China's domestic political institutional architecture (which is rather conducive to economic statecraft), the immense scale of economic interaction between the United States and China, and the strategic competitive elements present in Sino-American relations, I still find it somewhat surprising to discover so little evidence of economic statecraft. This may tell us something interesting regarding Sino-American relations. Perhaps with the United States, China pursues a strategy of economic statecraft that is fundamentally different from its strategies with other partners. Maybe China is significantly more conservative in its use of economic statecraft. This difference may be driven by the sheer size of the US economy, making it difficult for China to wield coercive economic power in a meaningfully asymmetric way. It may also be driven by the physical distance separating the United States from China. Or perhaps the security/competitive dimension of Sino-American relations relegates the economic relationship to a historically mitigating role — something that acts as a firebreak to political tension. When such tensions rise, the economic aspect of the relationship serves to remind the leaders of the mutual benefits of cooperation. Whatever the reason, China seems to be pursuing relatively less intense forms of economic statecraft in its relations with the United States than with some of the other partners discussed in this book.

China does face a number of constraints in its attempts to pursue economic statecraft in its relations with the United States. First, the American
legalistic business climate and political landscape is an inhospitable and
largely foreign operating environment for Chinese firms.[18] Chinese firms
struggle to navigate the unfamiliar political minefields amid legal obstacles.
Second, public distrust of Chinese intentions and the disillusionment of the
once-supportive US business community have created a more challenging atmosphere for China's activities in the United States. Finally, Chinese
weakness in domestic innovation continues to hinder long-term economic
competitiveness. Current attempts to leverage overseas intellectual property may help China make the leap to a new generation of productivity.
But China's attempts to rely on imported intellectual property and copy-
ing state-of-the-art processes may just as easily contribute to a long-term
structural dependency. To make matters worse, the state's attempts to pick
winners may ironically squelch China's truly innovative firms.

Despite the significant short- and medium-term economic challenges
facing it, China has a number of strengths supporting its future economic
power. China has been the world's success story for the last 35 years. It is
a rising power whose corporate balance sheets are flush with cash. Moreover, China has a very high national savings rate (even though much of this
seems to be designed for self-insurance) with a rather unproductive return
on savings. These features, in conjunction with signs of capital account liberalization, suggest that China will have increasing assets to deploy internationally. If China implements the proposed liberalization and deepens
market reforms, it could significantly add to its growing economic clout
over time.

Conclusion

In this chapter, I examined how China has used economic statecraft in
its relations with the United States. I suggest that one must conceptualize

---

[18]Lorraine Eden and Stewart Miller, 'Revisiting Liability of Foreignness: The Socio-
Political Hazards facing Chinese Multinationals in the United States of America', in *Is the
United States Ready for Foreign Investment from China?* Karl Sauvant, ed. (Cheltenham,
UK: Edward Edgar, 2010), pp. 122–141.

Chinese economic statecraft beyond simple coercion. We did not see very much simple coercion — at least not yet — in Sino-American relations. Rather, we observed a Chinese economic statecraft strategy that is predicated on *bolstering* and *strategic transfer* logics. In this chapter, I presented a number of possible instances of such episodes of Chinese economic statecraft.

As I reflect on long-term trends for Chinese economic statecraft in the US relationship, I am struck by three observations. First, my cases reflect an intense politicization of China's inbound investment and trade practices in the United States. CFIUS featured heavily in many of these cases and I cannot help but think it will have (or already may be exercising) a deterrent effect on Chinese economic statecraft. While this may prevent some of the most egregious efforts of *strategic transfer*, it may also circumscribe mutually beneficial cross-border investment. Such investment might otherwise generate new jobs and inject needed capital into local communities in the United States. Although it may be unrealistic to entirely depoliticize Chinese ODI, there seems to be a need for policy-makers to more clearly distinguish between cases that present genuine security concerns and those that do not. The framework presented in this chapter should aid in specifying such distinctions.

Second, China's ODI is likely to increase in the coming years. It seems that a significant portion of this growing ODI will naturally be attracted to the US economy. The US short-medium term outlook for the world's largest economy is relatively promising. If previous patterns are an indication, we should then expect more of these *strategic transfer* and *bolstering* types of security externalities being generated. To the extent the recent past serves as a guide, we should also expect to see Chinese economic statecraft seeking to facilitate such externalities. Chinese ODI to the United States doubled from 2012 to US$14 billion in 2013. In the first quarter of 2016, there were already more than US$30 billion of pending deals and new projects. Although this growth is impressive, it is still paltry compared to the underlying GDPs of both the United States and China. China's ODI is still less than 1% of China's GDP. That figure should eventually head toward 2% of Chinese GDP — which means that there is still a lot of room for absolute levels of Chinese ODI to grow, particularly if one assumes China's GDP will continue to grow.

Lastly, I think that the key to successful FDI endeavors for China in the United States will revolve around structuring genuine partnerships which benefit both sides. China needs to escape from the limitations of a zero-sum mentality when it comes to business negotiations and partnerships. Just as when international companies were first entering China, the most successful joint ventures were premised on a long-term, mutually beneficial, value-added approach. These ventures found ways to ensure that incentives of all partners aligned. The same spirit will be needed to keep China's ODI going forward. One interesting trend to keep an eye on is the recent effort on the part of individual states in the United States to create investing climates conducive for Chinese partnerships. Even as the national atmosphere may have become caustic toward China, many states have individually embarked upon innovative attempts to seek out partnerships with Chinese investors to facilitate mutually advantageous opportunities in their locales.

Today, the Chinese and American economies are intimately linked. This economic complementarity provides a stabilizing influence on what can sometimes be a tumultuous security relationship. This chapter provides greater clarity on the question of how economics relates to security concerns. A more precise understanding of such ties should improve measures like CFIUS that are designed to safeguard against security concerns while also helping to clear the way for constructive, commercial activity that benefits both the United States and China.

Chapter 9

China's Economic Statecraft in Africa: The Resilience of Development Financing from Mao to Xi

Ana Cristina Alves

The People's Republic of China (PRC) has very little record of making use of military force[1] or even negative economic statecraft tools (sanctions) in both bilateral and multilateral settings[2] since its founding in 1949. This trend was consolidated in the years following the introduction of economic reforms by Deng Xiaoping, becoming a very distinctive trait of China's foreign policy in an international context still dominated by the Cold War militarism. This is explained largely by the imperative of creating a friendly international environment favorable to its economic development. Unlike the sporadic use of military force and economic sanctions, the use of economic inducements to pursue foreign policy goals has been relatively consistent throughout the successive leaderships since the founding of the PRC, particularly in its dealings with the southern hemisphere.

Chinese economic statecraft toward fellow developing countries falls thus mainly under the foreign aid umbrella. According to the official

---

[1]The few exceptions are mostly confined to the Maoist period, namely Support provided to North Korea in the Korean War in the 1950s; the military training of African independence movements in the 1960s, and military intervention in Cambodia in the late 1970s.
[2]Since its accession to the UN Security Council (UNSC) in 1971, it has typically abstained from voting on economic sanctions resolutions.

narrative, Chinese foreign assistance dates back to the early days of the PRC in the 1950s, when Beijing started channeling economic aid and technical assistance to neighboring communist countries first (Vietnam and North Korea) and then newly independent African countries.[3] While China's aid during much of the second half of the 20th century was limited by its meagre financial resources, its span and impact has grown exponentially since the turn of the century. The hasty expansion of China's foreign aid coupled with the complexity/opacity of the underlying operational system and increasing international scrutiny, urged Beijing to repackage its foreign assistance. To this end, two white papers on foreign aid were issued in recent years (2011 and 2014) illustrating well China's urge to make it more intelligible, not only to its recipients but also within an international cooperation framework dominated by the Western paradigm. While the various forms of aid provided by China have remained mostly the same since 1949,[4] its volume, geographical footprint, and the internal mechanism have changed significantly since the turn of the century.

According to the 2014 Foreign Aid white paper, China's foreign assistance amounted to US$14.41 billion between 2010 and 2012, with African countries now receiving the bulk of it (52%) followed by Asia (31%). China's foreign assistance is funded mainly through three financial instruments: grants, interest-free loans, and concessional loans. The first two target mostly social welfare, human resources development, technical coop, humanitarian aid, public facilities and projects, and are sourced from China's state finances. They accounted for 36% and 8%, respectively, of the amount mentioned earlier. Conversely, concessional loans, which are sourced on the market by the Export-Import Bank of China (China Exim Bank),[5] accounted for 56% (US$8 billion) and were primarily earmarked

---

[3]Information Office of the State Council of the People's Republic of China, 'China's Foreign Aid' (white paper issued in April 2011) (accessed 5 May 2011), available at: http://news.xinhuanet.com/english2010/china/2011-04/21/c_ 13839683_20.htm.

[4]Namely complete projects, goods and materials, medical aid, emergency humanitarian aid, overseas volunteer programs, human resource development, technical cooperation, debt relief, and financial assistance.

[5]China Exim Bank was created in 1994. It is fully owned by the Chinese government, and is under the direct leadership of the State Council. It plays an important role in promoting foreign trade and economic cooperation, acting as a key channel to finance Chinese export

for large- and medium-sized infrastructure.[6] While providing assistance to fellow developing countries, this particular economic statecraft tool has been implemented by China to pursue economic and political goals overseas. Concessional loans, for instances, have been systematically used by China to open the gates for Chinese construction and resources companies in African markets since the 2000s and also to secure resources supply and assets (such as oil, minerals, and other commodities) in the continent.[7]

While various cooperation instruments have been consistently used since the founding of the PRC in its relations with Africa, this chapter argues that soft loans for infrastructure have proven to be particularly consequential in pursuing Chinese foreign policy goals, and naturally came to be the dominant and most resourceful instrument of Chinese economic statecraft in the continent in the 21st century.

Michael Mastanduno[8] distinguishes between two types of positive economic statecraft goals. The first one which he termed tactical linkage (also called specific positive linkage) envisages an immediate outcome through the provision of a specific economic inducement. The second one, structural linkage (or general positive linkage), involves a long-term engagement providing a steady stream of economic inducements. The ensuing economic interdependence gradually transforms domestic interests in the target country, leading to a growing influence over the policy options of the weaker state, ultimately consolidating a coalition with the sanctioning states.[9] This type of economic inducement is in a way linked to the concept of 'soft

---

of mechanical and electronic products, equipment and technologies, and in undertaking offshore construction contracts and overseas investment projects by Chinese companies.

[6]Information and figures in this paragraph according to the white paper on China's foreign aid issued by China's Information Office of the State Council on 10 July 2014. (Xinhua/ China's Information Office of the State Council), available at: http://news.xinhuanet.com/ english/china/2014-07/10/c_133474011_ 2.htm (accessed 19 June 2015).

[7]Ana Cristina Alves, 'China's oil Diplomacy: Comparing Chinese Economic Statecraft in Angola and in Brazil' (PhD dissertation, London School fo Economics, 2012).

[8]Michael Mastanduno, 'Economic Statecraft', in *Foreign Policy: Theories, Actors, Cases*, S. Smith, A. Hadfield and T. Dunne, eds. (Oxford: Oxford University Press, 2008).

[9]M. Mastanduno, 'Economic statecraft, interdependence and national security: Agendas for research', in *Power and the Purse: Economic Statecraft, Interdependence and National Security*, J.F. Blanchard, E.D. Mansfield and N. Ripsman, eds. (London: Frank Cass, 2000), pp. 306–309.

power', developed by Joseph Nye ('getting others to want the outcomes that you want').[10]

Departing from Mastanduno's dichotomy, it is possible to identify two distinct layers of goals underlying China's economic incentives toward Africa. The first encompasses a long-term political goal, in the spirit of what he termed structural linkage. By fostering economic interdependence, China hopes to expand its political clout over the continent, so as to enact a coalition that will favor its interests in the long run. Soft loans targeting infrastructure are one among a set of many other positive economic statecraft instruments (such as trade promotion, the setting up of multilateral mechanisms such as the Forum of China–Africa Cooperation [FOCAC], free trade agreements, currency swaps, bilateral strategic partnerships, investment protection agreements, etc.) being currently implemented by China envisaging this outcome. The second layer of goals refers to more immediate ends, which can be economic or political in nature.

This chapter proposes to assess how successful Chinese soft loans for infrastructure have been in achieving Beijing's foreign policy goals in Africa since the founding of the PRC, with reference to tactical and structural goals. It also aims at unpacking relevant shifts that have occurred in this particular positive economic statecraft instrument overtime, and finally analyze its wider implications. The study will focus on two main time periods: before and after the establishment of the FOCAC in 2000, as this marks a radical shift in China's foreign policy goals toward the continent from primarily political to predominantly economic.

Pursuing Political Goals in Africa from the 1950s to the 1990s[11]

The founding of the PRC coincided with the onset of the Cold War and the dawn of the independence tsunami that swept the African continent in the following decades. The newly independent African countries rapidly

[10]J.S. Nye, *Soft Power: The Means to Success in World Politics* (New York: Public Affairs, 2004), p. 5.
[11]This section draws on: Chris Alden and Ana Alves, 'History and Identity in the Construction of China's Africa Policy', *Review of African Political Economy*, 35, no. 115 (2008), pp. 43–58.

emerged in the communist regime's radar as a potential solution to its legitimacy problem. With Taipei occupying China's permanent seat in the United Nations Security Council (UNSC) backed by most Western powers, harnessing the increasing voting weight of new African members in the UN General Assembly (UNGA) offered Beijing the possibility of turning the odds in its favor.

The initial contacts with Africa in this period happened in the framework of the 1955 Bandung conference, where Zhou Enlai met several African leaders, including Gamal Abdel Nasser from Egypt, which became in 1956 the first African country to establish diplomatic ties with the PRC. China's courtship to Africa in this period was, however, under the shade of the alliance with the Soviet Union (SU) and hence limited to somewhat shy diplomatic contacts, guided by China's anticolonial solidarity and the dissemination of its self-reliance development model, mainly through the Afro-Asian People's Solidarity Organization (AAPSO) created in 1957. By the end of the decade, only four other African countries had established ties with China (Morocco, Algeria, Sudan, and Guinea).

The ideological rift with the SU in the late 1950s changed China's stance in Africa and as a result, Beijing became much more assertive in the following decade. China's foreign policy in Africa was now two-pronged: in addition to gaining wider international diplomatic recognition and replacing Taiwan in the United Nations as the legitimate government of China; Beijing was also now competing with the SU for the leadership of the world socialist revolution and the lead of the Third World.[12] It was with these two aims in mind that China started to consistently deploy economic incentives in its dealings with Africa. These came mostly in the form of aid and technical assistance agreements and the provision of financial assistance.[13] Chinese loans — mostly to fund turn-key projects in various areas — were provided with no conditions attached, interest-free or low interest, contemplating long repayment schedules, some guaranteed by African exports to China.[14]

---

[12]George T. Yu, 'China's failure in Africa', *Asian Survey*, 6, no. 8 (1966), pp. 464.

[13]George T. Yu, 'Sino-African Relations: A Survey', *Asian Survey*, 5, no. 7 (1965), pp. 324–331.

[14]*Ibid.*, p. 325.

Guinea under Sekou Toure, was the first African country to benefit from China's financial assistance in the form of a RMB100 million interest-free loan (roughly US$25 million) in 1960.[15] The loan funded the construction of a number of factories (peanut and palm kernel oil-pressing, cigarette and match, and bamboo processing), agriculture projects (rice and tea plantations and irrigation), and prestige buildings (Conakry's Freedom Cinema and the People's Palace and Conference Hall).[16] During Zhou Enlai's celebrated tour to 10 African countries (December 1963–February 1964), China pledged a total of US$120 million in aid to five countries (Congo-Brazzaville, Ghana, Kenya, Mali, and Tanzania).[17] Although much of the aid extended during the 1960s came in the form of economic and technical agreements, Chinese loans gained some traction in the region. According to Yu, in 1964 China alone was responsible for over half of the loans extended to the continent.[18] The volume and footprint of Chinese aid continued to expand in the following years[19] in tandem with the increasing number of African independent countries. By 1966, its total aid commitments were estimated at US$428 million[20] spread across nine countries.

During this period, China's foreign policy in Africa also included a variety of controversial covert instruments, namely financial and technical assistance to liberation and rebel movements (i.e., guerrilla training and arms transfers),[21] in a clear attempt to win the hearts and minds of African leaders in the making. By the end of 1965, 17 out of the 38 existing African states had established ties with Beijing (compared to 14 with Taipei) and the PRC had linkages to 12 liberation movements.[22]

---

[15]Deborah Brautigam, *The Dragon's Gift: The Real Story of China in Africa* (Oxford: Oxford University Press, 2009), p. 32.

[16]*Ibid.*

[17]*Ibid.*, pp. 32–33.

[18]George T. Yu, 'Sino-African', p. 325.

[19]Deborah Brautigam, 'Chinese Development Aid in Africa', in *Rising China: Global Challenges and Opportunities*, eds. Jane Golley and Ligang Song (ANU, 2011), p. 209, available at: http://press.anu.edu.au?p=113721.

[20]George T. Yu, 'Africa in China's Foreign Policy', *Asian Survey*, 28, no. 8 (1988), p. 853.

[21]See Mohamed A. El-Khawas, 'China's Changing Policies in Africa', *Issue: A Journal of Opinion*, 3, no. 1 (1973), pp. 25–26.

[22]George T. Yu, 'Africa in China's', p. 853.

The onset of the Cultural Revolution in 1966 dictated, however, a contraction in all forms of China's assistance to Africa in the years that followed, with Beijing concentrating its attention in a few selected allies: Congo-Brazzaville, Guinea, Mali, Tanzania, and Zambia.[23] Despite this retrenchment and the many diplomatic debacles produced by PRC's subversive activities in the continent,[24] Beijing succeeded in maintaining some degree of influence in Africa and in laying long lasting friendship foundations with a number of African states. This was the case namely of Tanzania and Zambia, with which the PRC signed a US$400 million loan agreement in 1967 to build its first backbone infrastructure project on the continent — a 1870 km railway linking the rich copper belt in Zambia to Dar Es Salam port in Tanzania, the famous Tazara Railway.[25] The loan was interest-free and to be repaid over a 30 years period with five years of grace.[26] The decision to construct the railway grew out of a direct request from Zambian president Kenneth Kaunda, seconded by his Tanzanian counterpart, Julius Nyerere. Despite the financial and political limitations at the time, Mao embraced this mega project with great enthusiasm as it was perceived as a unique opportunity to raise China's profile on the continent. In the post-independence period, the funding for the railway had been denied or dismissed as unfeasible by the World Bank and a number of Western powers.[27] What is more, this project became then the largest economic assistance project granted to an African state by a communist country. The construction started in 1970 and was completed in 1975, two years ahead of schedule. All equipment and materials were shipped from China along with thousands of Chinese technicians.

This type of soft loan (with no conditions attached and offering easier terms for the borrower) became very appealing in the African eyes, especially in the face of the reluctance of Western donors to fund similar projects.

---

[23] *Ibid.*, pp. 853–854.

[24] See Mohamed A. El-Khawas, 'China's Changing', pp. 25–26.

[25] For an in-depth study, see George T. Yu, 'The Tanzania-Zambia Railway: A Case Study in Chinese Economic Aid to Africa', in *Soviet and Chinese Aid to African Nations*, Warren Weinstein and Thomas H. Henriken, eds. (New York: Praeger, 1980), pp. 117–144.

[26] Mohamed A. El-Khawas, 'China's Changing,' p. 27.

[27] Deborah Brautigam, *Dragon's Gift*, p. 40.

Many African countries ran to Beijing in search for support, including traditional SU allies in eastern Africa: in 1971 Ethiopia received a $84 million interest-free loan for agriculture development to be repaid with exports; and Sudan a $40 million loan to build a weaving and textile factory and build two roads.[28]

The Tazara Railway was, however, the only mega-infrastructure project funded by China during this period. Notwithstanding its patent economic failure[29] it stands out to this day as a landmark in China–Africa friendship, frequently cited as the epitome of China–Africa solidarity in public speeches by both Chinese and African leaders. This fact attests to the success of Beijing's economic statecraft in pursuing long-term political goals.

China's development financing also paid off in regards to more immediate foreign policy objectives during this period, namely in expanding its diplomatic ties and winning African votes in the UN Assembly to oust Taiwan. Although the rapprochement with the US around this period undoubtedly set a more favorable international context, African delegates at UNGA played a critical role in restoring the PRC as the legitimate founding member and lawful occupier of the permanent seat in the UNSC and ensuing expulsion of Taiwan on 25 October 1971. That day, five African states (Botswana, Cameroon, Senegal, Sierra Leone, and Togo) changed their stance to defeat the procedural motion that qualified this issue as important and thus requiring 2/3 majority — the reason why the 21 previous attempts to change the status quo had failed. This opened the floor for the direct voting of the motion that became UNGA Resolution 2758 and encouraged other countries to change their stance. The resolution passed with 76 votes (notably three votes over 2/3 majority), having seven African states changed their vote to favor China: Rwanda, Sierra Leone, and Togo changed from 'no' to 'yes', and Botswana, Cameroon, Senegal, and Tunisia switched from abstention to

---

[28] El-Khawas, 'China's Changing,' p. 27.

[29] Mostly due to bad management and poor maintenance by local authorities, not only did the railway fail to serve the purpose for what it was built: transporting Zambian copper to the Indian Ocean; but also to this day the loan has not been repaid. What is more, additional Chinese funding had to be channelled to this project throughout the years to avoid its complete collapse and hence loss of face.

'yes'.[30] Meaningfully, according to D. Brautigam's records,[31] with the sole exception of Tunisia, all these countries seemed to have received Chinese assistance that same year or in the following two years.

From this point on, Chinese economic and technical assistance flows to Africa intensified significantly. According to CIA records cited by Yu, China's aid commitments between 1970 and 1977 totaled $1.9 billion spread across 29 countries.[32] Not surprisingly, the number of countries that established or restored diplomatic ties with China rose considerably during this period. By end of 1975, 37 out of 48 African countries had diplomatic ties with Beijing while only eight still recognized Taiwan.

By the twilight of Mao's rule, China's foreign policy had achieved major political goals set at the founding of the PRC: gain wider recognition and replace Taiwan in the United Nations. Although many other factors may have also concurred to this outcome, China's aid and financial assistance to African countries have undoubtedly played a significant role. Less successful, however, was China's attempt to organize an African front against the Soviet Union and supersede its influence on the continent and become the uncontested leader of the Third World — which may be explained by Moscow's much larger financial and logistic resources.

With the onset of economic reforms by Deng Xiaoping in 1978, Chinese foreign policy shifted away from ideological competition with the SU in Africa to focus on attracting capital and technology from Western developed countries, crucial for its domestic modernization. Nonetheless, China did not let go of its non-aligned credentials and ambitions to lead the Third World. In the midst of the normalization of relations with the US and the SU, Beijing launched in 1982 the guidelines of its new independent foreign policy, stressing the enduring validity of the 'Five Principles of Peaceful Coexistence'. This was followed by Zhao Ziyang's Africa tour to 11 countries, where he expounded China's new Africa policy. Much of the ideological baggage of the past was scrapped in favor of a much more pragmatic approach embedded in South–South cooperation narrative. Chinese aid in Africa became then focused on low profile projects requiring

---

[30]Mohamed A. El-Khawas, 'China's Changing,' pp. 26–27.
[31]Deborah Brautigam, *Rising China*, p. 210.
[32]George T. Yu, 'Africa in China's', p. 855.

smaller investments and quicker returns, with an emphasis on self-reliance and mutual benefit.[33] As a result China–Africa relations entered a period marked by small scale projects, reassessment of existing aid projects and the ensuing attempt to move away from one-way aid projects and concentrate instead on mutually beneficial arrangements involving namely the setting up of joint ventures, compensatory trade agreements and linking aid to investment.[34] Although this period may have been uneventful from a foreign policy outcome perspective, it was an important laboratory for the incubation of new policies and instruments marrying aid and investment[35] that would become the blueprint of China's development financing in the new century.

The Tiananmen massacre in 1989 brought this dormant period to a sudden end. In the aftermath of Tiananmen, China was faced with two major challenges in its foreign policy. First, how to circumvent western condemnation and sanctions and avoid becoming the new pariah as the last standing communist power in the post-Cold war setting. And second, how to counter Taiwan's increasingly efficient cheque book diplomacy in the battle for diplomatic recognition.

In response, China immediately launched a diplomatic offensive targeting the developing world. Chinese foreign minister Qian Qichen toured six African countries barely a month after the Tiananmen incident. The fact that this was the first Chinese high level visit to the continent in 25 years (Zhao Ziyang in 1963–1964) confirms the sudden upgrading of Africa in China's foreign policy in face of this new framework. From then on Qian visited Africa every year in January (by 1995 he had visited 36 African countries), a tradition that was followed by his successors.[36] Numerous African leaders were also invited to Beijing.

Aid to African states was promptly boosted, particularly to states that stood by China after the Tiananmen incident. In 1990, China–Africa aid reportedly totaled US$375 million spread across 46 states, up from

---

[33] See George T. Yu, 'Africa in China's', pp. 855–858; Deborah Brautigam, *Dragon's Gift*, pp. 52–66.
[34] For more detail on this phase, see Deborah Brautigam, *Dragon's Gift*, pp. 52–66
[35] Deborah Brautigam, *Dragon's Gift*, pp. 52–66.
[36] *Ibid.*, p. 68.

US$60 million across 13 states in 1988.[37] In the years that followed, framed by the on-going transformation from a planned economy to a socialist market, Beijing restructured the sources of funding of China's assistance. First, through the creation of a foreign aid fund with part of the interest-free repayments from developing countries, to help small and medium Chinese enterprises to form joint ventures or undertake cooperation projects in recipient countries; and more significantly through the extension of concessional loans by the China EXIM Bank from 1995 onwards,[38] which had been established the year before to promote Chinese imports and exports. This Bank would become in the new century the most prominent vehicle of Chinese development funding in Africa.

The boost in Chinese aid flows in the 1990s were warmly welcomed by Africans as they came at a time marked by SU's sudden collapse, the US withdrawal and Europe's disenchantment with the continent. Furthermore, Beijing's cause resonated with their own struggles against the developed world regarding democracy and human rights issues, so most African governments responded positively to Chinese economic statecraft, gladly rallying behind China. The swift revival of China's economic statecraft in Africa and other developing regions in the aftermath of the Tiananmen crisis enabled Beijing to evade the isolation imposed by the West and preempted a number of UN resolutions against China on human rights (and the Taiwan missile crisis) throughout the 1990s.

As for the diplomatic dispute with Taiwan, the winning of African hearts was not as clear cut with allegiance pragmatically following the highest bidder. While Taipei won back a number of African countries throughout the decade,[39] by the end of it, Beijing had recaptured half of them[40] plus a major

---

[37]Ian Taylor, 'The all-weather friend? Sino–African interaction in the 21st century', in *Africa in International Politics: External Involvement on the Continent*, Ian Taylor and Paul William, eds. (London: Routledge, 2004), p. 87.

[38]White paper on China's foreign aid issued by China's Information Office of the State Council on 21 April 2011 (Xinhua/China's Information Office of the State Council), available at: http://news.xinhuanet.com/english2010/china/2011-04/21/c_13839683_5.htm (accessed 19 June 2015).

[39]Burkina Faso, CAR, Chad, The Gambia, Guinea Bissau, Liberia, Lesotho, Niger, Senegal, Sao Tome & Principe.

[40]Guinea-Bissau, Lesotho, Liberia, Niger, Senegal.

weight on the continent: South Africa, all thanks to generous cooperation packages. The fact that only a handful of countries, all strategically unimportant, remained with Taipei, indicates that Beijing's economic incentives paid off well in this regard too.

Pursuing Primarily Economic Goals since the Turn of the Century

The formal establishment of the FOCAC in 2000 in Beijing inaugurated a new phase in China's foreign policy towards Africa, now increasingly driven by economic interests.

This dramatic remaking of relations was largely the result of the exponential growth of China's financial resources applied to the new foreign policy objectives driven by the Going Out policy. The immediate tactical goals were now primarily economic: open doors for Chinese companies and services overseas; find new markets for its exports, and last but not least facilitate access to much needed commodities (base metals and fossil fuels). In the political realm, the recognition battle with Taiwan continued to be the most immediate objective along with African support in multilateral fora. The underlying structural goal remained largely unchanged: to foster China's image as a key promoter of the developing world agenda and a major player in South–South cooperation.

By the turn of the century, China's exchange reserves totaled US$166 billion, up from US$30 billion, a decade earlier. By 2006, its FOREX reserves had reached one trillion and as of March 2016 it stands at US$3.3 trillion.[41] These unmatched financial resources enabled China to deploy economic statecraft instruments in an unprecedented scale to facilitate its new foreign policy goals on the continent.

These instruments naturally draw on China's past experiences, and hence most of the economic incentives targeting Africa in the early 2000s continued to be deployed under the foreign aid umbrella. Among them are numerous grants in kind (mostly funding prestige projects in Africa such as government buildings, stadiums, hospitals, and schools built with Chinese

---

[41] SAFE, FOREX Reserves, available at: http://www.safe.gov.cn/wps/portal/english/Data/Forex (accessed 20 April 2016).

materials and by Chinese companies), debt relief as well as interest-free loans, and generous low interest credit lines for much needed infrastructure development in Africa. While grants and debt forgiveness served mostly the purpose of improving China's image, garnering political capital on the continent and showcase their companies' work in an initial phase; soft loans for infrastructure enabled China to, in addition, open the African markets for its companies and goods as well as pursue resource security goals (namely, secure long term supply contracts and facilitated access to assets).[42]

China's growing financial might and search for new markets for its goods and companies coupled with the daunting infrastructure deficit on the African side,[43] contributed largely to the swift consolidation of development financing as China's most prominent positive economic statecraft tool on the continent in the new century.

Development Financing: The Paramount Economic Statecraft Instrument

As mentioned previously, the use of soft loans as an economic state-craft instrument resurfaced in the 1990s[44] in the wake of Tiananmen, and expanded rapidly after the establishment of China EXIM Bank. The EXIM was created in 1994, along with China Development Bank (CDB), to facil-itate China's domestic development, but as China's economy globalized they increasingly assumed the function of supporting China's developmen-tal policies overseas. China EXIM Bank holds the exclusive mandate for extending concessional loans[45] and preferential export buyers credit on

---

[42]Alves, SAJIA.

[43]According to World Bank estimates, by early 2000s Africa needed an annual investment of US$90 billion to bridge its infrastructure gap.

[44]See Peter Hubbard, 'Aiding transparency: What we can learn about China's Exim Bank concessional loans', Center for Global development Working Paper 126, 4 September 2007, available at: http://www.cgdev.org/files/14424_file_Aiding Transparency.pdf.

[45]In concessional loans the difference between the interest rate negotiated and the bench-mark of the People's Bank of China is subsidized by the Chinese state, enabling very low interest rates (Libor + 1.5% to 3%). These kind of loans are usually extended to low income countries.

behalf of the Chinese government as foreign aid.[46] As most African states are low-income countries, EXIM Bank came to hold the bulk of Chinese loans portfolio to Africa, while CDB occupied a prominent position in Latin America.

Drawing from figures released by Chinese authorities in 2011 and 2014 Foreign Aid white papers, Chinese concessional loans totaled roughly US$10.8 billion in the 15 years between 1995 and 2009, and an astonishing US$8 billion in the following three years (2010–2012). The figures also show a substantial growth in relative terms as in the second period concessional loans represented 56% of total aid up from 29% in the previous period, signaling the increasing importance of this particular economic statecraft instrument.

But, how much of these concessional loans actually went to Africa? The actual figure is difficult to establish as existing data is scarce and uneven, with Chinese official figures being in general more modest and regarded as less credible. For example, according to a recent independent study, China EXIM Bank alone lent $30.5 billion to African countries from 2001 to 2010 — triple the Chinese official figure for the period 1995–2009.[47] Chinese official sources (White Paper on China Africa Economic and Trade Cooperation, published in 2013) state that between 2010 and 2012 China approved $11.3 billion[48] in concessional loans to Africa (total of 92 projects), which does not tally with the official total figure of $8bn mentioned above and thus raises questions about its reliability.

Along with China EXIM Bank, CDB also has played a major role in extending countless commercial loans to African countries for infrastructure development, which in general still carry very competitive interest rates. Although commercial loans to developing countries are not formally included in its foreign aid sources, Beijing is very adamant in emphasizing

---

[46]China EXIM Bank, Preferential Facilities, available at: http://english.eximbank.gov.cn/tm/en-TCN/index_640.html.

[47]Jyhjong Hwang, Deborah Brautigam and Janet Eom, How Chinese Money is Transforming Africa: It's Not What You Think', China Africa Research initiative, policy Brief No. 11, April 2016, pp. 1–2.

[48]The word 'approved' may explain the evident discrepancy with the total figure provided earlier for the same period. This kind of incongruences and the lack of published aggregated data contribute toward the poor reliability of Chinese sources abroad.

the developmental ends they pursue. In Africa, China often combines commercial and concessional loans in one package, frequently reported in the media as one single loan. Quantifying and mapping Chinese commercial loans to Africa is even more complicated than concessional credit lines as in addition to the aforementioned misreporting, China has not published any official figures of these. The few existing estimates aggregate concessional and commercial credit lines and draw mostly on media surveys and an array of cross-validation techniques involving primary and secondary sources, which by its conservative nature are likely to underestimate the real figures. Brautigam and Gallagher[49] estimate that in the period 2003–2011, China has committed around US$53 billion in Africa in 317 loans across 43 countries. Among other interesting data in this short but very rich study comparing Chinese financing in Africa and LA reveal that most Chinese loans to Africa come from EXIM Bank; the bulk (56%) of these credit lines are backed by commodities[50]; and that nearly half of the credit lines were extended after the 2008 economic crisis to a handful of countries. This figure would place China's development financing roughly on par with the World Bank, which loans to Africa in the period 2000–2010 are estimated at US$54.7 billion.[51]

A more recent study led by D. Brautigam estimates that '(. . .) from 2000 to 2014 Chinese government, banks, and contractors extended US$86.9 billion worth of loans to African governments and state-owned enterprises (SOEs)'.[52] According to the same study, nearly US$60 billion (68%) originated from EXIM Bank and US$14 billion from CDB. Five countries alone account for over half of the loans: Angola (US$21 billion), Ethiopia

---

[49]Deborah Brautigam and Kevin P. Gallagher, 'Bartering Globalization: China's Commodity-Backed Finance in Africa and Latin America', *Global Policy*, 5, no. 3 (2014), pp. 348–349.

[50]*Ibid.*

[51]Fitch Ratings cited by Michael Cohen, 'China Exim loans to Sub-Sahara Africa exceed World Bank funds Fitch says', 28 December 2011, available at: http://www.bloomberg.com/news/articles/2011-12-28/china-exim-loans-to-sub-sahara-africa-exceed-world-bank-funds-fitch-says.

[52]Jyh Jong Hwang, Deborah Brautigam, and Janet Eom, 'How Chinese Money is Transforming Africa: It's not what you think', *Policy Brief*, no. 11 (China Africa Research Initiative, SAIS, Johns Hopkins University, 2016), p. 1.

(US\$12.3 billion), Sudan (US\$5.6 billion), Kenya (US\$5.2 billion), and the DRC (US\$4.9 billion).[53]

Regardless of what the real figure may be, the point of the matter is that the extension of infrastructure loans to Africa seem to have increased steadily since the turn of the century and appears to be intensifying since 2010. Evaluating by China's increasing financial support pledges within the FOCAC structure,[54] development financing (concessional and non-concessional) seems set to continue as a major resource in China's Africa foreign policy in years to come. Chinese concessional and non-concessional loans to Africa are structured in similar ways. They are in general ear-marked for economic and social infrastructure development, normally mega projects, and as corroborated above, repayment is often secured by commodities' exports to China. This formula derives from China's own past experiences, namely infrastructure-for-oil loans Beijing received from Japan in the 1970s[55] and its own loans to Africa in the 1960s and 1970s. Besides the different nature of the goals they pursue at present, the main differences are that the bulk of the loans conceded then by China were inter-est free while the present ones are concessional or commercial and much larger in volume and footprint.

China–Africa infrastructure loans (concessional and commercial) are normally rooted in two legal instruments: a framework cooperation agree-ment signed by the two governments stating the general terms (volume, pur-pose, interest rate, and maturity) and a loan agreement signed by a Chinese policy bank (China EXIM Bank or CDB) and the borrower (normally the Ministry of Finance of the recipient state). The repayment period of these loans in Africa are in general longer than in South America (most between

---

[53]*Ibid.*

[54]After committing \$5 billion in concessional loans and preferential export credits to Africa in the 2006 FOCAC summit, China has substantially expanded this fund in every subsequent meeting: to \$10 billion in 2009, \$20 billion in 2012, \$30 billion during Li Keqiang's visit to the headquarters of the African Union (AU) in May 2014, and to \$60 billion during the sev-enth FOCAC in Johannesburg in December 2015 (\$35 billion of which in preferential loans). Available at: FOCAC website: http://www.focac.org/eng/ltda/dwjbzjjhys_1/t1322068.htm (accessed 20 April 2016).

[55]D. Brautigam, *Dragon's Gift*, p. 47.

10 and 20 years).[56] They come often tied to a large quota of procurement of services and goods in China. The amount negotiated with African recipients is in general above 50% and the practice sometimes includes the import of Chinese labor. It is administered on a project basis through the borrower's account with China EXIM Bank in Beijing, and payments are made directly to Chinese contractors after completion of the construction project, meaning the capital never actually leaves China, reducing the chances of embezzlement.

These infrastructure loans are often secured by commodities to mitigate repayment risks in countries with low creditworthiness. This works by locking proceeds from the sale of commodities from the borrowing country to a Chinese SOE to service the loan. Oil is the most used collateral, but other commodities have been used as well (Cocoa-Ghana, Sesame-Ethiopia, copper-DRC, diamonds-Zimbabwe, etc.).[57] Although most contracts refer to a given volume of the selected commodity to service the loan, in most cases it is agreed that this figure will in fact fluctuate according to market prices oscillation, which may imply adjustments to the term of the loan.[58]

Africa was no stranger to this kind of deal as Western private banking institutions had been implementing this formula since the early 1990s to mitigate the risk of lending to resource-rich African governments (i.e., Angola) with low creditworthiness but strong background as commodities exporters.[59] Moreover, there are other states using the same facility, namely the Brazilian Development Bank (BNDES) with Angola, which it is seeking to replicate in Mozambique (coal) and Ghana (oil).[60]

The key difference of the Chinese version is that this mechanism is not used as a mere financing vehicle to support one specific project but a

---

[56]D. Brautigam and K.P. Gallagher, 'Bartering Globalization', p. 350.

[57]*Ibid.*

[58]Personal interview, Angolan oil sector expert, Luanda, Angola, 1 February 2011.

[59]For a detailed study on commodity-backed finance in Africa, see JBIC London Office, 'Commodity backed finance in sub-Saharan Africa', Research papers on Africa and Development, 20 October 2006.

[60]Personal interview, BNDES International Department, Rio de Janeiro, Brazil, 23 May 2012.

full-fledged economic statecraft instrument designed to pursue a number of foreign policy goals, most of which is in tandem with its Going Out policy agenda.

Over the past decade, this specific Chinese economic statecraft instrument has become a paramount feature in China–Africa relations, having greatly contributed to change the geopolitical, economic, and even the physical landscape of the continent. But how has it performed in relation to the immediate and structural foreign policy goals it was designed to pursue? For this purpose, a number of such deals in Africa are discussed in more detail below. The first countries to receive large loans in Africa in the early 2000s were oil-rich countries with established producing capacity, namely Angola, Sudan, and Nigeria. Angola was the first to receive a large scale soft loan from China to kick start the country's reconstruction after a nearly three decade conflict. The initial US$2 billion deal for infrastructure was signed with China EXIM Bank in early 2004.[61] The concessional loan (LIBOR + 1.25), was guaranteed by oil sales (equivalent to 10,000 barrels of oil per day) from Sonangol (national oil company) to a subsidiary of Sinopec (China's second largest national oil company) and tied to the sourcing of up to 70% of companies, materials (and labor) in China. Chinese construction companies disembarked in Angola soon after and, tellingly, Sinopec acquired its first asset in the Angolan oil industry (50% of Block 18) around the same time the loan was inked.[62] A disagreement, however, between Beijing and Luanda regarding the construction of a refinery led to souring of relations in 2007. Although additional multi-billion-dollar loans were signed with EXIM Bank and CDB in 2010 for infrastructure and agriculture development, Sinopec only managed to acquire more assets in the Angolan Oil industry after the extension of Chinese commercial loans to Sonangol in 2013–2015.

In Nigeria, Chinese National Oil Companies (NOCs: the China National Petroleum Corporation [CNPC], China National Offshore Oil Corporation [CNOOC], and Sinopec) were initially very successful in obtaining access to stakes in the oil industry in exchange for engaging in major infrastructure projects (Kaduna oil refinery, the Lagos–Kano 1350 km

---

[61] Followed by a second batch of $2.5 billion in 2007.

[62] Ana C. Alves, *The Oil Factor in Sino-Angolan Relations at the Start of the 21st Century*, Occasional Paper 55 (Johannesburg: SAIIA, 2010).

railway and Mambilla hydroelectric station).[63] The oil backed loans Obasanjo signed with China EXIM Bank for that purpose in 2006 reportedly totaled US$12 billion.[64] Most Chinese oil exploration contracts awarded by Obasanjo and loans signed under his rule were, however, frozen by his successor, Umaru Musa Yar'Adua, immediately after the elections in 2007, followed by a review of the Nigerian oil industry regulatory framework under Goodluck Jonathan. In a similar way, Chinese interests in Sudan suffered a major drawback with South Sudan's independence in 2011.

In an initial phase, China extended similar loans to minerals producers aimed at funding Greenfield mining projects and related infrastructure in exchange for mining concessions and secured by minerals supply. The largest ones were signed with Gabon and the DRC.

In Gabon, a Chinese consortium was granted in 2006; the concession to develop Belinga mine (among the largest known untapped iron ore deposits) and the off-taker rights in the sequence of a US$3 billion loan from China EXIM Bank signed with Omar Bongo.[65] The infrastructure to be developed included a new 560 km railway line linking Belinga to the Transgabonais, a deepwater mining harbor, a hydroelectric dam, and a steel mill. In September 2007, China signed a US$5 billion loan deal with the DRC, which was increased to US$9 billion in January 2008. The projects to be developed included a 3400 km highway, a 3200 km railway, and other social infrastructure. Sinohydro and the China Railway Engineering Corporation (CREC) were to undertake the infrastructure and the development of two mining concessions (copper and cobalt) in Katanga province, plus the off-taker rights.[66] Both loans were to be repaid with revenue obtained from the exploration of these concessions.

---

[63] For a detailed study on China's engagement in Nigeria, see G. Mthembu-Salter, *Elephants, Ants and Superpowers: Nigeria's Relations with China*, Occasional Paper 42 (Johannesburg: SAIIA, 2009).

[64] Personal interview, China Exim Bank Risk Analyst, Beijing, China, 26 August 2009.

[65] For a detailed study on China's engagement in Gabon, see Romain Dittgen, *To Belinga or Not to Belinga: China's Evolving Engagement in Gabon's Mining Sector*, Occasional Paper 98 (Johannesburg: SAIIA, 2011); Ana C. Alves, *China and Gabon*, China in Africa Project Policy Report 5 (Johannesburg: SAIIA, 2008).

[66] J. Bavier, 'China's DRC Investment $9 billion – $3 billion for mining', *Reuters-Kinshasa*, 16 February 2008, available at: http://www.mineweb.com/mineweb/view/mineweb/en/page67?oid=47452&sn=Detail.

In most cases, in addition to the long-term supply contracts, Chinese SOEs managed to acquire assets directly or indirectly through these loans, sparing them from having to compete with the more experienced and much better equipped (in terms of technology and expertise) international resource companies.[67]

While China's eagerness to provide cheaper and unconditional loans and willingness to embrace large infrastructure projects neglected by Western donors represented at first a valuable competitive advantage for Chinese extractive and construction companies in Africa (helping to offset their latecomer status on the continent), it did not always produce the desired outcome. This is the case with the DRC, where project development was delayed by traditional donors' pressure over Kinshasa to renegotiate the non-concessional contract, having the loan revised and downsized to US$6 billion in 2009. At the time of writing, the loan was only partially under implementation and the bulk of the loan yet to be released.[68] In Gabon, the Belinga project was postponed repeatedly due to persistent disagreements (regarding labor and environmental issues) and calls for renegotiation of the contract perceived by civil society as too favorable to China. The global commodity price volatility and the changing domestic political landscape (following Omar Bongo's death) have also added new risks and costs for the Chinese.[69] The contract has been revised twice (2009 and 2012)[70] and rumors have been circulating in the media that Gabon is on the lookout for an alternative partner.

Although those experiences have clearly exposed the vulnerabilities of this economic statecraft instrument in the volatile African context, this tool has performed relatively well, particularly in oil producing countries in regards to its immediate goals, in that it has produced long-term supply contracts and important oil equity (i.e., Angola and Sudan) as well as opened

---

[67]For details see Alves, Sinopec (Power & Alves).

[68]For more detail, see Johanna Jansson, 'The Sicomines Agreement Revisited: Prudent Chinese Banks and Risk-Taking Chinese Companies', *Review of African Political Economy*, 40, no. 135 (2013), pp. 152–162.

[69]See R. Dittgen, *To Belinga*.

[70]Agence France Press, 'Gabon renegotiating China mining deal', *News 24* (12 June 2012), available at: http://www.news24.com/Africa/News/Gabon-renegotiating-China-mining-deal-20120607.

the gates for Chinese construction companies, equipment, materials, and labor, which now dominate the construction market in most African countries that received these kind of credit lines. In sharp contrast, the loans structured around Greenfield mining projects (i.e., DRC and Gabon) seem to have become particularly problematic since production (and hence long-term supply and repayment) turned out very unpredictable. From a more structural point of view, China's initial political capital gains were to some extent eroded by a number of setbacks, namely, pressure from traditional donors (DRC), regime change and waning of political support (Nigeria), contract revision, and growing civil society criticism (Nigeria, Gabon).

The difficulties discussed and the increasing volatility of commodities markets following the onset of the global economic crisis at the end of 2008 led to a temporary halt in large-scale lending. That no large credit lines were extended by China to African countries in 2009 and 2010 (contrasting with the massive loans that China extended to NOCs in Brazil, Russia, and Kazakhstan during this same period) suggests that Beijing took a step back to reflect on the usefulness of this economic statecraft instrument in Africa. However, the downturn of commodities prices severely impacted African economies and compelled its leaders to knock at China's door for more funding, leading to a new wave of infrastructure loans from 2011 onwards, this time pushed largely by African demand. A number of shifts are, however, noticeable in regards to the general pattern of previous loans.

Among the first to rush to Beijing was Ghana, which approached CDB in 2009 to request a loan to fund the infrastructure necessary to develop the newly found Jubilee oil field in its offshore. The US$3 billion loan secured by crude sales (13,000 barrels per day — with UNIPEC as the offtaker)[71] took two years to negotiate. Its disbursal has been slow, hindered mostly by risk considerations on the Chinese side in the context of persistent low commodity prices. Although Chinese oil companies did not obtain any assets upstream parallel to the loan, the deal did enable Sinopec to enter the sector downstream as the contractor for the gas pipelines.

---

[71]Ministry of Finance, Republic of Ghana, 'US$ Billion Term Loan Facility Agreement Between China Development Bank and Government of Ghana — Summary', (accessed 20 May 2014), available at: http://www.mofep.gov.gh/?q=reports/cdb-loan-summary-050112.

The sharp dip in oil prices in 2008 also severely impacted the Angolan economy right when its large-scale infrastructure rehabilitation programme was at full steam. Being China's major partner in this endeavor, Dos Santos rushed to Beijing in December 2008 to ensure further Chinese funding. Despite the positive answer, this time around the new loans negotiations took two years, a sharp contrast with the few months that preceded the signing of the first loan in 2004. In 2011, Angola secured three infrastructure credit facilities with Chinese banks: US$3 billion with China EXIM Bank; US$2.5 billion with Industrial and Commercial Bank of China (ICBC) and US$1.5 billion with CDB, the latter allegedly not secured by oil sales but by a sovereign warranty.[72] As before, most of the projects are to be developed by Chinese construction companies with materials and labor sourced in China. Furthermore in December 2014[73] Sonangol, the country's oil parastatal, concluded a US$2 billion loan from CDB for asset development, logistics, and downstream operations.[74] Little is known, however, about the specifics of the deal, namely whether any Chinese NOC is to undertake any contract downstream or get a partnership with Sonangol in any oil blocks. This particular loan suggests that the model already applied in South America and Central Asia — direct loans to NOCs at higher interest rates (i.e., 6.5% in the loan to Petrobras) and tied to an oil collateral — is now being transferred to Africa. The reprise of the sharp dip in oil prices in the second half of 2014 led to another official visit to Beijing by Dos Santos in June 2015, allegedly to finalize a US$4.5 billion loan to build a much needed hydropower scheme (to be built by a Chinese construction company), and look for funding for other infrastructure projects.[75] These loans still entail

[72]Ana C. Alves, 'Taming the dragon: Sinopec's interests in Angola', *China and Angola: A Marriage of Convenience*, Ana C. Alves and Marcus Power, eds. (Cape Town: Fahamu, 2012).

[73]According to news circulated in Lusophone media this loan had been in the pipeline since mid-2013.

[74]Portal Angop, 'China concede credito de 2 bilioes de dolares a Sonangol', Portal de Angola, 12 December 2014, available at: http://www.portaldeangola.com/ 2014/12/china-concede-credito-de-dois-bilioes-de-dolares-a-sonangol/.

[75]Reuters, 'Angola's dos Santos in China Seeking cash for ailing economy', 9 June 2015 (accessed 15 June), available online at: http://uk.reuters.com/article/ 2015/06/09/angola-china-idUKL5N0YV1R220150609.

procurement of majority of construction services and equipment in China and Sinopec has since been able to acquire two additional oil stakes.

Nigeria is also part of this list. In February 2012, Lagos announced it was negotiating a US$3 billion loan with China Exim Bank and the CDB for the completion of various infrastructure projects in the fields of oil and gas, energy, transportation, aviation, education, and agriculture.[76] The final agreement, however, contemplated only a US$1.1 billion low interest credit line, which was signed in July 2013.

While this new batch of loans has been pushed mostly by African leaders demand, China has been very keen to reassure its African peers of its willingness to help in times of need so as to consolidate its credentials as an all-weather friend. In May 2014, Premier Li Keqiang announced in a speech at the African Union that another US$10 billion had been added to the US$20 billion African loans fund announced at the 2012 FOCAC interministerial conference,[77] and during the 2015 FOCAC in South Africa, Xi Jinping announced that the figure had been increased to US$60 billion.

In tandem with the unfolding of Xi Jinping's 'One Belt, One Road' initiative, the latest batch of infrastructure loans have been struck in Eastern Africa, contemplating mega-transportation and energy projects. Kenya signed in August 2013 an MoU with China for a loan facility of US$5 billion, allegedly to fund 85% of a railroad linking the port of Mombasa to Uganda and some power projects, which contracts have been granted to Chinese companies. In May 2014, during Premier Li Keqiang's visit to Kenya, a MoU was signed with Kenya, Rwanda, Uganda, and South Sudan to extend the railway line to the neighboring countries in an effort to improve transport links and facilitate access to sea routes to landlocked countries in the region.[78] Uganda has in the meanwhile signed MoUs with Chinese companies to undertake the job within its frontiers and is currently courting

---

[76] Nse Anthony-Uko, 'Nigeria: President Jonathan Finalises US$1.1 Billion Loan Deal With China', all Africa, 21 July 2013 (accessed 20 May 2014), available at: http://allafrica.com/stories/201307110351.html.

[77] The BRICS Post, 'China increases African loan to $30 billion', 6 May 2014, available at: http://thebricspost.com/china-increases-african-loan-to-30-bn/#.VZzHGRuqqko.

[78] Reuters, 'China east African leaders sign up for new rail link', 11 May 2014, available at: http://www.reuters.com/article/2014/05/11/us-kenya-china-idUSBREA4A03F20140511.

China for an US$8 billion concessional loan to that effect.[79] Museveni has already secured US$1.4 billion (part concessional, part at 4% interest rate) from China EXIM Bank to fund 85% of the construction of Karuma hydropower project to be built by Sinohydro.[80] The loan that had been in negotiation since 2013 was signed with EXIM bank in 2014 and approved by Ugandan parliament in March 2015.[81] Uganda is expecting its first oil output from Lake Albert in 2016, where CNPC is one of the main developers. Ethiopia has also signed a loan agreement with China for another railway line linking Addis to Djibouti.

This growing African appetite for Chinese cheap infrastructure loans may, however, represent a double edge sword for Beijing as it attempts to improve the transportation infrastructure in this part of Africa. While these loans allow China to tighten the bows with African elites in need, they are increasingly under scrutiny by African civil society regarding, namely, the terms of the deal, debt sustainability, environmental, and social impact. Moreover, some Chinese loans that are earmarked for contentious dams and irrigation projects in highly volatile border regions (i.e., Lake Turkana) threaten to drag China into African regional conflicts, which could seriously harm its interests on the continent in the long term.[82]

Assessing the Performance of China's Development Finance since the Founding of the PRC

Until the turn of the century, Chinese economic incentives in Africa pursued a manifest political agenda, namely to gain wider international recognition

---

[79] James Kynge, 'Uganda turns East: China will build infrastructure says Museveni', *Financial Times*, 21 October 2014, available at: http://www.ft.com/ intl/cms/s/0/ab12d8da-5936-11e4-9546-00144feab7de.html#axzz3fHzKRRom.

[80] Bloomberg, 'China's Xi finds eight good reasons to host Uganda's president', 1 April 2015, available at: http://www.bloomberg.com/news/articles/2015-04-01/china-s-xi-finds-eight-good-reasons-to-host-uganda-s-president.

[81] Samuel Nabwiiso, 'Ugandan MPs approve loan for new dam', available at: East Africa Business Week, http://www.busiweek.com/index1.php?Ctp=2&pI=3030&pLv=3&srI=68&spI=107.

[82] Peter Bossard, 'Chinese loans could fuel regional conflict in East Africa', China Dialogue, 14 January 2013, http://www.chinadialogue.net/article/show/single/en/5601-Chinese-loans-could-fuel-regional-conflict-in-East-Africa.

and replace Taiwan at the UNSC; outrun the Soviet Union in the leadership of the international socialist movement and the Third World; and in the 1990s to circumvent Western criticism in the wake of Tiananmen and counter Taiwan's cheque book diplomacy on the continent. As discussed earlier, Chinese economic incentives appear to have been instrumental in achieving immediate political goals. As for the long-term goals, while it may not have turned the balance in its favor in regard to the competition with the Soviet Union, it did, nonetheless, grant the PRC solid anti-colonialist and third world champion credentials as a key promoter and defender of the developing world agenda in the eyes of successive generations of African leaders. The fact that to this day African leaders frequently mention in their official speeches their gratitude for China's support to liberation movements and its selfless commitment to African projects neglected by the West, attest to the immense political capital China has garnered through economic incentives in previous decades.

As emphasized earlier, the economic agenda has gained increasing weight in Chinese foreign policy toward Africa since the turn of the century. At the tactical level, Chinese infrastructure loans in Africa have had mixed results so far. If on the one hand, they did successfully open the gates for Chinese companies, technology and goods to penetrate African markets in the construction sector and increasingly in the oil industry upstream and downstream, ensuring China's energy security has been less consequential. A significant part of the assets acquired in parallel to these deals is yet to start producing or was lost (particularly the mining deals); and the bulk of the oil produced by Chinese companies or acquired as collateral through loan guarantee mechanisms end up sold in international markets (better priced) instead of being shipped back to China (lower profit margins owing to subsidized prices and transport costs).[83]

At the structural level, although success remains uncertain at this early stage, Chinese infrastructure loans have clearly been a critical tool in consolidating Beijing's political capital among the continent's elites particularly

---

[83]The State Council Information Office, PRC, *China's Energy Policy 2012*, October 2012, http://www.china.org.cn/government/whitepaper/node_7170375.htm (accessed 20 April 2016); Chi Zhang, *The Domestic Dynamics of China's Energy Diplomacy* (Singapore: World Scientific Press, 2015), pp. 198–199; Bo Kong, *China's International Petroleum Policy* (Santa Barbara, CO: Praeger Security International, 2010), p. 93.

in the current financial contraction context inducing greater reliance on Beijing. China's economic statecraft has also been instrumental in facilitating Africa's geopolitical turn to the East and away from Western donors and development finance institutions, as Beijing's development financing come with no political or macroeconomic stability impositions and is in general perceived as offering easier repayment terms. Attesting to its growing clout, China has largely enjoyed African support in its Global South leadership role. The loans have been, however, less consequential in winning the hearts and minds of regular Africans who remain wary of China's collusion with corrupt elites in power, and the negative social and environmental impact or lack of positive spillovers of these loans in their daily lives. This has increasingly affected China's image on the continent in recent years.

As for noticeable shifts, Chinese development financing seem to be moving away from mega-mining greenfield projects and partnerships with local state companies, to favor established oil-producing countries, but also new producers (Uganda, Niger, and Mozambique) as they appear to offer a more leveled playground for latecomers like China. Infrastructure-for-oil loans appear to be much easier to manage, more effective in terms of locking in supply and therefore more reliable as a resource-backed financing instrument. The longer negotiating periods of this new batch of loans and the fact that it was triggered by the borrowers also suggests that Chinese banks have become more wary of African business risks and therefore more cautious and thorough when negotiating new credit lines.

Notwithstanding, other Chinese banks have joined China EXIM Bank in financing infrastructure in Africa in this second phase, namely CDB (until recently most active in South America and Central Asia). As a result, concessional loans (a privilege of EXIM Bank) seem to be gradually giving way to the extension of credit lines in more commercial terms, or packages combining the two formats. In addition, an increasing quota of the projects are to be funded by the recipient country (10%–15%), indicating a drive to share responsibilities and risks with the borrower. Oil backed loans seem to have also dropped the goal of facilitating the access of Chinese SOEs to equity assets. Chinese companies appear to be increasingly confident in venturing out on their own on the continent. Through mergers and acquisitions, they have gathered a significant portfolio in Africa in recent years, benefitting from the financial contraction and ensuing divesting strategies of Western resource companies.[84] The new loans seem to focus instead in securing mid and downstream contracts (i.e., Ghana and Nigeria) for its oil companies.

The shifts highlighted earlier in the new batch of infrastructure loans indicate that some of the shortcomings at the tactical level have been acknowledged by Beijing and are already being addressed in an effort to fine-tune this economic statecraft tool. On the other hand, little seems to have been done to address challenges at the grassroots level, which may undermine China's image as a reliable development partner in the long run.

Concluding Remarks

The earlier analysis demonstrates that despite some failures (i.e., outcompeting SU influence over the continent in the 1960s and 1970s), the use of economic incentives has been relatively successful in pursuing Chinese foreign policy tactical goals mentioned above over the two periods. Not only did it win African support for most its political struggles in the 20th century as it succeeded in opening the gates for its companies, services and goods in the continent in the 2000s. Moreover, while it may have lost the battle with the SU in Africa, it has been much more consequential than Moscow[85] in mobilizing at present the political capital accumulated in those years, not only to promote its economic interests on the continent but also its image as a peer and a viable alternative to Western-dominated financial institutions.

Although many argue that Chinese and Western capital complement rather than compete with each other in Africa owing to the massive infrastructure gap, one cannot ignore that there are underlying doctrinal and operational tensions. Chinese capital privileges the development of hard economic and social infrastructure with no conditions attached, whereas traditional donors tend to privilege the strengthening of public financial management systems, anticorruption institutions, transparency and other good-governance initiatives. There are also stark differences in regards to environmental and procurement standards. The fact that over the past

---

[84]Ana C. Alves, *China's economic statecraft and African mineral resources: Changing Modes of Engagement*, SAIIA Occasional Paper (Johannesburg: SAIIA, January 2013).
[85]Ana C. Alves, Russia in Africa, SAIIA, 2013.

15 years, China has established itself as a prominent development financing provider on the continent, clearly indicates African siding on this matter. Attempts to smooth out the differences between the two paradigms such as the Busan dialogue on aid effectiveness in 2011, have served only to demonstrate how African and other developing countries rally behind Beijing to uphold the values and practices of South–South cooperation, which development financing practices have been spearheaded by Chinese infrastructure loans.

While Chinese development financing rules have been largely implemented on a bilateral basis so far, the establishment of alternative Chinese-led multilateral developmental banking institutions in 2015[86] such as the Asia Infrastructure Investment Bank (AIIB), the BRICS New Development Bank (NDB), and the Silk Road fund indicate China's readiness to take its quest to reform international development finance landscape to the next level. These alternative Chinese development banking institutions are expected to fund major infrastructure projects linking Asia to Europe, Middle East, and East Africa in the framework of Xi Jinping's 'One Belt, One Road' vision, which is increasingly regarded as China's 'Marshall Plan' and way out of the current economic slowdown. China's development financing in Africa is thus not only a tool to expand Beijing's clout over the continent and the developing world in general but also carry the seeds that may revolutionize global financial governance and international economic and information routes that have been so far dominated by Western interests and doctrine.

---

[86]Instead of just giving more resources to existing banking institutions dominated by Western donors.

Part Four
China's Economic Statecraft
in the Global Context

Chapter 10

China's Economic Power and the Global Financial Structure

Gerald Chan

This chapter aims to capture the evolving relationship between a rising China and the global financial structure. It does so in two main parts: the first part deals with China's involvement in the global financial structure, with a primary focus on the country's relations with the International Monetary Fund (IMF) and a secondary focus on its relations with the Group of 20 industrialized countries (G20); the second part analyzes China's regional involvement, focusing on the Chiang Mai Initiative Multilateralization (CMIM). The theme running through the chapter addresses these questions: What has China done to enhance its standing in the financial world? Why has it achieved only moderate success so far? The chapter begins by introducing China as a rising economic power and by placing it within the current global financial structure.

China's Economic Power

China's economic power has risen very rapidly in the recent past. A brief account suffices to attest to this: the country is as of early 2014 the second largest trading nation after the United States, with Japan standing at number three. According to the IMF, the Gross Domestic Product (GDP) figures for these three countries in 2012 were US$16,244,575 million;

US$8,221,015 million; and US$5,960,269 million.[1] In November 2012, the OECD forecasted that China would surpass the United States as the largest economy by 2016, measured in purchasing-power-parity terms.[2] On 30 April 2014, however, the *Financial Times* reported that the United States was on the brink of losing its status as the world's largest economy, and that it would slip behind China in 2014, according to the World Bank.[3] The United States had been the global leader since overtaking the United Kingdom in 1872.[4] Bloomberg reported that China surpassed the United States as the world's biggest trading nation in 2012 when measured by total trade: the sum of exports and imports.[5] In early 2013, the US Commerce Department said that America's exports and imports in 2012 totaled US$3.82 trillion, while China's customs administration said that their country's total trade in 2012 amounted to US$3.87 trillion.

In addition, China has become one of the most important investors in the world. According to United Nations Conference on Trade and Development (UNCTAD) in 2012, the United States topped the list of the total amount of inward and outward foreign direct investment flows amounting to US$167.62 billion; China was second with US$121.08 billion; and Hong Kong was third with US$74.584 billion.[6] The combined total of China and

---

[1] 'World economic outlook database (October 2013 edition): report for selected countries and subjects', *IMF Data and Statistics*, available at: https://www.imf.org/external/pubs/ft/weo/2013/02/weodata/index.aspx (accessed 26 December 2013).

[2] 'Balance of economic power will shift dramatically over the next 50 years, says OECD', *OECD* (9 November 2012), available at: http://www.oecd.org/newsroom/ balance-ofeconomicpowerwillshiftdramaticallyoverthenext50yearssaysoecd.htm (accessed 28 April 2016).

[3] Chris Giles, 'China poised to pass US as world's leading economic power this year', *Financial Times* (30 April 2014), available at: http://www.ft.com/intl/cms/s/2/d79fff8-cfb7-11e3-9b2b-00144feabdc0.html#axzz47iFRoaZa.

[4] *Ibid.*

[5] 'China eclipses US as biggest trading nation', *Bloomberg News* (11 February 2013), available at: http://www.bloomberg.com/news/2013-02-09/china-passes-u-s-to-become-the-world-s-biggest-trading-nation.html (accessed 28 April 2016).

[6] 'Inward and outward foreign direct investment flows and stock, annual, 1970–2012', *Knoema* (9 July 2013), available at: http://knoema.com/UNCTADFDI2013/inward-and-outward-foreign-direct-investment-flows-and-stock-annual-1970-2012; http://unctadstat.unctad.org/TableViewer/tableView.aspx (assessed 27 December 2013).

Hong Kong would then in theory have overtaken that of the United States. Above all, China has the largest foreign exchange reserves, some US$3.21 trillion in March 2016.[7] Although these economic indicators and forecasts must be read with extreme caution for various obvious reasons, they do point to the fact that the existing economic system is severely challenged by China's rapid rise.

The Global Financial Structure

The current global economic structure inherits the legacies of the Bretton Woods system set up shortly after the Second World War. The tripartite system consists of the World Bank, the IMF, and the World Trade Organization (WTO, which replaced the General Agreement on Tariffs and Trade in 1995). China joined the World Bank and the IMF in 1980 and the WTO in 2001. In the global financial structure, the IMF is the most important institution. The G20 also plays an important part in paving the way for the development of global finance in recent times. The G20 is an expanded group of the Group of Eight industrialized countries (G8) led by the United States and its allies. The G8, beginning to take proper shape since 1994, found it necessary in 2008 to include the emerging economies (including the BRICS countries consisting of Brazil, Russia, India, China, and South Africa) to discuss global economic issues. The relationship between the G8 and the G20 is one of coordination. The interdependent relationship is such that policy influence flows from the G8 to the G20 much more than the other way round. In a way, the 12 middle economic powers and the emerging economies have been successfully absorbed by the highly industrialized eight to form the G20.

Apart from this mainstream development, there are many regional financial institutions, which look after the financial affairs in their respective regions, mostly in coordination with the IMF. These include the Asian Development Bank, the European Central Bank, the Islamic Development Bank, and others. In Asia, China plays a significant part in the formation

---

[7] 'China foreign exchange reserves: 1980–2016', *Trading Economics* (2016), available at: http://www.tradingeconomics.com/china/foreign-exchange-reserves (accessed 27 April 2016).

and development of the Chiang Mai Initiative Multilateralization (CMIM), a mechanism dubbed as a mini-IMF in Asia. A more recent development is China's establishment of the Asian Infrastructure Investment Bank (AIIB) in early 2015, with 57 countries signing up as founding members, including many industrialized countries in the West.[8] The major exceptions are the United States and Japan. Both have reservations about China's financial rise and its standard of financial governance with regard to operational transparency, labor standards, and environment protection.

Since 1980, China has increased its participation in the activities of the world financial structure, even though the size and efficacy of China's involvement have remained limited, for domestic as well as external reasons. China's own capabilities and policy preferences account for some of the domestic constraints, while the embedded interests of the established powers in the global financial system put an external limit to what China can do. Figure 10.1 captures the main features of China's involvement in the global and regional financial structures, including the CMIM and the AIIB.

China and the IMF

In commensuration with its rising economic power, China strives to enhance its influence in the IMF, as part of an overall effort to boost its global politico-economic standing. It wants to raise its voice and increase its voting power in the organization. China's effort in this respect can be seen from three ways: its monetary contributions, its personnel contributions, and its policy inputs to the organization.

China's monetary contributions can be assessed in two streams: one is its regular contributions as a member state; the other is its additional contributions made through the purchase of IMF bonds or other products. The regular contributions are very much tied to the existing system of quota rights and voting rights. Reforms in these quota and voting rights are at present ongoing, even though running into obstacles (discussed later in the

---

[8]For a succinct commentary on the AIIB, see June Teufel Dreyer, 'The Asian Infrastructure Investment Bank: who will benefit?', *Foreign Policy Research Institute* (April 2015), available at: http://www.fpri.org/article/2015/04/the-asian-infrastructure-investment-bank-who-will-benefit/.

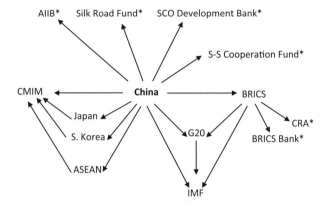

Figure 10.1. A model of China's multilateral financial involvement.

⟶ Direction of China's desired flow of its influence

*These are new initiatives made by China since 2013.

Abbreviations: AIIB, Asian Infrastructure Investment Bank; CMIM, Chiang Mai Initiative Multilateralization; CRA, Contingency Reserve Arrangement; SCO (Shanghai Cooperation Organization) Development Bank.

Source: Author's own drawing.

Notes: G20 holds 65.8% of the quotas and 64.7% of the votes of the IMF.[9] The establishment of the South–South Cooperation Fund was announced by President Xi Jinping in his first address to the UN General Assembly on 28 September 2015; China has formed more than a dozen or so bilateral financial arrangements with individual countries or groups of countries. It has also exercised its loan extension through such big state-owned banks as the China Development Bank and the Export-Import Bank of China.

chapter). Regarding additional contributions, China has come under some external pressure to help a few member states, but it is subject to domestic pressure to devote resources to internal financial development, in addition to the need to justify the exchange of such contributions for a greater say in the IMF. For example, to tackle the global financial crisis, some rich countries pledged to contribute US$500 billion to the IMF in 2009: the European Union and Japan each pledged US$100 billion and China pledged US$40 billion.[10] At the G20 Summit held in Los Cabos, Mexico, in 2012,

---

[9]C. Randall Henning, 'Coordinating regional and multilateral financial institutions', Peterson Institute for International Economics Working Paper No. 11-9 (March 2011), p. 3.

[10]Gerald Chan, Pak K. Lee, and Lai-Ha Chan, *China Engages Global Governance: A New World Order in the Making?* (London and New York: Routledge, 2013), p. 66.

China revised its contribution up to US$43 billion, while other emerging economies such as Brazil, India, Russia, and Mexico each offered US$10 billion.[11]

China's personnel and policy contributions have been very limited, compared with major powers in the West. In 2013, the IMF staffing situation shows that about 70% of managerial staff (economists and specialized career posts) come from advanced economies, while 30% come from developing countries.[12] The representation of Asians among the IMF staff is relatively low given the region's fast-growing economic size, despite an increase from around 15% in 2006 to about 20% in 2010.[13] China's highest-ranking official in the IMF is Zhu Min. He was appointed special advisor to the then-managing director Dominique Strauss-Kahn of the IMF in 2010. When Christine Lagarde became the new managing director in mid-2011, Zhu was made one of the three deputy managing directors, ranking after the first deputy managing director.[14] Zhu was the first Chinese national to make it to such a high position in the IMF. Before he joined the IMF, he was a deputy governor of the People's Bank of China, China's central bank. Zhu has spoken on a number of media occasions in the recent past, including a BBC interview in Davos at the 2014 World Economic Forum,[15] on the need to increase the quota and voice of emerging economies in the IMF. Apart from that and other commentaries on the global economy and the state sector influence on the Chinese economy, it is not clear from available public sources what he has done to introduce major policy changes in the IMF.

---

[11]Ding Yifan, 'China's IMF contribution, a move of multiple-layered meaning', *China US Focus* (13 July 2012), available at: http://www.chinausfocus.com/foreign-policy/chinas-imf-contribution-a-move-of-multiple-layered-meaning/ (accessed 28 April 2016).

[12]See 'Web Table 5.3: distribution of IMF staff by developing countries and advanced economies', *IMF* (30 April 2013), available at: http://www.imf.org/external/pubs/ft/ar/2013/eng/pdf/webtable53.pdf (accessed 28 April 2016).

[13]Deepanshu Bagchee, 'Asia remains under-represented at the IMF: experts', *CNBC* (2 September 2011), available at: http://www.cnbc.com/id/44504069 (accessed 28 April 2016).

[14]'Senior Officials of the International Monetary Fund', *IMF* (6 April 2016), available at: https://www.imf.org/external/np/sec/memdir/officers.htm (accessed 28 April 2016).

[15]'Davos 2014: what does "reshaping the world" theme mean?', *BBC News* (22 January 2014), available at: http://www.bbc.co.uk/news/business-25842811 (accessed 28 April 2016).

On the quota and voice reform in the IMF, Zhu pointed out during a BBC interview that US Congress had been stalling the reform process by blocking the government's proposal to adjust the quota and voting shares, thus rendering any future reform more distant. It seems that it is not only the United States which is doing so; parliaments of other countries in the developed West are inclined to do likewise, because established powers are reluctant to give away their vested interests and privileges. An often-cited example of this uneven distribution of voice and vote is Belgium — a relatively small economy in Europe, whose share of vote and voice is greater than that of Brazil, a relatively huge rising economy. In 2012, Belgium's GDP, measured in nominal terms, ranked 25th in the world, according to the IMF. However, it currently has 1.86% of the total votes in the IMF, larger than Brazil's 1.72%,[16] though Brazil ranked seventh in the world's GDP in that year.

So far the Chinese government does not seem to have made any open, concrete suggestion as to exactly what China wants in the reform of the voting powers in the IMF, apart from saying that it needs to be changed to reflect more accurately the current economic power situation in the world. China's official view is in line with the views of many other emerging economies like India, Brazil, and Russia. Speaking in the Asia Society Hong Kong Center on 10 September 2012, Arvind Subramanian, an economist from the Peterson Institute of International Economics in Washington DC, suggested something tangible. He said that China should be empowered to contribute to the open economy of the world. If China is given a veto power in the IMF, it can make greater contributions to the global economy.[17] China's share of the votes in the IMF should at least be more than 15% (as major decisions in the IMF need to have 85% of votes to pass, according to its constitution). This would translate into a hefty rise from China's

---

[16]'IMF members' quotas and voting power, and IMF board of governors', *IMF* (4 May 2016), available at: http://www.imf.org/external/np/sec/memdir/members.aspx (assessed 28 April 2016).

[17]Wendy Tang, 'Subramanian: renminbi will become world's reserve currency', *Asia Society* (10 September 2012), available at: http://asiasociety.org/hong-kong/subramanian-renminbi-will-become-world%E2%80%99s-reserve-currency (accessed 28 April 2016).

holding of around 3.9% at present.[18] Established powers would have to forego substantial existing voting powers, and these powers would include not only the United States but also many European countries. The United States may not have to give up some of its voting powers, since it is a net contributor to the IMF based on its GDP strength. It is the Western European powers which have to sustain the bulk loss of voting powers if a realignment of voting powers according to GDP strengths is to take place. Subramanian's suggestion, pleasant to the ears of leaders in China and in other emerging powers, is unlikely to be accepted by decision-makers in Europe, apart from those in the United States and some oil-rich countries in the Middle East. Perhaps a progressive increase over an extended period of time might be a way out to partially satisfy the demands of the rising powers, but certainly a lot of bargaining and negotiations would be needed over a long stretch of time to come to that sort of fair situation.

Figure 10.2 shows the projected result, if the 2010 agreed governance reform were to be adopted by 2012. That projected result would have put China behind the United States and Japan as the third largest holder of quota and voting shares in the IMF. Besides, the 2010 reform would have doubled the IMF quota to raise its equity capital to US$720 billion. It would have shifted 6% of total quota to developing countries, and moved 2 of 24 IMF directorships from European to development countries.[19] However, up till early 2016, the agreed reform had not been implemented, as pointed out earlier. In actual practice, China's quota and voting shares had fell behind the United States, Japan, Germany, France, and the United Kingdom in early 2016. Its respective shares stand at 3.994% and 3.803%.[20] The fact that previous reform agreements made in 2010 have not been implemented means that any future reform program would be further delayed.

One of the measurements suggested for making adjustments to the IMF quotas and shares is based on the GDPs of member states. If such a single

---

[18] 'Quota and voting shares before and after implementation of reforms agreed in 2008 and 2010', *IMF*, available at: http://www.imf.org/external/np/sec/pr/2011/pdfs/quota_tbl.pdf (accessed 28 April 2016).

[19] Robert Harding, 'US fails to approve IMF reforms', *Financial Times* (14 January 2014), available at: http://www.ft.com/intl/cms/s/0/8d4755ee-7d43-11e3-81dd-00144feab dc0.html#axzz47iFRoaZa.

[20] 'Quota and voting shares'.

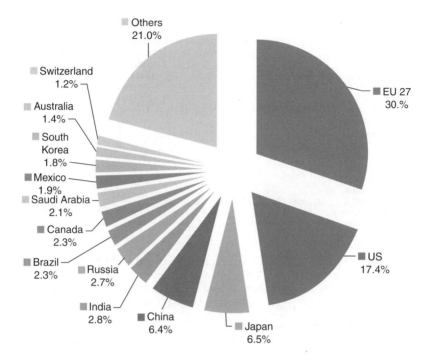

Figure 10.2. Projected quota shares in the IMF after the reform agreed in 2010 for implementation by 2012.

Source: 'Quota and voting shares before and after implementation of reforms agreed in 2008 and 2010', IMF (2011), p. 1.

measurement were to be adopted to make changes, then a picture of the subsequent winners and losers would look like those shown in Fig. 10.3. The winners, apart from China as a lead beneficiary, would include the United States as the second beneficiary. Oil-rich Saudi Arabia and many European countries would lose their shares.

The Asian Financial Structure

The Asian economic structure comprises the financial, developmental, and trading parts. China's involvement in this structure can be viewed from the perspective of the Chiang Mai Initiative, the Asian Development Bank, and various trading pacts in the region such as the Asia-Pacific Economic Cooperation, the Pacific Economic Cooperation Council, the Trans-Pacific

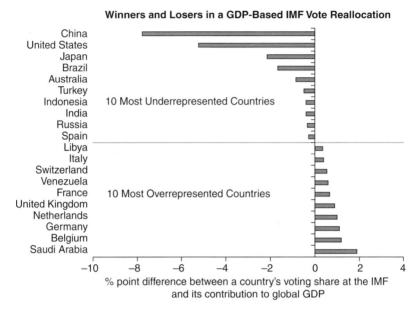

Figure 10.3. A hypothetical change based on using GDPs to distribute voting powers.

Source: Benn Steil and Dinah Walker, 'A GDP-based IMF would boost China's voice …and America's', *Council on Foreign Relations* (22 January 2013), available at: http://blogs.cfr.org/geographics/2013/01/22/gdpimf/ (accessed 28 April 2016).

Partnership, the Regional Comprehensive Economic Partnership, and many other free trade agreements. Figure 10.4 shows the major components of this structure.

China was slow to take part in the making and shaping of the Asian economic structure. This is partly due to its initial slow economic growth in the first three decades after the Second World War; partly due to its relatively timid diplomatic style; and partly due to Japan's much more active engagement in trade and investment in Asia before and during China's recent rise. It was Japan which initially proposed some form of financial integration in the region in the 1980s, but the country's proposal initially received lukewarm responses from the United States and China. The US concern was that it might lose its influence in Asia to others, including Japan. China, however, was concerned about Japan's dominance in Asia.

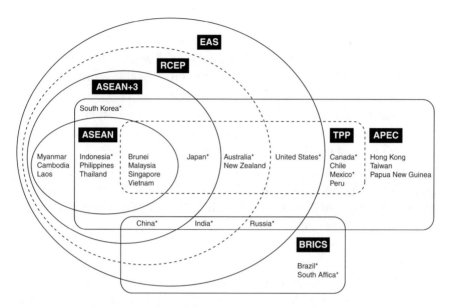

Figure 10.4.   The Asian economic structure.

Notes: *G20 members — Trade agreement/negotiation group.

Source: Theresa Robles and Kaewkamol Pitakdumrongkit (eds.), 'Governance of East Asian regional economic architectures', RSIS Policy Report (November 2013), adapted from Australian Government Department of Foreign Affairs and Trade.

China changed its attitude gradually as it rose in economic prominence after adopting a reform and opening up policy in the late 1970s and as it faced the demand for regional collective action subsequent to the Asian financial crisis of 1978–1979. China's more active involvement in the Chiang Mai Initiative can be seen against this backdrop.

China and the CMI[21]

The CMIM is the only such organization in Asia, which performs some functions similar to that of the IMF, but on a much smaller scale and within the Asian region. It aims to help member countries to combat possible

---

[21] For a more detailed background, see Gerald Chan, 'China's response to the global financial crisis and its regional leadership in East Asia', *Asia Europe Journal*, no. 9(2), (2012), pp. 197–209.

shortfalls in financial liquidity, as an insurance policy subsequent to the Asian financial crisis of the late 1990s. China, Japan, and South Korea are the large contributors to the funding of the CMIM, with the ASEAN 10 countries contributing in different sliding scales by groups roughly according to their different economic sizes. Their borrowing limits are also tied roughly in proportion to their financial contributions to the organization. China and Japan play major roles in the organization, in terms of contributions in money and personnel, if not in policy inputs.

The organization is yet to be tested on several grounds. First, it is still relatively young, being institutionalized in 2010 as the CMIM. Second, the collective pool of funds is still very small, US$120 billion rising to US$240 billion in late 2014. Third, since its formation, Asian countries have not been really challenged by any major economic crisis. The side effects of the global financial crisis in 2008–2009 affected European countries the most, leaving Asian countries largely unscathed. Fourth, and more recently, because of the political disputes between China and Japan, progress in the further development of the CMIM might have been slowed down. Furthermore, the borrowing from the CMIM is at present tied to the IMF: the amount of delink was 30% in 2012 rising to 40% by 2014. Many members of the CMIM have also set up currency swaps with major trading partners outside the grouping. This situation can be interpreted in two rather contradictory ways: one is that the role of the CMIM is being diminished; the other, currency swaps serves as a supplementary means to ameliorate possible financial difficulties.

To address the perceived imbalance in representation in the existing global financial system, China's relative dominant position in the CMIM notwithstanding, the country seemingly adopts a three-thronged approach. First, it aims to strengthen the collective bargaining position of the emerging economies. This is being done in several ways, including the pulling of resources of the BRICS countries to form a development bank and to create currency swaps to help developing countries. Second, the BRICS countries are considering enlarging their group to include other emerging economies such as Mexico and Turkey, both members of the G20. Third, China works with other emerging economies to try to reform the representation issue within major international financial institutions like the IMF and the World Bank. However, China's drive is hampered by some difficulties, as the BRICS countries are not totally united. India and Russia may have reservations about China's rise. Moreover, the progress of development of the CMIM suffers from the political fallouts between China, Japan, and South Korea over some island territorial disputes. Furthermore, these countries suffer from economic slowdown and political difficulties.

Apparently, China is not happy with the slow progress of voting reforms in the IMF and the World Bank. It has therefore taken initiatives since late 2013 to mount a new Silk Road plan, consisting of a maritime component and a land component in order to drastically boost regional and global trade, infrastructure development, and social connections.[22] To help finance these projects around the world, especially in developing countries and regions, China has proposed the establishment of a Silk Road Fund (with an initial capital of US$40 billion), apart from the AIIB (capital: initially US$50 billion, rising to US$100 billion) and the BRICS Development Bank (capital: US$100 billion) aforementioned (Fig. 10.1). Bilaterally, China can make use of its financial reserves through its Export-Import Bank and other state-owned banks such as the Bank of China, the China Development Bank, and the China Construction Bank to finance these projects with other countries and institutions based on a win–win formula. The development of its high-speed rail diplomacy is a case in point. As a result, China has the potential to change significantly the face of global development in the near future, barring unforeseen circumstances and inter-state political difficulties.[23]

Conclusion

This chapter has tried to tackle these questions: How has China used its economic power to enhance its position in the global financial structure? What are China's objectives and how to assess China's success or its effort to achieve those objectives? What are China's strengths and constraints in

---

[22] See Gerald Chan, 'Can China connect the world by high-speed rail?', *YouTube video*, 19:10, posted by TedxTalk on 15 September 2015, available at: https://www.youtube.com/watch?v=uRdQ_2sjF2s (accessed 28 April 2016).

[23] For further elaboration, see Gerald Chan, 'China's high-speed rail diplomacy: its impacts on global development', paper presented at the Shanghai Forum, 23–25 May 2015, and 'China's high-speed rail diplomacy: global impacts and East Asian responses', EAI (Seoul) Working Paper (15 February 2016).

its endeavor? What are the long-term trends as a consequence of all these developments?

To sum up the answers to these questions: China has apparently utilized its aggregate economic power to enhance its position in the global financial structure, including the regional financial structure. The change has been slow, more so at the global level than at the regional level. The country has attained better results regionally, but progress has been stymied by its political complications with some major regional powers such as Japan and to a lesser extent, India. China has pursued its quest through the global channel and the regional channel as well as other avenues. However, China does not seem to be very eager to take on a leadership role to bring about these changes. It still plays a relatively low profile in international political affairs, with occasional strong rhetoric statements on issues of injustice in the existing system as China sees it. This relatively low profile is brought about by its relatively weak diplomatic and political capabilities. Its aspirations to do more are hampered by domestic difficulties and external constraints.

The United States remains the dominant force in the international system. It has made adjustments to revitalize its politico-economic strength. It has withdrawn its troops from active combats in Iraq and Afghanistan. It has decided to cut its defense spending in the coming years. Its balance of payment has improved. It has found a relatively new source of energy from shale oil on home soil. Above all, with a huge margin over any potential competitor, the country has remained a mighty military power. Its soft powers have continued to attract investments and bright brains from around the world to its shores, from political allies as well as rivals. It has remained a staunch supporter of its allies and friends, in Asia and in Europe. And its political system has remained a shining light to many aspiring democracies.

On the other hand, China does not seem to have any concrete grand objective or strategy to rise in the hierarchy of the global financial structure. The occasional flash of strong statements and the limited number of Chinese diplomats in high-ranking positions in some of the major international institutions do not seem to amount to any major push for change. The balance sheet of China's strengths and weaknesses still shows quite a big deficit in China's drive to address the imbalance in the global financial structure, which favors the West rather than the rest in the developing world, including China. Major changes to the current situation do not seem to have appeared on the horizon yet. China still has a long way to go before any meaningful change could take hold.

As far as China and the United States are concerned, a process of mutual learning has been taking place. The United States is socializing China into the existing global economic system, while China is providing economic lessons to others through its own developmental experiences. In a way, there is some sort of coordination going on, not necessarily borne out of a situation in which one country has to comply with the norms and rules of powerful states and institutions. In this process of mutual learning, the United States, being the superpower with a lot of hard and soft powers at its disposal, is able to influence and affect China more than the other way round. The overall situation can be understood as a process of coordination in a fragmengrated system,[24] one that professor James Rosenau a few decades ago envisaged as consisting of two opposing trends — fragmentation and integration — each criss-crossing the other to produce a complex development that is the hallmark of today's global financial structure.

---

[24]For an elaboration of 'fragmengration', see James N. Rosenau, 'The governance of frag-mengration: neither a world republic nor a global interstate system', paper presented at the Congress of the International Political Science Association, Quebec City, 1–5 August 2000, available at: http://aura.u-pec.fr/regimen/_fich/_pdf/pub_002.pdf (accessed 28 April 2016).

Chapter 11

Hunting for Food: A New Driver in Chinese Foreign Policy

Hongzhou Zhang and Mingjiang Li

In September 2013, numerous international media reported that China was planning to purchase large farmlands in Ukraine. It was reported that China's Xinjiang Production and Construction Corps (XPCC) signed an agreement with Ukraine's KSG Agro to lease 5% (three million hectares) of Ukraine's land.[1] Very soon, both the XPCC and KSG Agro denied such reports and claimed that they were only discussing agricultural cooperation on a much smaller scale.[2] Meanwhile, international attention was drawn to the US$4.7 billion takeover of Smithfield Foods by one of the

---

[1] 'Ukraine to become China's largest overseas farmer in 3 m hectare deal', *South China Morning Post* (23 September 2013), available at: http:// www.scmp.com/news/china/ article/ 1314902/ukraine-become-chinas-largest-overseas-farmer-3m-hectare-deal (accessed 28 September 2013); 'China to invest in 3 mln hectares of Ukrainian farmland – media', *Reuters* (22 September 2013), available at: http://www.reuters.com/article/2013/09/22/china-ukraine-idUSL3N0HI04620130922 (accessed 28 September 2013).

[2] 'Xinjiang Bingtuan: shang weiyu wukelan jiu nongye kaifa qianding renhe hetong huo xieyi'[Xinjiang Production and Construction Corp: no contract or agreement with Ukraine on agricultural development yet], *Xinhua News* (27 September 2013), available at: http://news.xinhuanet.com/world/2013-09/27/c_117542888.htm (accessed 28 September 2013); 'Refutation of information', *KSG Agro* (23 September 2013), available at: http://www.ksgagro.com/en/2013/09/23/refutation-of-information/ (accessed 28 September 2013).

leading meat supplier in China named Shuanghui.[3] Furthermore, in the first quarter of 2014, Chinese state-owned grain trader China National Cereals, Oils, and Foodstuffs Corporation (COFCO) made a back-to-back purchase of controlling stakes in two global agricultural commodities traders — Netherlands-based Nidera BV and the agribusiness division of Singapore-listed commodities trader Noble Group.[4]

Business deals like these could always easily generate much attention throughout the world because of the age-old international concern that feeding China — a nation with one-fifth of the global population but only 9% of the world's arable land — would pose daunting food security challenges for the rest of the world. China's fast-growing economy has accelerated consumer demand to the point that aggravates an already alarming food security situation. On the one hand, China's total food consumption is rising rapidly partly due to the rapid expansion of the population, and partly due to the growing affluence and demand for increasing food amount, quality, and diversity. On the other hand, China's industrialization and urbanization have exacerbated China's resource shortages, greatly weakening China's agricultural production capacity.

In response to these challenges, China's food security today is gradually moving away from the strategy of self-sufficiency to a new strategy. At the Central Rural Work Conference convened in December 2013, Chinese policy-makers defined the country's new food security strategy as one that relies on domestic supply with 'moderate imports'. Under the new food security strategy, China will be increasingly active in securing food sources from other parts of the world through trade, purchase, and lease of foreign land, as well as mergers and acquisitions (M&A) of foreign agricultural businesses. Given the strategic importance of food resources, and worsening outlook for food security globally, this shift in China's food security strategy is likely to have a profound impact on China's foreign relations.

---

[3] 'Shuanghui, Smithfield complete merger deal', *Xinhua News* (27 September 2013), available at: http://news.xinhuanet.com/english/business/2013-09/27/c_132755541.htm (accessed 28 September 2013).

[4] George J. Gilboy and Eric Heginbotham, *Chinese and Indian Strategic Behavior: Growing Power and Alarm* (London: Cambridge University Press, 2012).

In the field of Chinese foreign policy, one question comes under intense debate: What drives China's foreign policy? Some scholars believe that Beijing's international policy has been primarily motivated by realist considerations such as the pursuit of power and other national interests.[5] Some analysts maintain that China's foreign policy has had deep roots in its domestic context, including the political elite,[6] bureaucratic politics,[7] and public opinion.[8] There is also a growing body of literature that identifies

---

[5]Robert G. Sutter, *Chinese Foreign Relations: Power and Policy Since the Cold War* (Lanham: Rowman & Littlefield Publishers, 2012); Yong Deng and Fei-Ling Wang, eds., *China Rising: Power and Motivation in Chinese Foreign Policy* (Lanham: Rowman & Littlefield Publishers, 2004); John J. Mearsheimer, *The Tragedy of Great Power Politics* (New York and London: W.W. Norton and Company, 2014); David M. Lampton, *The Three Faces of Chinese Power: Might, Money, and Minds* (Berkeley: University of California Press, 2008); George J. Gilboy and Eric Heginbotham, *Chinese and Indian Strategic Behavior: Growing Power and Alarm* (London: Cambridge University Press, 2012).

[6]Yun-han Chu and Chih-cheng Lo, eds., *The New Chinese Leadership: Challenges and Opportunities After the 16th Party Congress* (London: Cambridge University Press, 2004); Sujian Guo and Jean-Marc F. Blanchard, eds., *Harmonious World and China's New Foreign Policy* (Lanham: Lexington Books, 2010); M. Taylor Fravel, 'Regime insecurity and international cooperation: explaining China's compromises in territorial disputes', *International Security*, 30 (2005), pp. 46–83; M. Taylor Fravel, *Strong Borders, Secure Nation: Cooperation and Conflict in China's Territorial Disputes* (Princeton: Princeton University Press, 2008); Wang Gungwu and Zheng Yongnian, eds., *China and the New International Order* (London: Routledge, 2008); Yong Deng, *China's Struggle for Status: The Realignment of International Relations* (London: Cambridge University Press, 2008).

[7]Hongyi Lai and Yiyi Lu, eds., *China's Soft Power and International Relations* (London: Routledge, 2012); Michael Dalton McCoy, *Domestic Policy Narratives and International Relations Theory: Chinese Ecological Agriculture as a Case Study* (Lanham: University Press of America, 2000).

[8]James Reilly, *Strong Society, Smart State: The Rise of Public Opinion in China's Japan Policy* (New York: Columbia University Press, 2011); Peter Hays Gries, *China's New Nationalism: Pride, Politics, and Diplomacy* (Berkeley: University of California Press, 2005); Biwu Zhang, *Chinese Perceptions of the U.S.: An Exploration of China's Foreign Policy Motivations* (Lanham: Lexington Books, 2013); Yufan Hao, *China's Foreign Policy Making: Societal Force and Chinese American Policy* (Farnham: Ashgate Publishing, 2006); Christopher Hughes, *Chinese Nationalism in the Global Era* (London: Routledge, 2006); Zheng Wang, *Never Forget National Humiliation: Historical Memory in Chinese Politics and Foreign Relations* (New York: Columbia University Press, 2012); Simon Shen and Shaun Breslin, *Online Chinese Nationalism and China's Bilateral Relations* (Lanham: Lexington Books, 2010).

soft power as a driving force in China's foreign policy.[9] Business interests have also been regarded as an important factor in China's international politics.[10] Others argue that Chinese culture and tradition play a significant role in shaping China's foreign relations.[11]

This paper aims to provide a fresh perspective on the motivations behind China's foreign policy: food security has become one of the main drivers in China's foreign policy. The rest of the paper is organized as follows: The first section provides a comprehensive overview of China's evolving food security situation. With abundant data, we demonstrate that China is facing daunting challenges in meeting its growing domestic food demand. In the next section, we discuss China's emerging new food security strategy that increasingly attempts to utilize international resources. We explore in detail China's major initiatives in its international food policy. The extent to which China has been involved in international agribusiness and global food security indicates that food security has indeed become a significant driver in China's foreign relations. We conclude that food security concerns will have tremendous positive and negative consequences on China's relations with the outside world.

China's Food Security: Growing Concerns

In the past three decades, China's food demand-and-supply pattern has undergone dramatic changes. On the one hand, the country's total food

---

[9]Joshua Kurlantzick, *Charm Offensive: How China's Soft Power Is Transforming the World* (New Haven: Yale University Press, 2007); Sheng Ding, *The Dragon's Hidden Wings: How China Rises with Its Soft Power* (Lanham: Lexington Books, 2008); Hongyi Lai and Yiyi Lu, eds., *China's Soft Power and International Relations* (London: Routledge, 2012); Mingjiang Li, *Soft Power: China's Emerging Strategy in International Politics* (Lanham: Lexington Books, 2011); Kenneth King, *China's Aid and Soft Power in Africa* (Woodbridge, UK and Rochester, NY: James Currey, 2013).

[10]Yongjin Zhang, *China's Emerging Global Businesses: Political Economy and Institutional Investigations* (Basingstoke: Palgrave Macmillan, 2003); Ho-fung Hung, *China and the Transformation of Global Capitalism* (Baltimore: Johns Hopkins University Press, 2009); Sigfrido Burgos Cáceres, *The Hungry Dragon: How China's Resource Quest is Reshaping the World* (London: Routledge, 2013).

[11]Huiyun Feng, *Chinese Strategic Culture and Foreign Policy Decision-Making: Confucianism, Leadership and War* (London: Routledge, 2007); Alastair Iain Johnston, *Cultural Realism* (Princeton: Princeton University Press, 1995).

demand has been rising rapidly due to demographic change, economic development, and dietary shift. On the other hand, China's food production has also experienced phenomenal growth after the introduction of the rural Household Responsibility System (HRS) and a series of other agricultural policies. Yet, in recent years, China's food supply has increasingly fallen short of demand. China's current high level of food producing capacity also appears to be unsustainable.

Rapidly rising food demand

In 1978, after the 10-year Cultural Revolution, the Chinese economy was at the brink of collapse. Food was in short supply: 250 million out of the 800 million rural residents were impoverished.[12] With rapid economic development and social liberalization, hundreds of millions of Chinese were lifted out of poverty and a large middle class emerged in China. As the Chinese became richer, their diet and food preferences dramatically changed. They began to move up the food chain, from primary products (such as grains, roots, and pulses) to secondary food commodities (such as meat, fish, and milk) and processed food (such as sweeteners). Both rural and urban residents' direct consumption of grain dropped notably, whereas their demand for meat, poultry, as well as both aquatic products and dairy products increased significantly, resulting in a surge in indirect grain consumption. At the same time, the Chinese are consuming more fruits and other agricultural products.

What is also noteworthy is that there are huge dietary differences between rural and urban residents. The urban residents are consuming less grain but more animal products (meat, fish, milk, and eggs), fruits, and other agricultural products. As China underwent rapid urbanization from 2000 to 2012, the Chinese rural population decreased by over 150 million, whereas the number of urban residents increased by more than 250 million.[13] This resulted in a significant impact on China's food consumption. When people from the rural areas migrated to the cities, they began eating less staple grain and more meat. Considering that seven kilograms of grain is needed

---

[12] Ruisheng Du, *The Course of China's Rural Reform* (Washington, DC: The International Food Policy Research Institute, 2006).

[13] *2013 China Statistical Abstract*, National Bureau of Statistics of China (Beijing: China Statistics Press, 2013).

to produce one kilogram of beef and four kilograms of grain is needed for one kilogram of pork, mass migration to cities would create a dramatic increase in China's total food demand.[14]

Furthermore, a 40% increase in the Chinese population over the past three decades[15] led to a significant increase in per capita food demand that caused the surge in the country's total food demand for grain and non-grain foodstuff. Owing to rapid industrialization and rising demand for processed food, the country's industrial demand for agricultural products is growing rapidly. Take, for example, industrial demand for grain: China's total industrial consumption of grain increased by more than 60% from 2000 to 2010.[16] This is a stark contrast to the slight decrease of the country's grain consumption.

As China's economy rapidly grows, the country's future demand for food will continue to rise. As more people move into cities and towns, food demand will rise and exhaust the supply of farm products; thus in the coming years, China will face severe food challenges. This situation is aggravated by declining rural labor productivity, worsening natural environment, and weather extremities.

Troubling trends in food supply

While the demand for food has grown rapidly, China's agricultural production has also grown substantially in the past three decades. Since the 1978 reform and opening up, various factors — the introduction of the HRS, the increase in government purchasing price, liberalization of the market, and financial support by the government — have triggered the rapid growth of China's agricultural sector and enabled domestic production to meet the shifts in consumer demands.

---

[14]Zhang Hongzhou, 'Feeding the Asian: Agricultural R & D and Food Security'. *RSIS Commentary*, No. 075 (2012), available at: https://www.rsis.edu.sg/wp-content/uploads/2014/07/CO12075.pdf.

[15]*2013 China Statistical Abstract*, National Bureau of Statistics of China (Beijing: China Statistics Press, 2013), p. 39.

[16]'Xiwang qianye banlan huajuan-tanxun zhongguo nongye xiandaihua daolu'. [Search for the path of modernizing China's agricultural sector], *The Central People's Government of the PRC*, 18 November 2010, available at: http://www.gov.cn/jrzg/2010-11/18/content_1747796.htm (accessed 28 September 2013).

Table 11.1. Outputs of major agricultural products (10,000 tons).

	Grain	Cotton	Oil Bearing Crops	Fruits	Fishery Products	Meats	Milk
1978	30,476.5	216.7	521.8	657.0	465.4	NA	NA
1980	32,055.5	270.7	769.1	679.3	449.7	NA	136.7
1985	37,910.8	414.7	1578.4	1163.9	705.2	1926.5	289.4
1990	44,624.3	450.8	1613.2	1874.4	1237.0	2857.0	475.1
1995	46,661.8	476.8	2250.3	4214.6	2517.2	5260.1	672.8
2000	46,217.5	441.7	2954.8	6225.1	3706.2	6013.9	919.1
2010	54,647.7	596.1	3230.1	21,401.4	5373.0	7925.8	3748.0
2011	57,120.8	658.9	3306.8	22,768.2	5603.2	7957.8	3810.7
2012	58,958.0	683.6	3436.8	24,056.8	5907.7	8387.2	3868.6
Change	93%	215%	559%	3562%	1169%	335%	2730%

Source: China's *Statistical Yearbook 2013*, p. 117.

The country's agricultural production increased dramatically by 93% between 1978 and 2012 while remarkable increases in the production of fruits (35.6 times) and fishery products (11.7 times) were recorded (see Table 11.1). Furthermore, China's meat production increased by more than three times from 1985 to 2011, and the country's milk production increased 27.3 times (from 13.6 million tons in 1980 to 387 million tons in 2012). Relying on merely 9% of the world's arable land, China has not only managed to meet the demand of over 1.3 billion people for grain and other agro-products, but has also provided raw materials, manpower, and market demand for industries, services, and other sectors. The remarkable development of the agricultural sector enabled China to achieve basic food self-sufficiency through domestic production.

However, in spite of the nine consecutive years of grain production increase since 2003, China's domestic food production has fallen short of the country's rapid growing demand. China's import of grain increased dramatically in the last decade. Total grain import, including imports of soybeans and cereals, increased from 16 million tons in 2002 to over 80 million tons in 2012 (see Table 11.2). What is more alarming is that, due to rapid urbanization and industrialization, the quantity and quality of China's total arable land is plummeting. Large areas of fertile arable land and fresh

Table 11.2.   China's grain imports (10,000 tons).

	Grain	Cereal	Wheat	Rice	Maize	Barley	Soybeans
1992	1182	1152	1058	10	0	0	0
1993	16	1	1	0	0	0	0
1994	925	913	730	51	0	0	0
1995	2083	2036	159	164	518	0	0
1996	1106	1078	825	76	44	0	0
1997	738	410	186	33	0	187	288
1998	742	382	149	24	25	152	319
1999	809	334	45	17	7	227	432
2000	1391	312	91	24	0	196	1042
2001	1950	344	74	27	4	237	1394
2002	1605	285	63	24	1	191	1131
2003	2526	208	45	26	0	136	2074
2004	3352	974	726	76	0	171	2023
2005	3647	627	354	51	0	218	2659
2006	3714	358	61	72	7	213	2824
2007	3731	155	10	49	4	91	3082
2008	4131	154	4	33	5	108	3744
2009	5223	315	90	36	8	174	4255
2010	6695	571	123	39	157	237	5480
2011	6390	545	126	60	175	178	5264
2012	8025	1398	370	237	521	NA	5838

Source: Li Jingmou, *China Grain Market Report.*[17]

waters have been channeled from agricultural production to commercial use. China's intensive use of chemical fertilizers and pesticides to sustain high crop yield has led to land degradation and water pollution, seriously undermining sustainable agricultural production.

Given the country's agricultural production factor endowment, China does *not* have a comparative advantage in land and water-intensive agricultural production, grain and cotton in particular. As a result, land-intensive agricultural production cost much more in China than in other countries.

---

[17]Jingmou Li, *China Grain Market Development Report 2012* (Beijing: China Finance and Economic Press, 2012); the data for 2012 is from the news report by Jingyi Zhang, 'Zhongguo damijinkoujizeng, weixieliangshianquan?' [Surge in rice imports: a threat to food security?] *International Finance News* (5 February 2013), available at: http://finance. people.com.cn/n/2013/0205/c1004-20434376.html.

Moreover, with the dramatic outflow of the rural labor force, as well as the surge in prices of energy and land, China's agricultural production cost has risen radically. As a result, Chinese agricultural products are losing favor in the eyes of agribusiness leaders and consumers. Also, China's major food-consuming regions are located in the south and near the coast while its agricultural production center, particularly the grain production center, is shifting north. Given the severe lack of water and the vulnerability of the ecosystem in China's northern and western regions, the shift of the agricultural center to the north subjects China's food supply to greater risk. Furthermore, the inefficient, poorly coordinated food transportation system makes cross-region food transportation more tedious and costly. Consequently, importing food from abroad through marine transportation becomes a more attractive option to coastal regions.

In the past few years, China was beset by a series of high-profile food safety scandals, such as the melamine-tainted milk, exploding watermelons, addictive-tainted pork, illegally recycled waste cooking oil, and contaminated rice. China's agricultural sector is dominated by millions of small household farms. Each small household farm's average land holding is 0.515 hectare.[18] For decades, the overuse of fertilizers, pesticides, and insecticides in agriculture has seriously depleted the soil. Furthermore, rapid industrialization and urbanization have led to increasing levels of metal pollution, water pollution, and air pollution culminating in serious crop contamination.[19] Contamination is even worse in the food processing (food-handling and transport) sector engaging at least 400,000 food processing companies and millions of people and businesses, as well as many informal and unregistered food producers and processors. With increasing food suppliers, the government faces intensifying challenges in disseminating standards, monitoring production, and troubleshooting.[20] As the general public raises

---

[18]Z. Tian, 'Whether migration of rural labor force lead to land circulation', *China Reform Daily* (27 October 2008).

[19]'Jingji Guancha: gongye wuran gei nongye da guo dailai tudizhishang', *Xinhua News Agency* [Economic watch: land disaster brought by industrial pollution to the major agricultural country] 9 June 2013, available at: http://news.xinhuanet.com/2013-06/09/c_124839488.htm (accessed on 29 September 2013).

[20]F. Gale and J. C. Buzby, *Imports from China and Food Safety Issues* (Washington, DC: USDA, 2009).

concern over local food safety, their demand for imported food also continues to rise.

Therefore, with consumers' growing dietary emphasis on greater variety and better quality, China's domestic production cannot fully meet its increasing food demand. The supply-demand gap has to be filled by food imports. China's agricultural imports jumped from US$12.5 billion in 2002 to US$117.9 billion in 2013. The balance in China's agricultural trade has tumbled from a surplus of US$5.6 billion in 2002 to a deficit of over US$50 billion in 2013 (see Table 11.3).

Rapid growth of grain and food imports naturally means declining grain and food self-sufficiency rate. China's grain self-sufficiency rate has long breached the official red line of 95%. In 2012, it dropped to nearly 86% (see Figure 11.1).[21] Some Chinese scholars estimate that China's current food self-sufficiency rate is only around 70%.[22]

Table 11.3.   China's agricultural trade (US$ billion).

	Total	Export	Import	Net
2002	30.6	18.2	12.5	5.6
2003	40.3	21.3	19.0	2.4
2004	51.4	23.4	28.1	−4.7
2005	56.4	27.6	28.8	−1.2
2006	63.6	31.4	32.2	−0.8
2007	78.2	37.0	41.2	−4.2
2008	99.3	40.5	58.8	−18.3
2009	92.3	39.6	52.7	−13.1
2010	122.0	49.4	72.6	−23.2
2011	155.7	60.8	94.9	−34.1
2012	174.0	62.5	111.4	−48.9
2013	185.0	67.1	117.9	−50.8

Source: Agricultural Trade Office of the Ministry of Agriculture of China, 2012; Ministry of Commerce of China, 2014.

---

[21]The grain self-sufficiency rate is an estimated number which represents the share of China's total domestic grain production in the country's total grain supply: domestic grain production plus net grain import.

[22]Xiaohua Yu and Puning Zhong, 'Ruhe baozhang zhongguo de liangshi anquan' [How to safeguard China's food security), *Journal of Agrotechnical Economics,* 2 (2012), pp. 4–8.

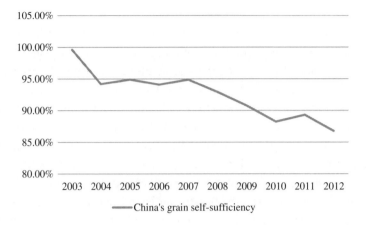

Figure 11.1.   China's grain self-sufficiency rate in recent years.

Source: Calculation based on data from the National Bureau of Statistics.

Demand-supply gap continues to widen

Looking forward, China's food demand and supply gap will continue to be driven by population growth, urbanization, and economic development. Although China's 2010 census shows that its population growth rate has reduced by half within a decade, its total population will continue to grow at least in the short to medium term and peak at 1.4 billion by 2030.[23] Given the current size of the Chinese population of around 1.35 billion, China will have to increase food supply by 2030 to feed an additional 50 million people.

Yet, as China's population growth rate drops, the country ages rapidly. It is projected that China's over-60 population will almost double over the next 20 years, from 178 million in 2010 to over 350 million in 2030.[24]

---

[23]'World Population to reach 10 billion by 2100 if fertility in all countries converges to replacement level', *United Nations Press Release* (2010); Chengxing Shao, 'Woguo renkou 2025 niandai fengzhi'[China population to reach its peak in 2025], *West China City Daily* (1 October 2012); 'Zhongguo xianru chaodi shengyulv xianjing' [China falls into the trap of extremely low fertility rate), *Infzm* (24 May 2011), available at: http://www.infzm.com/content/59364 (accessed 29 September 2013).

[24]'China under pressure to cover aging population: official', *Xinhua News* (24 June 2013), available at: http://news.xinhuanet.com/english/china/2013-06/24/c_132482514.htm (accessed 29 September 2013).

The aging problem will be more severe in the rural areas. The number of elderly people in the countryside will be 1.69 times of those in the cities. Due to China's incomplete urbanization, the elderly population will serve as the main labor force for China's agriculture, and severely tax China's agricultural production.[25] As China's rural population ages at an even faster rate, China's agricultural production will come under mounting pressure.

Aside from the continuous expansion of China's total population, more and more Chinese will be living in cities. As China's new leadership views urbanization as a major reform and the main driver of China's future economic growth, the pace of urbanization will certainly accelerate in the coming years.[26] The Chinese government projected that China's urbanization rate will reach 60% in 2020.[27] With more people moving into the cities and towns, the supply of farm products will be limited by declining rural labor productivity, environmental degradation, and more importantly, shrinking arable land. According to Chinese scholars, for every 1% increase in China's urbanization rate, 127,000 hectares of arable land will be in demand.[28] By 2020, around one million hectares of arable land (mostly highly fertile land) will be lost, given that China's urbanization rate is likely to reach 60%, up from current level of around 52.5%.[29] Meanwhile, rapid urbanization will

---

[25] Zhang Hongzhou, 'China's Food Conundrum: Insecurity of the Rural Abandoned', RSIS Commentary No. 182 (2011), available at: https://www.rsis.edu.sg/wp-content/uploads/2014/07/CO11182.pdf.

[26] 'Duihua quanwei zhuanjia: tuijin zhengzhenghua xujia kuai pochu zhidu zhangai' [Dialogue with the experts: to push for faster urbanization, institutional barriers need to be cleared], *Xinhua News* (25 May 2013), available at: http://news.xinhuanet.com/fortune/2013-05/25/c_124763505.htm (accessed 23 October 2013).

[27] 'Meiti cheng zhongguo chengshihualv guoban yinghuan suixing xufang fazhan shiheng' [Media says risk comes with China's urbanization rate exceeded 50%, needs to prevent imbalance development], *People.com*, (25 May 2012), available at: http://politics.people.com.cn/GB/70731/17968454.html (accessed 20 October 2013).

[28] Huibo Wang, 'Chengshihua jingcheng zhong de shi di nongmin yu zhengce paichi wenti yanjiu' [Research on the conflicts between landless farmers and government policies during the urbanization process], *Agricultural Economics*, 3 (2008), pp. 5–8.

[29] 'Chen Xiwen: chengzhenhua wenti tuxian jincheng nongmin bixu you xiangying baozhang' [Chen Xiwen: problems arise during the urbanization process, migrated farmers need to be protected], *China News* (26 January 2013), available at: http://big5.chinanews.com:89/gate/big5/finance.chinanews.com/cj/2013/01-26/4522876.shtml (accessed 28 September 2013).

also create additional demand for food. According to Chinese vice minister of agriculture Chen Xiaohua, more than half the population will be living in cities and towns during 2011–2015. This will create an additional demand of 4 million metric tons of grain, 800,000 tons of vegetable oil, and 1 million ton of meat every year.[30]

Besides, the Chinese are becoming richer. In spite of numerous challenges facing China, according to some international institutions and economists, China's economy will continue to boom.[31] Although China is the world's second-largest economy in 2010, it is categorized as a developing country because it remains poor in per capita terms. As China sets per capita income growth targets for its economic development,[32] its people will have higher disposable income that will dramatically change their food demand. While the Chinese food consumption structure has diversified (from consuming staple grain to consuming more animal protein), China's per capita meat consumption is still quite low compared to the United States and other developed countries. The Chinese per capita annual meat consumption is less than 60 kilograms whereas the American per capita annual meat consumption hits 160 kilograms.[33] With higher disposable income, the Chinese will demand more animal protein, raising the demand for feed grain.

However, China's achievement of high-grain production increment over nine consecutive years appears unsustainable. Its 2012 grain production of nearly 600 million tons well exceeded the 540 million tons target set by Chinese government in its 'Medium and Long-term Planning Outline

---

[30]'China faces more difficulty meeting food demand, official says' *Bloomberg* (31 January 2011), available at: http://www.bloomberg.com/news/2011-01-31/china-faces-more-difficulty-meeting-food-demand-official-says.html (accessed 29 September 2013).

[31]*OECD Economic Outlook* (Paris: OECD, 2012); Vivian Chen, Ben Cheng, Gad Levanon, Ataman Ozyildirim, and Bart van Ark, 'Projecting Global Growth',Conference Board Economics Program Working Papers No. 12–02 (2012); 'Long term economic and demographic projections', *Deloitte Access Economics ADF Posture Review* (24 November 2011).

[32]'China adds resident's per capita income into economic growth target', *Xinhua News* (8 November 2012), available at: http://news.xinhuanet.com/english/special/18cpcnc/2012-11/08/c_131959039.htm (accessed 29 September 2013).

[33]Stefan Schwarzera, 'Growing greenhouse gas emissions due to meat production', *UNEP Global Environmental Alert Service* (October 2012), available at: http://www.unep.org/pdf/unep-geas_oct_2012.pdf.

of National Food Security' (2008–2020) released in 2008.[34] According to Cheng Guoqiang, professor at Tsinghua University, the Chinese government has already realized that the continuous push for higher grain production could be too costly and unrealistic; effort will have to be spent in maintaining the production level at 5.5 billion tons, while working on the long-term sustainability of the sector.[35]

Considering the outlook on both demand and supply, it is certain that China's food demand and supply gap will widen in the future. More food needs to be sourced from overseas; but the amount of imported food cannot be determined because of the vast discrepancies between projections.[36] Fan Shenggen, director-general of the International Food Policy Research Institute (IFPRI), suggested that by 2020, China would need to import 100 million tons of grain each year.[37] Xu Xiaoqing, head of the rural department at the State Council's Development and Research Center, a government think tank, projected that China could import between 20 million tons and 30 million tons of corn a year to address growing supply shortages.[38] And according to the latest joint forecast by the Organization for Economic Cooperation and Development (OECD) and Food and Agriculture Organization (FAO), the country's imports of coarse grains (mostly used for fattening herds) are

---

[34] 'Guojia liangshi anquan zhongchang qiguihua gangyao, 2008–2020' [National mid-to long-term grain security plan guidelines, 2008–2020], *The Central People's Government of the PRC* (13 November 2008), available at: http://www.gov.cn/jrzg/2008-11/13/content_1148414.htm (accessed 21 September 2013).

[35] Interview with a Chinese official, 6 June 2013.

[36] Verity Linehan, Sally Thorpe, Neil Andrews, Yeon Kim, and Farah Beaini, 'Food Demand to 2050 Opportunities for Australian Agriculture', paper presented at the 42nd ABARES Outlook Conference ABARES, Canberra, March 6–7 (2012); Xiaohong Zhang, 'Comparative study of projection models on China's food economy', *Journal of Peasant Studies, 30* (2003), pp. 192–223; Jikun Huang, Scott Rozelle, and Mark W. Rosegrant, 'China's food economy to the twenty-first century: supply, demand, and trade', *Economic Development and Cultural Change*, 47 (1999), pp. 737–66.

[37] 'Food self-sufficiency no longer option for China', *South China Morning Post* (28 January 2013) http://www.scmp.com/news/china/article/1137897/food-self-sufficiency-no-longer-option-china (accessed 12 October 2013).

[38] Emiko Terazono, 'China sees rising appetite for corn imports', *Financial Times* (11 September 2013), available at: http://www.ft.com/intl/cms/s/0/4d738f8e-19f5-11e3-93e8-00144feab7de.html#axzz2lH1HkFUb (accessed 29 September 2013).

expected to double by 2022. Imports of soybeans are expected to grow by 40%, while beef imports are expected to nearly double.[39]

From Self-Sufficiency to a Dual Food Security Strategy

For a long time, China has regarded national food security as equivalent to food self-sufficiency, grain self-sufficiency in particular. Yet, with the widening supply and demand gap, a dual food security strategy which aims to utilize both domestic and international resources has emerged.[40]

Paradigm shift in China's food security strategy

At the Central Rural Work Conference convened in December 2013, a new food security strategy was formed. The Chinese policy-makers defined the country's food security strategy as one that relies on domestic supply with 'moderate imports'. Although self-sufficiency is still the cornerstone of China's food security strategy, with 95% of self-sufficiency rate as the bottom line for China's food security, some fundamental shifts in China's food security strategy have occurred. First, China has narrowed the scope of grains covered by the 95% self-sufficiency target. Soybeans and tuber crops are no longer covered under the self-sufficiency policy and corn is no longer considered as staple grain. Second, it is the first time that the term 'moderate imports' was explicitly stated. This indicates that 'moderate imports' now form part of the national food security strategy. Therefore, we are witnessing a policy shift from self-sufficiency to a dual strategy which aims to utilize both domestic and international food resources.

Improving agricultural ties with food exporters

In recent years, the need for stable food supply has led China to be very proactive in expanding agricultural ties with the world's top food exporters.

---

[39] *OECD-FAO Agricultural Outlook 2013–2022*, OECD/FAO (Paris: OECD, 2013).

[40] In a broad sense, China has long adopted a dual food security strategy: maintaining a high degree of cereal self-sufficiency while importing other food products from international market. With a widening food supply and demand gap, however, it appears that China is no longer able to achieve cereal self-sufficiency, particularly corn, and this will lead to an emergence of a dual food security strategy in the real sense.

Numerous agricultural deals were signed between China and major agricultural exporters in recent years. To name just a few, in September 2013, during Xi Jinping's visit to Tajikistan, both sides held talks on establishing a free trade zone in bordering countries to expand trade in agricultural products.[41] In June 2013, following a meeting between Argentine president Cristina Kirchner and Chinese vice president Li Yuanchao, China signed an agreement on agricultural cooperation with Argentina.[42] In May 2013, during premier Li Keqiang's visit to Germany, both countries agreed to establish a ministerial dialogue mechanism to reinforce guidance on agricultural cooperation.[43] In November 2012, during his visit to Thailand, former Chinese premier Wen Jiabao signed a Memorandum of Understanding in which Thailand agreed to supply China with rice when needed while the Chinese government agreed to support Thailand's private rice traders.[44] In February 2012, during Xi's visit to the United States, the two countries signed the Five-year Plan of Strategic Cooperation on food security, food safety, and sustainable agriculture.[45] At the same time, a series of new agricultural agreements was reached between Canada and China when Canadian prime minister Stephen Harper and minister of agriculture Gerry Ritz visited China. China signed the Agricultural Cooperation Agreement with Australia in 1984. In recent years, China has negotiated the Agricultural Free Trade Agreement with Australia to ensure stability in agricultural

[41] Pu Zhendong, 'China, Tajikistan eye free trade zone in agriculture', *China Daily* (5 September 2013), available at: http://www.chinadaily.com.cn/china/2013xivisitcenterasia/2013-09/05/content_16945022.htm (accessed 29 September 2013).

[42] 'China, Argentina sign agricultural accords', *Jakarta Post* (24 June 2012), available at: http://www.thejakartaglobe.com/archive/china-argentina-sign-agricultural-accords/ (accessed 28 September 2013).

[43] 'China, Germany issue joint statement, vow to deepen cooperation', *Xinhua News* (27 May 2013), available at: http://news.xinhuanet.com/english/china/2013-05/27/c_132409661.htm (accessed 29 September 2013).

[44] Sameer Mohindru, 'China, Thailand secure rice deals', *The Wall Street Journal* (25 November 2012), available at: http://online.wsj.com/article/SB10001424127887324469304578142091171909654.html (accessed 29 September 2013).

[45] Tan Yingzi, 'Xi champion's agricultural pact', *China Daily* (17 February 2012), available at: http://usa.chinadaily.com.cn/us/2012-02/17/content_14635006.htm (accessed 29 September 2013).

trade between Australia and China. China also signed agricultural agreements with countries such as Sudan, Mongolia, and Pakistan. As Ukraine emerges as a major global grain exporter, China started talks with Ukraine to improve food and agricultural trade. In July 2012, China agreed to provide Ukraine, an emerging corn supplier to China, a loan of US$3 billion in exchange for corn.[46]

Creating a favorable atmosphere for international opinion

There is long-lasting international concern that feeding China — a nation with one-fifth of the global population but only 9% of the world's arable land — will pose daunting food security challenges for the rest of the world. In his well-known book *Who Will Feed China? A Wake-Up Call for a Small Planet*, Dr. Lester Brown claimed that the increasingly affluent China would starve the world, and this incited debate about China's threat to global food security.[47] International concern about China's food security still continues to exist today.[48]

Since self-sufficiency is no longer an option, China understands that creating a favorable atmosphere of international opinion will be critical to allow the country to better utilize foreign agricultural resources. To counter the China threat narrative, China has zealously offered agricultural aid and assistance to famine-stricken developing countries. In terms of agricultural aid, China has mainly focused on building farms, agro-technology demonstration centers, and agro-technology experiment and promotion stations; constructing farmland irrigation and water-conservancy projects; supplying agricultural machinery and implements, farm produce processing equipment and related agricultural materials; and providing agro-technicians and

---

[46]Zhou Siyu, 'China, Ukraine to boost agricultural trade', *China Daily* (20 July 2012), available at: http://www.wantchinatimes.com/news-subclass-cnt.aspx?id=20120815000003&cid=1102 (accessed 29 September 2013).

[47]Brown Lester, *Who Will Feed China? A Wake-Up Call for a Small Planet* (New York: W.W. Norton & Co, 1995).

[48]'How China deal with the global food crisis', *Financial Times* (9 May 2008), available at: (accessed 29 September 2013); 'Food crisis is depicted as 'silent tsunami', *Washington Post* (23 April 2008), available at: http://www.washingtonpost.com/wp-dyn/content/article/2008/04/22/AR2008042201481.html (accessed 20 September 2013).

senior agricultural expertise to transfer agricultural production technologies and provide consultation services on rural development, and training for agricultural personnel in recipient countries.

By the end of 2009, China had aided various developing countries with 221 agricultural projects: 35 farms, 47 agro-technology experiment and promotion stations, 11 animal husbandry projects, 15 fisheries projects, 47 farmland irrigation and water-conservancy projects, and 66 other types of agricultural projects, in addition to providing a large amount of agricultural equipment and materials to them.[49] China has established agricultural R&D exchanges and economic cooperation with major international agricultural and financial organizations in over 140 countries. China has set up agro-technology demonstration centers in the Philippines, Cambodia, Indonesia, Malaysia, and some African countries. In 2010, at the UN High-Level Meeting on the Millennium Development Goals, China further pledged to dispatch 3,000 agricultural experts and technicians to establish 30 agro-technology demonstration centers in other developing countries, and invite 5,000 agricultural personnel from these countries to China for training.[50]

While providing agricultural aid helps improve China's image, it brings other benefits to China as well. Providing aid (agro-technological aid, education and training, and agricultural machineries, among others) to food-insecure developing countries with high potential for expanding agricultural production in certain aspects contribute to China's food security as well. Increasing agricultural production in those countries could effectively turn the international grain trade from a 'sellers' market to a 'buyers' market that would benefit China.

Investing in overseas agricultural resources

As China's food import, particularly grain import, continues to rise, China becomes increasing concerned that excessive reliance on the international grain market could worsen its food security situation. The US food embargo against China during the Cold War as well as grain export bans during the

---

[49] *National Plan for Development of Modern Agriculture, 2011–2015,* China State Council (Beijing: State Council Information Office of China, 2011).

[50] Katherine Morton, 'Learning by Doing: China's Role in the Global Governance of Food Security', Indiana University RCCPB Working Paper No. 30 (September 2012).

global food crisis in 2008 reminded China of the uncertainties of the international grain market. As the country's food imports grow, China becomes anxious because the international grain trade (particularly wheat, corn, and soybean trades) is tightly controlled either by the United States and other developed countries or their multinational food enterprises (such as Archer Daniels Midland ADM, Bunge, Cargill, and Louis Dreyfus). To strengthen food security, China has adopted a state-centered approach: using both national resources and state-owned enterprise investments to boost overseas agricultural assets, and tightening imports and exports of food products. China aims to build a global food supply network by diversifying agricultural investments in foreign countries.[51]

The Chinese government has issued many policy papers and regulations in order to encourage Chinese enterprises to invest in overseas agricultural projects. These policies and regulations offer support and guidance in terms of financial subsidies and financing concessions to Chinese enterprises that invest in overseas agricultural projects. In 2008, at the height of global food crisis, the Chinese policy circle even discussed the feasibility of foreign investment for agricultural production as a basic national strategy for China.[52]

With strong government support, China's overseas agricultural activities expanded dramatically in the past three decades. China is now the third largest source of foreign investment stocks in agriculture.[53] In 2012, China's agricultural Outward Foreign Direct Investment (OFDI) reached nearly US$1.46 billion and accumulated agricultural OFDI totaled nearly US$5 billion (see Table 11.4). In 2010, 468 Chinese agricultural corporations invested abroad while 768 agricultural corporations were registered

---

[51] Due to political reasons, the Chinese government has not officially announced that it is abandoning the long-held grain self-sufficiency policy; however, it has strived to build a global food supply network to safeguard its food security.

[52] Li Ping, 'Haiwai zhongliang huo liru jiben guoce, nongyebu lin wu nongkengjituan fenpian baogan'. [Overseas farming may be listed as basic national policy, Ministry of Agriculture asks five Nongkeng groups to target at different regions], *China Economic Observer* (30 June 2008).

[53] Carin Smaller, Qiu Wei, and Liu Yalan, 'The quest for commodities: Chinese investment in farmland', *Investment Treaty News*, 3, no. 4 (June 2003), available at: http://www.iisd.org/sites/default/files/publications/iisd_itn_june_2013_en.pdf (accessed 24 June 2013).

Table 11.4.   China's agricultural outward FDI (US$ billion).

	2004	2005	2006	2007	2008	2009	2010	2011	2012
Agricultural OFDI	0.29	0.11	0.19	0.27	0.17	0.34	0.53	0.80	1.46
Total OFDI	5.50	12.26	21.16	26.51	55.91	56.53	68.81	74.65	87.80
Share	5.25%	0.86%	0.87%	1.03%	0.31%	0.61%	0.78%	1.07%	1.66%
Agricultural OFDI Stock	0.83	0.51	0.82	1.21	1.47	2.03	2.61	3.42	4.96
Total OFDI Stock	44.78	57.21	90.63	117.91	183.97	245.76	317.21	424.78	531.94
Share	1.86%	0.89%	0.90%	1.02%	0.80%	0.83%	0.82%	0.80%	0.93%

OFDI, outward foreign direct investment.
Source: China National Bureau of Statistics 2013.

Table 11.5. China's agricultural major OFDI destinations.

	EU	US	Russia	ASEAN	Others
Agricultural OFDI	149.05	13.68	147.47	190.72	296.83
Share in total OFDI	19%	2%	18%	24%	37%
Agricultural OFDI Stock	357.37	47.99	883.94	709.36	1417.78

Source: China National Bureau of Statistics, 2013.

by the Chinese in foreign countries.[54] Major destinations of China's agricultural investment now include Russia, Southeast Asia, and Europe (see Table 11.5).

China's overseas agricultural expansion is undertaken in two different forms. First, more Chinese firms are purchasing or leasing land in foreign countries for agricultural production. The 2008 global food crisis has caused a rapid surge in foreign land acquisitions by countries with insufficient domestic food production, including South Korea, Japan, Saudi Arabia, UAE, China, and some western investment entities. Second, China has built production bases for cereal, soybean, rubber, palm oil, sisal, and other agricultural products in Russia, Southeast Asia, Central Asia, South America, and other areas (see Table 11.6).

Yet till now, what should also be noted is that, China's agricultural products from its overseas agricultural investment is mainly sold on the international market instead of being shipped back to China for domestic consumption. There are several reasons for it. First, as far as cereal is concerned, China's domestic production is still sufficient given a marginal demand and supply gap. Therefore, China still does not need to produce cereal abroad for domestic consumption. Second, it is not economically viable for Chinese companies to ship agricultural products produced overseas back to China because of domestic infrastructural bottlenecks and high transport costs. Third, owing to the extremely inefficient domestic agricultural production, the Chinese government still controls the agricultural trade, particularly grain trade, to protect its farmers. For instance, a Chinese company has to

---

[54]Chen Wei, 'Zhongguo nongye zou chuqu de xianzhuang wenti ji duice' [China's agricultural going-out: current status, problems and solutions], *International Economic Cooperation*, 1 (2012), pp. 34–39.

Table 11.6.   China's overseas land acquisitions.

Host Country	Company	Size	Crops	Status
Angola	CAMC Engineering Co. Ltd	1500	Rice	Done
Argentina	Beidahuang	320,000	Maize, soybeans, wheat	Suspended
Australia	Beidahuang	80,000	Dairy and grain farms	In process
Australia	Chinese interests	2800	Cattle	Done
Australia	Nanshan Group	30,000	Superfine wool	In process
Australia	Nexis Holding	1705	Cattle, nuts	Done
Australia	Shaanxi Kingbull Livestock Co	5000	Cattle	In process
Benin	'Chinese investment group'	10,000	Oil palm	In process
Benin	COMPLANT	4800	Cassava, sugar cane	In process
Bolivia	Pengxin Group	12,500	Maize, soybean	Done
Brazil	Chongqing Grain Group	200,000	Soybean	In process
Brazil	Pengxin Group	200,000	Cotton, soybean	In process
Bulgaria	Tianjin State Farms Agribusiness Group	2000	Alfalfa, maize, sunflower	In process
Cameroon	IKO	10,000	Cassava, maize, rice	Done
Colombia	China	400,000	Cereal	Proposed
Congo	ZTE	100,000	Oil palm	Done
Ethiopia	Hunan Dafengyuan	25,000	Sugar cane	Done
Indonesia	'Chinese investors'	1000	Rice	In process
Jamaica	COMPLANT	18,000	Sugar cane	Done
Laos	ZTE	50,000	Cassava	Done
Madagascar	COMPLANT	10,000	Sugar cane	Done
Mali	ClIC for Foreign Economic and Technical Cooperation	20,000	Sugar cane	Done
Mozambique	Hubei State Farm Agribusiness Corp	1000	NA	Done
New Zealand	Pengxin Group	8615	Dairy farm	Done

(Continued)

Table 11.6. (*Continued*)

Host Country	Company	Size	Crops	Status
Nigeria	Chinese investors	6000	Cassava	Done
Pakistan	China Green	4000	Fruit, vegetable	In process
Philippines	China	1,280,000	Various crops	Suspended
Russia	Heilongjiang Province	426,667	Crops	Done
Senegal	China	100,000	Peanut	In process
Senegal	Datong Trading Enterprise	60,000	Sesame	Done
Sierra Leone	COMPLANT	8100	Cassava, sugar cane	Done
Sierra Leone	Shanghai Construction Investment	30,000	Rice	Done
Sudan	ZTE	10,000	Oil seed	Done
Tajikistan	China	110,000	Cotton, rice	Done
Tanzania	Chongqing Seed Corp	300	Rice seed	Done
Uganda	Hebei Company	540	Fruit, livestock, others	In process
Uganda	Liu Jianjun	4000	NA	Done

Source: GRAIN Database, 2012.[55]

undergo a series of administrative procedures if it wishes to export grain produced overseas back to China. Fourth, shipping agricultural products back to China is not the only way to contribute to China's food security. As echoed by agricultural official Chen Xiwen, if China's overseas agricultural operations could help to harness the potential of global food production, the increase in global food supply could become the bulwark against China's food insecurity.[56]

---

[55] Some data from the GRAIN Database is not verified.

[56] 'Chen Xiwen: Zhongguo de liangshi anquan shi you baozhang de' [Chen Xiwen: China's food security is safeguarded], *China Daily* (2 February 2012), available at: http://www.chinadaily.com.cn/hqgj/jryw/2012-02-02/content_5064055.html (accessed 21 September 2013).

Nonetheless, as China's domestic food demand and supply gap continues to widen, it is inevitable that China's agricultural enterprises will transport more agricultural products from overseas farms back to China. Being fully aware that owning land in foreign countries cannot fully guarantee China's food supply because of disruptions in food transportation, China is always actively investing in infrastructural projects in countries that supply food sources to China. Food security concern is one of the key drivers behind China's rising investment in transportation of crops from Africa, Brazil, and other countries to China.[57]

In spite of widespread suspicions and concerns over China's growing overseas land acquisitions, China will still increase investment to boost agricultural production in foreign countries. Led by the Chongqing Grain Group, the China National Agricultural Development Group (CNADC), Heilongjiang Nongken Bureau, and Chinese state-owned agribusinesses are planning to acquire more land in foreign countries for agricultural production.[58] In addition to the Chongqing Grain Group's US$375 million investment in Brazil for soybean production, the Chongqing municipal government announced that during the 12th Five-Year Plan (2011–2015), it would build five overseas soybean and oil seed production bases in Brazil, Argentina, Canada, and other places.[59] In addition, the Heilongjiang Nongken Bureau aims to build no less than 40 million *mu* (2.7 million hectares) of overseas farms in the Philippines, Russia, Brazil, and other parts of the world for grain production, livestock-raising, and logging by 2015.[60] Furthermore, the CNADC focus is on developing overseas farms in Africa, South America, Australia, and Southeast Asia. It targets to utilize

---

[57]Cheng Guoqiang and Zhu Mande, 'Zhongguo liangshi hongguan tiaokong de xianshi zhuangtai yu zhengce kuangjia' [The situation and policy frame work of Chinese grain macro-control], *Reform* 1 (2013).

[58]'Nongye buju "zou chuqu" san da yangqi quanding zhongdian' [Agricultural 'Going Out' plan structured: focus areas set for three major state-owned companies], *China Economic Observer* (11 February 2012), available at: http://www.eeo.com.cn/2012/0211/220696. shtml (accessed on 20 September 2013).

[59]Jiang Wenzhang, 'Zhongguo Nongye zouchuqu bufa jiakuai' [The pace of China agricultural going-out accelerated], *China Economic Observer* (13 February 2012).

[60]*Ibid.*

between 10 and 30 million hectares of farmland in foreign countries in the next three to five years.[61]

Apart from overseas land acquisition, Chinese agricultural enterprises — private agribusiness firms in particular — are also very active in expanding their operations overseas through M&A (see Table 11.7). In contrast to the country's overseas land acquisitions, the initial phase of China's agricultural firms' overseas M&A was driven by domestic food safety concerns and domestic demand for high quality food. For example, food safety scandals have led consumers, especially the urban affluent class, to pay premium prices for the imported food. This has motivated some Chinese agribusiness firms to shift their production overseas. A typical example is seen in China's dairy industry: Chinese consumers' demand for imported milk has motivated domestic enterprises to set up factories and speed up acquisition in New Zealand and Australia. Besides, driven by strong domestic demand for higher food quality and variety, more private agribusinesses are embracing overseas M&A to secure alternative supply, establish brand image, expand market share, and acquire advanced agricultural technology and management expertise.

However, with China's increasing desire to groom its own transnational agricultural enterprises in a scale close to the ABCD traders (Archer Daniels Midland ADM, Bunge, Cargill, and Louis Dreyfus), it is keen to support Chinese agribusiness firms' acquisition of foreign agribusinesses as part of its long-term strategy to safeguard food security. For instance, in the first quarter of 2014, Chinese state-owned grain trader COFCO made a back-to-back purchase of controlling stakes in two global agricultural commodities traders — Netherlands-based Nidera BV and agribusiness division of Singapore-listed commodities trader Noble Group.

Strengthening global food security

As the most populous country in the world and a major global food trader, China's food security is highly dependent on global food trade and global

---

[61] Lihao, 'Zhongguo haiwai nongye touzi jiang zaoyu juda zuli' [China's overseas agricultural investments will encounter huge resistances] *Caijing Magazine* (27 March 2012), available at: http://comments.caijing.com.cn/2012-03-27/111777586.html (accessed 20 September 2013).

Table 11.7.   Recent major overseas M&A by Chinese agricultural firms.

China's Agribusiness	Year	Targeted Firms
COFCO	2010	Obtained the winery in Colchagua production area at US$18 million
Bright Dairy & Food Co Ltd	2010	Bought a 51% stake in New Zealand milk processor Synlait Milk Ltd at RMB382 million
COFCO	2011	Acquired the Château de Viaud in the prestigious Bordeaux Lalande-de-Pomerol AOC wine region
Guangdong Haida Group	2011	Bought a 100% stake in Panasia Trading
China Fishery Group	2011	Acquired two Peruvian fishing companies, Consorcio Vollmacht SAC and Negocios Rafmar SAC for a total of US$26.16 million
Bright Dairy & Food Co Ltd	2011	Bought a 75% stake in Australia's Manassen Foods for US$416 million
Shanghai Pengxin Group Co Ltd	2012	Purchased 16 dairy farms in New Zealand at US$172 million
Bright Dairy & Food Co Ltd	2012	Bought a 60% share in British food processing company Weetabix Ltd at RMB7 billion, and covers part of Weetabix's debt
Wahaha Group	2012	Announced intention to spend GBP520 million (RMB5.19 billion) to acquire KP Snacks of United Biscuits
Chinese enterprises including Wahaha group	2012	Indicated it was keen to buy Western Australia's largest dairying business, Lactanz Dairies
New Hope Group and Blackstone Group LP	2012	Jointly presented bids for Australia's largest poultry producer, Inghams Enterprises
Shuanghui International	2013	Bought US-based pork producer, Smithfield Foods, Inc. for US$4.1 billion
COFCO	2014	Paid US$1.2 billion for a major stake in Dutch grain trader Nidera BV
COFCO	2014	Paid US$1.5 billion for major stake in Noble Group's agribusiness

Source: Multiple official news reports compiled by the authors.

food security trends. Therefore, China recognizes that its rising influence and growing economic power come with the responsibility of maintaining global food security. It is also aware that doing so is advantageous for safeguarding its own food security and for countering the China threat narrative. Besides providing agricultural aid to developing countries to improve their agricultural production, China has also adopted four major approaches to strengthen global food security.

To begin with, China is emerging as a global food donor. Right after China officially made the role transition from food recipient to food donor, it provided 577,000 tons of grain to the United Nations World Food Program (WFP). China provided a total of 2,467,782 metric tons of food aid between 2000 and 2010, with most of it channeled to North Korea. Increasingly, China's food aid is directed to countries in Asia and Africa. In August 2008, China provided a cash contribution of US$400,000 in response to the Ethiopian government's request for aid, while the Chinese Red Cross contributed US$30,000.[62] In 2011 when food security situation deteriorated in East Africa, China provided close to US$70 million. In 2011, as the first country that joined the Strategic Alliance for South–South Cooperation led by the FAO of the United Nations, China donated US$30 million to a trust fund to aid developing countries' agricultural development.[63]

For a long time, Chinese food aid has been provided on a bilateral basis, with limited triangular purchases that allow for grain to be purchased in third countries. This practice has changed. Chinese agencies are now working in partnership with the WFP, buying food locally and hiring local support to facilitate distribution. Such an approach has been used to advance food aid to Zimbabwe and Lesotho. Administrative responsibility for implementing agricultural aid projects lies with the Ministry of Commerce, the Ministry of Agriculture, and the Ministry of Foreign Affairs. Chinese agricultural projects are expected to reduce poverty, increase agricultural productivity, and build capacity over time. Providing food aid is important to China

---

[62] Deborah Bräutigam and Xiaoyang Tang, 'An Overview of Chinese Agricultural and Rural Engagement in Ethiopia', IFPRI Discussion Paper No. 01185 (2012).

[63] *China and FAO: Achievements and Success stories* (Rome: FAO Representation in China, 2011), available at: http://www.fao.org/fileadmin/templates/rap/files/epublications/ChinaedocFINAL.pdf.

for countering the narrative of China's threat to global security. It is also important for creating a favorable environment for Chinese agricultural investment in developing countries in Africa and other parts of the world.

Next, China is becoming increasingly active in participating in global food governance. The global food regime which emerged after the First World War has long been controlled by US-led major food exporting nations.[64] The current global food regime is deemed as unfair, unreliable, and unstable as it serves the interests of the grain-exporting countries at the expense of the grain-importing ones. The 2008 global food crisis and the very fact that close to 900 million people all over the world suffer from hunger[65] prove that the current global food regime has failed.

For decades, agricultural trade liberalization was mainly targeted at reducing grain importing tariffs and other trade barriers and opening more markets for the United States and other grain export giants. Unless more is done to monitor the behavior of the grain-exporting countries, countries dependent on the international grain market for food will become highly vulnerable amid weakening global food security. According to a report by the IFPRI, grain-exporting countries' issue of bans, quotas, and taxes could be a bigger contributor to spikes in grain prices than factors such as financial speculation, US dollar depreciation, low interest rate, and grain stock reduction.[66] As the Chinese government's distrust of the global food regime deepens, it will push for the reform of the global food regime. With increasing donation to the FAO, the WFP, and the International Agricultural Consultative Group, China now plays a more important role in the Committee on World Food Security (CFS) established in 1974 following the World Food Conference. The global food crisis in 2008 heightened the need for the reform of the CFS. China has been elected to the 12-member bureau of the CFS for the period 2012–2013. Two Chinese experts, Tang Huajun, professor and vice-president of the Chinese Academy of Agricultural Sciences

---

[64]Harriet Friedmann, 'From colonialism to green capitalism: social movements and emergence of food regimes', in *New Directions in the Sociology of Global Development*, Frederick H. Buttel and Philip McMichael, eds. (Bingley: Emerald, 2005), pp. 227–264.

[65]*The State of Food Insecurity in the World: The Multiple Dimensions of Food Security* (Rome: FAO, 2013), available at: http://www.fao.org/docrep/018/i3434e/i3434e.pdf.

[66]Derek D. Headey, 'Rethinking the Global Food Crisis: The Role of Trade Shocks', *Food Policy* (2011), pp. 136–146.

and Zurong Cai, professor from Nanjing Normal University, are now members of the new High Level Panel of Experts which is established to inform the committee of emerging trends.

Furthermore, China is more willing to cooperate with other countries to promote food security. At various international forums, China's top leaders call on international communities to cooperate on global food security matters. As a major player in informal institutional settings such as the G20, BRICs (Brazil, Russia, India, and China), and ASEAN Plus Three, APEC, and Shanghai Cooperation Organization, China is enjoying more prominent roles and better opportunities to shape the rules of international conduct. China has become partners with the United States, Japan, Korea, ASEAN countries, Australia, and European countries to promote food security.

In addition, despite its strong preference for food sovereignty, China firmly supports the establishment of regional and international strategic food reserves. For instance, at the China–Latin America and the Caribbean Agricultural Ministers' Forum held in Beijing in June 2013, both parties agreed to set up a joint food reserve to offer humanitarian aid during disasters.[67] China is also one of the major contributors to ASEAN Plus Three Rice Emergency Reserve.[68]

Besides, as China's dependence on the international market for food grows and as its overseas agricultural investment increases, China's great interest in reshaping international trade and investment rules will soon be evident. One of the main tasks repeatedly advocated by Chinese officials and scholars and also outlined in China's 'National Plan for Development of Modern Agriculture (2011–2015)' by the State Council and the '12th Five-Year Plan for International Agricultural Cooperation' by the Department of International Cooperation, Ministry of Agriculture of China is this: China should actively participate in the negotiation and drafting of the rules

---

[67] '"Zhongguo-Ladingmeizhou he Jialebi nongyebuzhang luntan Beijing xuanyan" tongguo' ['China-Latin America and Caribbean Agricultural Minister Beijing Form Declaration' passed in China], *Xinhua News* (9 June 2013), available at: http://news.xinhuanet.com/world/2013-06/09/c_116107262.htm (accessed 1 December 2014).

[68] Roehlano M. Briones, 'Regional Cooperation for Food Security: The Case of Emergency Rice Reserves in the ASEAN Plus Three', ADB Sustainable Development Working Paper No. 18 (2011).

of international agricultural trade and investment in order to facilitate the country's overseas agricultural expansion. China believes that the deadlock in the Doha Round of trade talks is the main barrier to global agricultural trade liberalization and it could derail its food trade and food security. Consequently, China is very supportive of the Doha Round talks. China's Minister of Commerce Chen Deming has said that the country will continue to push for trade negotiations in the Doha Round of the World Trade Organization (WTO).[69] Chen urged the rich countries to agree to substantially cut their trade-distorting farm support, given favorable conditions of soaring global food prices. He added that China is willing to help these nations improve their deep processing capabilities of agricultural products to increase their value-add for the benefit of their people.

Lastly, as China's overseas investment (including agricultural investment) grows rapidly in recent years, the country is particularly concerned with rising investment protectionism. Unlike global trade which is managed by WTO, the world does not have an exclusive mechanism of global investment. Global investment rules are mainly based on bilateral investment agreements. China has signed bilateral investment agreements with over 150 countries; yet bilateral investment agreements face many obstacles because many countries are wary of China investing in politically-sensitive areas such as agriculture and energy sectors under the guise of safeguarding national security. Without a clear definition of the term 'national security', China's investment remains highly vulnerable. Therefore, China aims to increase its influence in the formulation of global investment rules to protect Chinese companies' cross-border investment.[70]

---

[69] 'China to push forward Doha Round of negotiation: minister', *People's Daily* (8 September 2011), available at: http://english.peopledaily.com.cn/90883/7592261.html (accessed 20 December 2013); Sun Zhenyu, 'A successful completion of the Doha Round benefits all', *China–US Focus* (20 December 2011), available at: http://www.chinausfocus.com/foreign-policy/a-successful-completion-of-the-doha-round-benefits-all/ (accessed 12 December 2013).

[70] 'China calls for int'l cross-border investment rules', *People's Daily* (27 November 2012), available at: http://english.people.com.cn/90778/8035044.html (accessed 20 December 2013); Li Jiabao, 'China "needs say" on investment rules', *China Daily* (12 January 2013), available at: http://www.chinadaily.com.cn/china/2013-01/12/content_16107338.htm (accessed 5 December 2013).

To facilitate China's agricultural 'Going Out' effort, China has formed a working group of 10 ministries such as the Ministry of Agriculture, the Ministry of Foreign Affairs, the Ministry of Commerce, and the Ministry of Finance; the inter-ministerial working mechanism comprises 14 ministries or departments that manage overseas agricultural resource development. However, the lack of effective coordination between different departments has hindered overseas agricultural expansion. Both academia and government officials have proposed to establish a unified management and coordination mechanism under the direct leadership of the State Council to guarantee effective support for China's agricultural 'Going Out' strategy. Moreover, China should also learn from US experience of safeguarding agricultural interests overseas by providing diplomatic support: setting up overseas agricultural offices and assigning agricultural attachés to overseas embassies.[71]

Conclusion: China's Food Security and Its Impact on Foreign Policy

Clearly, food security has become part of China's foreign policy agenda. Compared to the role of energy security in China's foreign policy, the food security-driven foreign policy is still in its infancy stage. Nonetheless, it has negative and positive effects on China's foreign relations with many other countries in the world.

On the negative side, China's growing food security challenges may prompt Beijing to adopt a more heavy-handed approach in managing various cross-border resources. When faced with severe water shortage, China may be more prepared to build dams to divert water flow in the Tibetan plateau which is the origin of several major rivers: the Mekong River, Yarlung Zangbo River (known as Brahmaputra in India), and the Indus River (which irrigates the crops of Vietnam, Myanmar, India, Pakistan,

---

[71] Zhang Yunhua, 'Woguo canyu haiwai nongye kaifa de jiyu yu duice' [China to participate in overseas agricultural development: opportunities and strategies], *Developmental Studies*, 9 (2009), pp. 52–54; Chen Wei, 'Zhongguo nongye zou chuqu de xianzhuang wenti ji duice' [China's agricultural going-out: current status, problems, and solutions], *International Economic Cooperation*, 1 (2012), pp. 34–39.

and other downstream countries). The water disputes between China and regional countries can adversely affect China's relations with these countries. With food security becoming a major concern in China, the importance of fishing resources in the Yellow Sea, East China Sea, and South China Sea will continue to grow. In future, China is likely to take a tougher stance on maritime disputes in these waters with regional countries.

China's global quest for food could also lead to greater rivalry between China and other major food importers such as Japan, South Korea, Gulf countries, and India. The rivalry was evident during the 2008 global food crisis when these countries also strained to purchase and lease land in Africa, Southeast Asia, and Latin America amid stiff competition with Chinese investors. Given China's growing appetite for foreign agricultural resources together with its enormous amount of financial resources, fierce competition is likely to prevail.

On the positive side, China's food security concerns may help improve relations between China and major food exporting countries, such as the EU, Australia, Canada, Brazil, Argentina, Central Asian countries, and some developing countries in Africa and Southeast Asia. In particular, China's emerging food security-driven foreign policy is likely to create opportunities for Sino–US cooperation, given the complementary nature of the two countries' agricultural sectors.

Moreover, China is committed to strengthening global food security through various policy initiatives: providing bilateral aid, contributing to world food programs, forging international and regional cooperation, pushing for reforms in the global food regime, and building strategic food reserves. Global food security has become an international policy area in which Beijing wants to dramatically increase its influence and ultimately play a leading role. As a result, China will appear to be even more active in international affairs.

Finally, with growing reliance on foreign countries for food, the security of China's food supply will become a significant concern for the Chinese government. China is encouraging its agricultural firms, particularly its state-owned agribusiness firms, to expand their global presence by means of overseas M&A. China will likely be seriously concerned about the domestic socio-political stability and may get entangled in the domestic politics of the host countries, which in turn will create severe challenges to

China's age-old non-intervention policy. As overseas food supply is mostly transported through sea-lanes, safeguarding maritime security — including safety of maritime navigation and countering terrorism and piracy — will eventually become an even more important issue in China's foreign policy.

Index